A Pastor's Field Guide

Ed Landry

**Essential
Guidelines,
Instructions,
and
Principles
Every
Pastor
Needs
to Know**

Uplifting Christian Books
Nashville, Tennessee 2022

A Pastor's Field Guide
Essential Guidelines, Instructions, and Principles, Every Pastor Needs to Know
Copyright © 2022 by Uplifting Christian Books

Published in Nashville, TN by Uplifting Christian Books
All rights reserved.

Printed in the Philippines by SAM Printing Press, Cebu City. 2022
Printed in the USA by Kindle Direct Publishin, 2022

Author - Ed Landry
Special thanks to our dedicated editorial team - Marcia P., Tom and Janet T., Dell W., Janet L., Carol S, Nelson R.

Book and cover design by Ed and Janet Landry.
Illustrations by Ed Landry.
Additional Development team - The Saturday Fellowship

ISBN: 978-0-9990931-6-0

Printed in the United States of America.

Dedicated

To all the pastors, church planters and faithful teachers of the Word of God. May this easy-to-read commentary be a wonderful inspiration to you and a help to you as you serve God.

Friends forever,
Ed Landry
Missionary, First Love International Ministries,
2022

Some free recommended resources to help in your studies

The Blue Letter Bible

This is a free App (BLB) for your phones which has a wide spectrum of Bible study tools. To use on your computers and laptops, go to:
https://www.blueletterbible.org/

The Bible Project

A very creative group have produced these imaginative animations and charts of the books of the Bible. Each animation is around 5-6 minutes long and gives a great overview of the Word of God. They allow free downloads of their quality materials.
https://bibleproject.com/all-videos/

Precept Austin

A massive commentary and Bible resource website. The site contains word by word commentary of the entire Bible with some 20,000 resources. This site is for serious Bible students. One of the best organized and helpful sites on the INTERNET. It will take a while to learn to navigate the site but worth the effort.
https://www.preceptaustin.org/

Got Questions

This online resource contains over 600,000 Bible questions and answers. Their leadership and staff represent some of the finest evangelical Bible colleges and seminaries in the USA. Comprehensive, yet concise.
https://www.gotquestions.org/

Bible.Org

A large collection of Bible commentaries and expostions arranged by topic, book, verse, words, etc. The site also has the NET Bible (2nd edition) with its 58,000+ notes, Greek, Hebrew, texts linked to Strongs numbers. It allows you to search all the translations of the Bible to find your favorite verses. The commentary section uses the works of hundreds of top theologians and evangelical authors. Find it at:
https://bible.org/

Bible Hub

A huge collecton of word studies, commentaries, Bible versions. Type in a verse and then choose what you want and you will have more resources than you can imagine. Like any web site, it will take a little time to understand it and take advantage of its power.
https://biblehub.com/

1 TIMOTHY

Paul's first letter to his faithful co-worker and son in the faith.

"Fight the good fight of faith; take hold of the eternal life to which you were called, and you made the good confession in the presence of many witnesses."

1 Timothy 6:12

Introduction

The world Timothy lived in. It was the best of times; it was the worst of times.

The world was changing. The church was born at one of the most amazing and strategic times in history. Let's set the stage.

1. The greatest empire in the world had taken center stage.

There are many different claims as to what empire on the earth was the greatest, so let's check the Guinness Book of Records:

> *"The Roman Empire is considered to have been the most enduring in history. The formal start date of the Empire remains the subject of debate. Most historians agree that the clock began ticking in 27 B.C. when the Roman politician Octavian overthrew the Roman Republic to become Emperor Augustus. Although Rome later fell to the Germanic "Barbarians" in A.D. 476, the ensuing "Eastern Empire" based at Constantinople is widely regarded as a continuation of the original Roman Empire. It wasn't until the fall of the city in A.D. 1453 that the curtain finally came down on the empire, ending a period of dominance across Europe and beyond that had lasted for almost 1,500 years."*
> (Guinness Book of Records)

The events of the entire New Testament happened when the Roman Empire was at its greatest. Rome had the most powerful emperor, Julius Caesar. The Empire provided the world with more advances than any other civilization. They assembled the most powerful military in history.

Rome developed the world's most intricate and complete road system which can still be seen 2,000 years later. They built 50,000 miles of hard-surfaced roadway (enough to circle the earth twice). The road system was constructed primarily for their enormous military. The process they developed remains a marvel today. After the military builders cleared the ground of rocks, trees, and other obstructions, they hand-dug a deep trench where the road was to go. They then filled the trench with a series of layers starting with large stones, then concrete mixed with broken tiles. Finally, they surfaced the stable underlayment with paving stones making a surface smooth enough for their equipment, chariots, and horses. In case you were wondering, the Romans invented concrete. The road system also helped the empire's commerce and more importantly, it helped the gospel expand to areas that formerly were almost impossible to reach.

Some other things the greatest empire introduced to the world:

- Architecture
- Engineering
- Water system
- Sewerage system
- City planning
- Parks
- Fountains
- Clothing styles
- Quality of life
- Arts
- Culture
- Inventions
- Innovations
- Education
- Philosophy
- Government
- System of laws

- Military strength
- Sports Colosseum

2. The greatest event in all of history had just happened.

God the Son became flesh, died for the sins of the world, and rose again from the dead. The Church was born in a political and religious storm. The Jewish world had been shaken by the presence of Jesus of Nazareth. The rulers of the Jews put Him to death, but the tomb was found empty three days later as He had promised. The disciples were emboldened. The long-awaited Messiah had come. The very existence of the Jewish system was crumbling. Many were being converted and following Christ. Christians were hated by the Jews.

The Roman religion and power structure were threatened. They also hated the Christians putting many of them to death. The Romans served Caesar as king, but the Christians acknowledged Jesus as the King of kings and Lord of lords. Both the Jewish leaders and Roman leaders wanted to extinguish the Christian threat. It was a time of great persecution by powerful forces.

3. The greatest team of Spirit-filled, God-glorifying church planters and evangelists was assembled by God.

It was God's dream team. Peter, John and the Apostles, Paul of Tarsus, Barnabas, Luke, Silas, Priscilla and Aquilla, Titus, Apollos, and many more too numerous to name. It was a team for the times and the world was beginning to shake. It was indeed "the *best of times*; it was the *worst of times.*"

A new player was added to the dream team, a teenager named Timothy. He lived in a small out-of-the-way town called Lystra in the Galatia region. Lystra was about 20 miles from the city of

Iconium. Today the city is called Kilistra and is in Turkey. Lystra was on a Roman road that ran from Ephesus at the sea and connected the towns of Sardis, Antioch Pisidia, Iconium, and Derbe and onward to Syria.

What do we know about Lystra?

Lystra, even though it was an insignificant town, became a military colony protecting the Roman Empire in 6 B.C. The population of Lystra consisted of a local band of Roman soldiers, Greeks, Jews (Acts 16:1, 3), and native Lycaonians (Acts 14:11). The city was built on a hill that the Roman army used to protect its empire from hostile invaders. Later, it was incorporated into the Roman province of Galatia, and shortly afterward the Romans built a road connecting Lystra to Iconium to the north.

The religious beliefs of the people of Lystra were diverse. The Romans carried on the mythologies of the Greeks, setting up images and temples for numerous Greek gods. It is evident from the narrative in Acts that the native Lycaonians (Acts 14:11) of the region were prepared to worship Paul and Barnabas as the gods, Zeus and Hermes. The Gentile population of the region followed pagan Greek mythology as their primary religion. This was the world that young Timothy saw every day. He was raised, however, to believe in the Laws of Moses and have faith in the God of the Old Testament Scriptures.

Paul later traveled into that region on his first missionary journey. His first contact with Timothy and his family was on that trip in 48 A.D. Three years later, at the beginning of Paul's second missionary journey, he revisited Lystra. It was then that he invited Timothy to join his growing team of disciples. The greatest gospel team the world has ever seen had acquired a new superstar. The name Timothy means "honored by God."

Events leading to the conversion of Timothy.

Acts chapters 13 and 14 chronicle the first missionary journey of Paul and Barnabas. After they preached on the island of Cyprus, they sailed to Perga in Pamphilia, then traveled north to Pisidian Antioch. Even though this was a Gentile, Roman city with Greek religious influence, it had a Jewish synagogue. It was always Paul's practice to go to the Jew first.

> *... and on the Sabbath day they went into the synagogue and sat down. [15] After the reading of the Law and the Prophets, the synagogue officials sent word to them, saying, "Brothers, if you have any word of exhortation for the people, say it."* (Acts 13:14,15)

Paul stood and gave a history of God delivering His people from Egypt. He described the story of redemption. He presented Jesus as the risen Messiah (Acts 13:16-41). Many believed and begged him to return the next Sabbath. Others, however, stirred the crowds and began persecuting Paul and Barnabas.

> *[44] The next Sabbath nearly all the city assembled to hear the word of the Lord. [45] But when the Jews saw the crowds, they were filled with jealousy and began contradicting*

the things spoken by Paul, and were blaspheming. ⁴⁶ Paul and Barnabas spoke out boldly and said, "It was necessary that the word of God be spoken to you first. Since you repudiate it and consider yourselves unworthy of eternal life, behold, we are turning to the Gentiles. ⁴⁷ For so the Lord has commanded us,

> *'I have appointed You as a light to the Gentiles,
> That You may bring salvation to the end of the earth.'"*

⁴⁸ When the Gentiles heard this, they began rejoicing and glorifying the word of the Lord; and all who had been appointed to eternal life believed. ⁴⁹ And the word of the Lord was being spread through the whole region. ⁵⁰ But the Jews incited the devout women of prominence and the leading men of the city, and instigated a persecution against Paul and Barnabas, and drove them out of their region. (Acts 13:44-50)

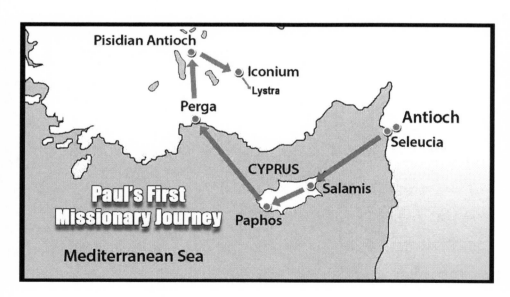

After being forced out of Pisidian Antioch, Paul and Barnabas traveled to the city of Iconium. There they preached at the synagogue where a large number of Jews and Gentiles heard and responded to the gospel. The unbelieving Jews, as in Pisidian

Antioch, became threatened and jealous. They stirred up the people and planned to stone Paul to death, but Paul heard about their plot and left town.

After leaving Iconium, Paul and Barnabas traveled south to Lystra. In that small Roman military outpost lived a family with a Gentile man and his Jewish wife, Eunice. Their son was a teenage boy named Timothy. Lois, the mother of Eunice, also lived with them. The women, along with young Timothy, were people of faith in the living God of the Old Testament and followed the ways of Moses. The Jewish population was too small to have a synagogue so Paul preached wherever he could find a crowd in Lystra. In a small town like that, everyone knew each other and what was going on. Lystra was the first recorded place Paul spoke where there was no synagogue. He went directly to the general crowds, both Jew and Gentile.

When Paul addressed the people that gathered, a man crippled from birth was present. Everyone in the small town knew his condition.

> *Paul looked at him intently and saw that he had faith to be made well, ¹⁰ and he said with a loud voice, "Stand upright on your feet!" And the man leaped up and began to walk. ¹¹ When the crowds saw what Paul had done, they raised their voice, saying in the Lycaonian language, 'The gods have become like men and have come down to us! ¹² And they began calling Barnabas, Zeus, and Paul, Hermes since he was the chief speaker.* (Acts 14:9-12)

Paul rebuked them when they tried to worship him, and he explained that the healing of the cripple was not because of the Greek false gods but through the power of the living God. The whole area was buzzing with the news and the events.

Word of the miracle and the preaching of Paul reached Pisidian Antioch, and Iconium. They gathered a group together and traveled to Lystra where they stirred up the people and stoned Paul and left him for dead on the road. There is no question that Timothy, Eunice, and Lois were witnesses of these events or at least heard about them. This was the big event in town. Although the details are not described in the Bible, God raised Paul back to health.

> **They stoned Paul and dragged him out of the city, thinking that he was dead. [20] But while the disciples stood around him, he got up and entered the city. The next day he left with Barnabas for Derbe. [21] And after they had preached the gospel to that city and had made a good number of disciples, they returned to Lystra, to Iconium, and to Antioch.** (Acts 14:19-21)

The crowd left him for dead because he was so beaten up they thought he was dead. Some think when Paul wrote 2 Corinthians 12:1-7 he was describing his death and being transported to God's presence in a vision where he heard things that he could not talk about. The passage in 2 Corinthians could have taken place while Paul was still in Antioch before his first journey.

One thing is certain. The faith of young Timothy, Lois, and Eunice was confirmed. They at some point came to salvation through the events of Paul's first visit to Lystra. When Paul returned three years later on the first part of his second missionary journey, here is what we are told:

> **[1] Now Paul also came to Derbe and to Lystra. And a disciple was there, named Timothy, the son of a Jewish woman who was a believer, but his father was a Greek, [2] and he was well spoken of by the brothers and sisters who were in Lystra and Iconium. [3] Paul wanted this man to leave with him; and he took him and circumcised him because of the Jews who were in those parts, for they all knew that his father was a Greek.** (Acts 16:1-3)

Timothy had become known as a strong disciple of Christ. One of the convincing proofs to Timothy during Paul's first visit to Lystra was the boldness and fearlessness that Paul demonstrated. After Paul's stoning, he was miraculously restored to health and went back into the city of Lystra and spent the night there. Later he returned from Derbe and he spent more time in the very town where he had been stoned. He even returned to Iconium and Pisidian Antioch and preached again. Paul was so confident in the power of God and his calling that he was courageous. Timothy saw this in Paul.

> [21] *And after they had preached the gospel to that city and had made a good number of disciples, they returned to Lystra, to Iconium, and to Antioch,* [22] *strengthening the souls of the disciples, encouraging them to continue in the faith, and saying, "It is through many tribulations that we must enter the kingdom of God."* [23] *When they had appointed elders for them in every church, having prayed with fasting, they entrusted them to the Lord in whom they had believed.* (Acts 14:21-23)

When Paul returned to Lystra three years later he heard about this young man who was now a disciple of Christ and *"he was well spoken of by the brothers and sisters who were in Lystra and Iconium"* (Acts 16:16:2, 3). Paul knew this was a young man he wanted on his dream team, a faithful worker with a strong reputation as a victorious disciple of Christ. Timothy's life calling had begun:

> [3] *Paul wanted this man to leave with him; and he took him and circumcised him because of the Jews who were in those parts, for they all knew that his father was a Greek.* [4] *Now while they were passing through the cities, they were delivering the ordinances for them to follow which had been determined by the apostles and elders in Jerusalem.* [5] *So the churches were being strengthened in the faith, and were increasing in number daily.* (Acts 16:3-5)

Paul would refer to Timothy from then on as his "true son" in the faith (1 Timothy 1:2,18; 2 Timothy 1:2; 2:1; 1 Corinthians 4:17). Paul and Timothy had a very special relationship until the death of Paul 18-20 years later in Rome. The two letters Paul wrote to his "true son" were the words of a loving father who disciplines, warns, and instructs his son. The last letter Paul wrote before he was beheaded by Nero was to Timothy.

> *² To Timothy, my beloved son: Grace, mercy, and peace from God the Father and Christ Jesus our Lord.³ I thank God, whom I serve with a clear conscience the way my forefathers did, as I constantly remember you in my prayers night and day, ⁴ longing to see you, even as I recall your tears, so that I may be filled with joy. ⁵ For I am mindful of the sincere faith within you, which first dwelled in your grandmother Lois and your mother Eunice, and I am sure that it is in you as well.*
>
> (2 Timothy 1:2-5)

If Paul had ever had a son, he would have wanted him to be Timothy. He loved him as his own flesh. In Paul's last words he said, *"You therefore, my son, be strong in the grace that is in Christ Jesus"* (2 Timothy 2:2). The next verses are the last recorded words of the Apostle Paul as he pleaded with Timothy to come to him in Rome during his final imprisonment:

> *²¹ Make every effort to come before winter. Eubulus greets you, also Pudens, Linus, Claudia, and all the brothers and sisters. ²² The Lord be with your spirit. Grace be with you.*
>
> (2 Timothy 4:21, 22)

The journeys of Timothy.

The story of Timothy can be reconstructed with the book of Acts and references to him in the various epistles.

During the second missionary journey of Paul, along with Silas, Timothy traveled with the team to Troas and then over to

Macedonia. Luke then joined them when they crossed over to Philippi. There, Lydia became the first convert in Europe. After Paul and Silas were imprisoned and miraculously rescued by God, the team went to Thessalonica for a three-week church plant and then on to Berea after agitators forced Paul to leave. Paul left Timothy and Silas in charge to minister to the believers (Acts 17:15). Thessalonica would become one of the strongest New Testament churches. Timothy ultimately helped Paul establish churches at Philippi, Thessalonica, and Berea (Acts 16:1 – 17:14).

Timothy helped Paul write six books of the New Testament including 1 Thessalonians. Here is what they wrote to that group of believers:

> *² We always give thanks to God for all of you, making mention of you in our prayers; ³ constantly keeping in mind your work of faith and labor of love and perseverance of hope in our Lord Jesus Christ in the presence of our God and Father, ⁴ knowing, brothers and sisters, beloved by God, His choice of you; ⁵ for our gospel did not come to you in word only, but also in power and in the Holy Spirit and with full conviction; just as you know what kind of men we proved to be among you for your sakes. ⁶ You also became imitators of us and of the Lord, having received the word during great affliction with the*

joy of the Holy Spirit, [7] so that you became an example to all the believers in Macedonia and Achaia. [8] For the word of the Lord has sounded forth from you, not only in Macedonia and Achaia, but in every place the news of your faith toward God has gone out. (1 Thessalonians 1:2-8)

On Paul's third missionary journey Timothy joined Paul in Ephesus (Acts 19:32).

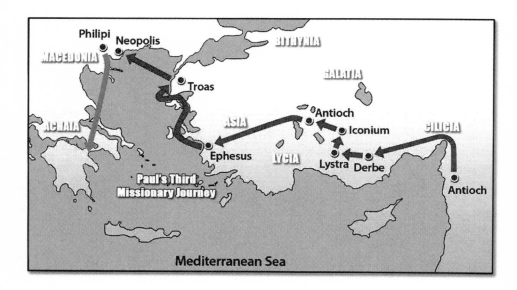

After news reached Paul about growing troubles in the church in Corinth, he sent Timothy to help teach and stabilize the struggling fellowship (1 Corinthians 16:10, 11). Paul later wrote a second letter to Corinth which he sent with Titus who also assisted the Corinthians. At the end of Paul's third missionary travels, Paul and Timothy would return to Corinth. Paul wrote Romans and Galatians at that time. Timothy was with him and would also help take relief funds to Jerusalem.

When Paul traveled to Rome for his hearing, Timothy was there with him (Col. 1:1, Phil. 1). While in house arrest in Rome, Paul wrote what we today call his prison epistles.

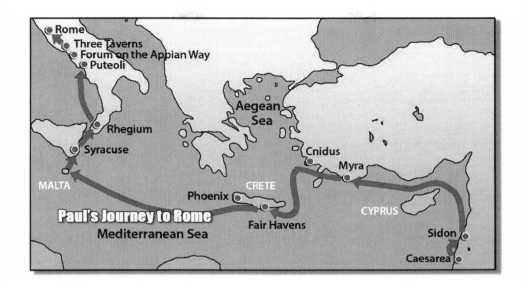

Timothy is generally believed to have hand-carried the letter to the Philippians (Philippians 1:1; 2:19). When Paul was released from prison in Rome, Timothy joined Paul to revisit friends in the churches they had founded. In Ephesus some in the church were confused about varous important doctrines of the faith. They were influenced by false teachers. Before Paul traveled back to Macedonia, he left Timothy behind in Ephesus to teach the truth to the church and pastor the house churches. Timothy helped rebuild and develop leaders in the Ephesian church (1 Timothy 2:1-15, 3:1-3). Paul later wrote to the Ephesian church:

> *15 For this reason I too, having heard of the faith in the Lord Jesus which exists among you and your love for all the saints, 16 do not cease giving thanks for you, while making mention of you in my prayers.* (Ephesians 1:15, 16)

The final years and death of Timothy.

The reconstruction of the final years of Paul's life is difficult. He may have fulfilled his desire to go to Spain (Romans 15:24). He certainly revisited the churches of Asia, Macedonia, and Achaia.

It is possible during this time Timothy was arrested and released (Hebrews 13:22, 23). Titus had been left on Crete to help organize the churches there and Paul intended to winter at Nicopolis. Paul, however, was arrested again and sent to Rome for the last time. Paul's final letter (2 Timothy), and the last mention of Timothy, was addressed from prison with his final wish that Timothy might *"make every effort to come before winter"* (Timothy 4: 21).

The death of Timothy.

> *"Timothy was the celebrated disciple of St. Paul, and bishop of Ephesus, where he zealously governed the Church until A.D. 97. At this period, as the pagans were about to celebrate a feast called Catagogion, Timothy, meeting the procession, severely reproved them for their ridiculous idolatry, which so exasperated the people that they fell upon him with their clubs, and beat him in so dreadful a manner that he expired of the bruises two days later."*
> (Foxe's Book of Martyrs, 1563)

The special relationship Paul had with Timothy.

In all of Paul's amazing life and ministry, there was no personal relationship he had with anyone closer than what he had with Timothy. Timothy had the privilege of being Paul's closest and best co-worker and friend. Paul wrote this in his letter to the Philippians:

> *[19] But I hope, in the Lord Jesus, to send Timothy to you shortly, so that I also may be encouraged when I learn of your condition. [20] For I have no one else of kindred spirit who will genuinely be concerned for your welfare. [21] For they all seek after their own interests, not those of Christ Jesus. [22] But you know of his proven character, that he served with me in the furtherance of the gospel like a child serving his father. [23] Therefore I hope to send him immediately, as soon as I see how things go with me; [24] and I trust in the Lord that I myself will also be coming shortly.*
> (Philippians 2:19-24)

20

Chronology of Timothy's travels.

A.D. 46 > > > **A.D. 97**

Paul's 1st journey

- **A.D.46-49** Timothy was most likely converted by Paul at Lystra. (See 1 Corinthians 4:17; 1 Timothy 1:2, 18; Acts 14:6-23).

Paul's 2nd journey

- **A.D. 50** At Lystra, Timothy joins the team of Paul and Silas (Acts 16:1-4).
  - Timothy with Paul, Silas, and Luke in Philippi, Thessalonica, and Berea.
  - Paul and Silas went to Thessalonica. Timothy stayed in Philippi but later went to Berea and Thessalonica when Paul went to Athens (Acts 17:13-15).
  - Paul sent for Timothy and Silas to come to Corinth to help him there.
- **A.D. 51-52** Timothy and Silas joined Paul at Corinth. Timothy helped Paul write 1 Thessalonians from Corinth (Acts 18:5).
  - Timothy was sent to Thessalonica to strengthen the faith of the believers (1 Thessalonians 3:1-2).
  - Timothy's unknown years. Timothy may have returned to Macedonia when Paul returned from his second missionary journey, but it's unknown.
  - Timothy joined Paul in Ephesus on his third missionary journey.

Paul's 3rd journey

- **A.D.53-58**
  During the three years Paul was in Ephesus teaching them about the amazing power of God, Timothy was there, too.
- **A.D. 57** Paul wrote 1 Corinthians while at Ephesus (1 Corinthians 15:8, 19; cf. Acts 18:18-19) and mentions

having sent Timothy to Corinth to help with problems in the church.

- **A.D. 57** From Ephesus, Paul sent Timothy to Macedonia (Acts 19:22), and Timothy presumably planned to proceed to Corinth from there (1 Cor. 4:17; 16:10-11).
- **A.D. 57** Paul wrote 2 Corinthians while in Macedonia (2 Corinthians 8:1-5). Timothy was once again with him, as evidenced by 2 Corinthians 1:1 and Acts 20:1.
- **A.D. 58** Timothy accompanied Paul to Corinth at the end of Paul's third journey, as is indicated in Paul's letter to the Romans (16:21). Romans was written while they were in Corinth (Romans 15:25-26; 16:23, cf. 1 Corinthians 1:14).
- Paul returned to Macedonia with his team, which included Timothy. They traveled to Troas and then sailed to Miletus to meet the Ephesian elders. (Acts 20)
- **A.D. 58** Timothy proceeded (perhaps in advance of Paul, Acts 20:5) to Troas, and was with Paul there (Acts 20:4-5).
- **A.D. 58-61** Paul returned to Jerusalem for trials and imprisonment at Jerusalem and Caesarea.

Paul's 4th journey – His first imprisonment at Rome

- **A.D. 62-63** Timothy was with Paul in Rome (Acts 28, Colossians 1:1, Philemon 1:1, and Philippians 1:1). When Paul was released he returned to his churches in Macedonia and Ephesus. In Ephesus, he left Timothy to pastor the church (1 Timothy 1:3).
- **A.D. 64** Paul wrote 1 Timothy (date uncertain) from Macedonia or Rome after he was arrested and imprisoned the final time in Rome.

Paul's arrest and final journey to Rome

- **A.D. 65 -67** Paul's second Roman imprisonment. Paul wrote his letters to Timothy with the help of Luke who was with him (2 Timothy. 4:11; see Colossians 4:14).
- **A.D. 67** Paul beheaded in Rome.
- **A.D. 97** Timothy died in Ephesus. While trying to stop a pagan procession to the goddess Diana, An angry mob beat and stoned him to death.

Timothy helped Paul write:

- 2 Corinthians
- Philippians
- Colossians
- 1 Thessalonians
- 2 Thessalonians
- Philemon

OUTLINE OF 1 TIMOTHY
Chapter 1

- Paul's Greeting (1:1-2).
- False teachers, divisive individuals, and fruitless discussions threatened to derail the church (1:3-7).
- The gospel, the Law, and the depraved conditions in the city of Ephesus. Standing for righteousness in a sinful world (1:8-11).
- No one is beyond saving. Paul shares his testimony of the grace and mercy of God shown to him (1:12-17).
- Paul's charge to young Timothy to press on in the fight. The opposition is great (1:18-20).

Chapter 2

- How to pray for the lost and the ones in authority (2:1-8).
- The godly woman in an ungodly world (2:9-15).

Chapter 3

- Appointing elders (3:1-7).
- Appointing deacons (3:8-13).

Chapter 4

- Some will fall from the faith and some will add to the gospel (4:1-5).
- Disciplines of a godly leader (4:6-16).
- The discipline of correction (4:6).

- The discipline of spiritual focus (4:7).
- The discipline of keeping balanced (4:8-11).
- The discipline of perseverance, steadfastness (4:12-16).

Chapter 5

- Treat older men and widows with honor (5:1-10).
- Respecting the elderly (5:1, 2).
- Honoring godly widows (5:3).
- Who is a true widow (5:4-10)?
- Instructions for younger widows (5:11-16).
- Selection and treatment of elders (5:17-22).

Chapter 6

- All believers should be respectful of those over them (6:1-2).
- The basis of true doctrine (6:3-5).
- Contentment – when enough is enough (6:6-10).
- Pursuing the greater things of God, not earthly values (6:11-16).
- Help the wealthy to be generous and rich in good works (6:17-19).
- Hang tightly on to that which God has given you avoiding worldly distractions (6:20-21).

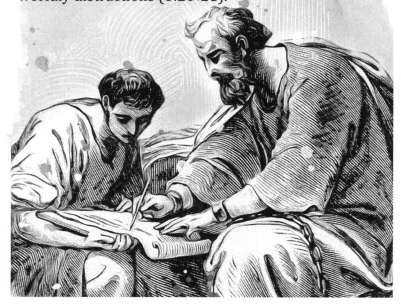

1 Timothy Chapter 1
Commentary

Paul's greeting (1:1-2).

¹ Paul, an apostle of Christ Jesus according to the commandment of God our Savior, and of Christ Jesus, *who is* our hope, ² To Timothy, *my* true child in *the* faith, "Grace, mercy *and* peace from God the Father and Christ Jesus our Lord.'

THE GREETING.

The Apostle Paul frequently used this greeting in the letters he wrote. *"Grace, mercy, and peace from God the Father and Christ Jesus our Lord."* When we realize his background and personal journey, we understand that these words were not just a common courtesy or standard greeting, but truly a heart-felt thanksgiving for what God had done in his life.

Paul was a pharisee, a persecutor of the church, even putting to death those who followed Jesus. He felt this made him a hero (among the Jews), a protector of the Law of Moses and the ancient path handed down from Abraham, Isaac, and Jacob. He was feared by the leadership of Judaism in the first century. He was a man of ambition. God, however, had a different plan! Forcefully and violently interrupted by Christ, Paul's entire life course was changed from being the head persecutor of the church to becoming the greatest church planter of the century. God broke him down in one crushing blow. Paul was ruthless, without mercy, and suddenly God flooded his life with truth, understanding, and grace. He was a man who formerly followed his own will and now was a man held captive by God's will.

When we first read Paul's greeting it is easy to miss just how important those words were to him. He was thankful he now followed the will of God, not his destructive path. He was thankful for the grace of God that rescued him from his former life, and he was thankful that his life was at peace with God. For Paul, this was not just a customary greeting, it was the deep expression of his heart. Paul was a zealous pharisee but it was God that transformed him into an Apostle. He would later tell one of his churches,

> *⁷ But whatever things were gain to me, these things I have counted as loss because of Christ. ⁸ More than that, I count all things to be loss in view of the surpassing value of knowing Christ Jesus my Lord, for whom I have suffered the loss of all things, and count them mere rubbish, so that I may gain Christ.* (Philippians 3:7, 8)

Grace, mercy, and peace describes Paul's life. His heart was filled with joy over what God had done for him. His co-laborers in the gospel shared the same all-consuming joy in Christ.

TIMOTHY, THE TRUE SON IN THE FAITH.

Paul wrote these words to the church he planted in Philippi:

> *¹⁹ But I hope, in the Lord Jesus, to send Timothy to you shortly, so that I also may be encouraged when I learn of your condition. ²⁰ For I have no one else of kindred spirit who will genuinely be concerned for your welfare. ²¹ For they all seek after their own interests, not those of Christ Jesus. ²² But you know of his proven character, that he served with me in the furtherance of the gospel like a child*

serving his father. [23] Therefore I hope to send him
immediately, as soon as I see how things go with me; [24] and
I trust in the Lord that I myself will also be coming shortly.
(Philippians 2:19-25)

Paul was Timothy's first contact with the gospel. Timothy had been raised by a God-fearing mother and grandmother to follow the laws of Moses and the ways of the prophets, but he needed the message of the gospel which he heard when Paul first came to Lystra. Timothy was in Lystra when Paul healed the cripple and presented the risen Christ to the people of that small town. Timothy was there when Paul was stoned and left for dead but rose to his feet and moved on to Derbe. Paul soon returned and preached again. Sometime during these events, Timothy became a committed believer and strong disciple. When Paul returned three years later on his second journey he heard about Timothy's strong reputation as a follower of Christ. Paul immediately invited him to join his team. After that, Timothy became the closest companion and fellow worker with the Apostle Paul. He had a bond with Paul as John had with Jesus.

PRINCIPLES TO LIVE BY

Trials are temporary but joy is eternal. There is no occupation, experience, achievement, position in life, award, or anything that can even approach the joy of being in the will of God and serving Him. No matter what will come into our lives to tempt us to give up, don't do it. Trials and attacks will come. Suffering is part of the job description of the follower of God's path. The ways of the world are empty, containing only hollow promises. The best the world can offer is but a mirage in the desert. Christ is the water of life.

Develop deep friendships with godly people. The relationship between Paul and Timothy lasted 18-20 years until the death of Paul. It was a source of joy for both men that carried them through the dark times. We all need those kinds of friends.

False teachers, divisive individuals, and fruitless discussions threatened to derail the church. (1:3-7)

³ As I urged you upon my departure for Macedonia, remain on at Ephesus so that you may instruct certain men not to teach strange doctrines, ⁴ nor to pay attention to myths and endless genealogies, which give rise to mere speculation rather than *furthering* the Administration of God which is by faith. ⁵ But the goal of our instruction is love from a pure heart and a good conscience and a sincere faith. ⁶ For some men, straying from these things, have turned aside to fruitless discussion, ⁷ wanting to be teachers of the Law, even though they do not understand either what they are saying or the matters about which they make confident assertions.

"*³ As I urged you upon my departure for Macedonia, remain on at Ephesus*" (1:3). The book of Acts does not describe a time when Paul traveled to Macedonia and left Timothy in charge of the church in Ephesus. When Paul went to Rome for his house arrest the book of Acts ends at that point. We know from books Paul wrote after he was released from his time in Rome that he revisited at least some of the churches he had helped plant. He must have visited Ephesus during that time or at least made sure Timothy, who was there, stayed on in his pastoral role while Paul went to the churches in Macedonia. The date is estimated around A.D. 63 or 64. Timothy would have still been a young man, around 30 years of age when Paul left him in Ephesus. Paul would later be re-arrested and taken to Rome where he would ultimately be beheaded during the reign of Nero. These events are not recorded in the New Testament but come from historical writings.

> *"The apostle had left Timothy to minister in Ephesus when he left that city and went to Macedonia. He was to remain behind to charge some that they teach no other doctrine. When Paul had met the elders of Ephesus at Miletus he had made this prediction, "For I know this, that after my departure shall grievous wolves enter in among you, not sparing the flock. Also, of your selves shall men arise, speaking perverse things, to draw away disciples after them" (Acts 20:29-30). Then he went to Jerusalem, where he was taken prisoner and sent to Rome. After his release, he must have visited Ephesus once more and found the very things in the assembly of Ephesus against which the Holy Spirit had sounded the warning. Timothy was with him at that visit between his first and second imprisonment."* (StudyLight.org)

We know Timothy was with Paul during his first Roman imprisonment. He was either:

- Sent ahead to Ephesus with Paul's instructions about the false teachers, or
- After Paul's release, both Paul and Timothy went to Ephesus.

The decision was made to split up, Timothy taking care of Ephesus and Paul returning to the churches in Macedonia to assist them.

TIMOTHY'S PRIMARY ASSIGNMENT IN EPHESUS.

We know from Paul's time in Athens in Acts 17 that *"the Athenians and the strangers visiting there used to spend their*

time in nothing other than telling or hearing something new"
(Acts 17:21). The Greek influence was strong across the region, including Asia Minor, where Ephesus was located. The Roman world had adopted the Greek Mythology religious system with its Parthenon of false gods. Temples for their gods covered the landscape. Conversations about religion and philosophy consumed much of the time.

Some in the church in Ephesus had slipped back into the cultural practices and teachers of these false religions. "Strange doctrines" had confused the Christians. There were also myths in some Rabbinical traditions that began consuming the conversations. Instead of talking about Christ and His redemption, the people became distracted and spent their time discussing useless Jewish false stories and Greek myths. Paul also warns about being preoccupied with "endless genealogies:"

> *"The Hebrews kept careful genealogical records, for this was necessary so that the distinction of their tribes might be kept up. Of course, in the lapse of centuries these tables would become very numerous, complicated, and extended - so that they might without much exaggeration be called 'endless.' The Jews attached great importance to them, and insisted on their being carefully preserved."* (Barnes Notes on the Bible)

Timothy's primary assignments were:

- Get the church back on track focusing on Christ.
- Turn away from the Jewish and Greek local myths; Christ alone is the truth.
- Love one another instead of arguing about useless things.
- Teachers had become false, ignorant teachers. They had neglected the Word of God and listened to wrong voices.
- Help the people to hold their leadership accountable and reject all these false paths they had taken.

Paul previously warned the Ephesians that a great danger was coming (Acts 20:28-30). He told them to be vigilant in his absence. The very thing he warned them about happened. Paul knew it would happen. In his first letter to Timothy, he prepared him because the Ephesian church would need to sort out the errors and become recommitted to Christ alone.

PRINCIPLES TO LIVE BY.

False teachings and empty discussions and speculations need to be handled carefully and quickly. These things are like cancer in the body. The longer you wait to treat it the more dangerous it becomes. Cancer has to be cut out of the body. False teaching requires radical, quick surgery. Like physical cancer, you can't leave any of it or it will regrow. The health of the physical body is at stake with untreated cancer. The health of the church is at stake with unanswered false teaching. Solid Biblical teaching is the treatment and the cure. False cults have been described as the unpaid bills of the church. If we don't answer false teachings, they will spread.

TIMOTHY WAS CHOSEN TO GUIDE THE PEOPLE BACK TO GODLY LIVING AND EDIFYING SPEECH.

Telling people to give up sin and live godly will change them it if your life is not an example of a dedicated Christian. The leaders in Ephesus had neglected the study of God's Word and had drifted into "fruitless discussion." They had become arrogant speaking with "confident assertions" about things they did not understand. As we have already seen, Timothy was genuine, unlike some of the teachers mentioned. Paul knew he was the kind of leader the Ephesian church needed. He was the godly man for the task. He lived it, not just talked about it.

"⁵ But the goal of our instruction is love from a pure heart and a good conscience and a sincere faith." (1 Timothy 1:5)

From what we know about Timothy he was a young man with a pure heart, a clear conscience, and his faith was rock solid. Paul was telling Timothy to instill these virtues in the Ephesian believers by showing them what a God-honoring Christian walk looked like. Ephesus needed to see the real thing. The people needed to see Jesus, not Zeus. Those who live God-honoring lives are like a refreshing breeze filling the house; false teachers are like a destructive storm ravaging everything they contact.

The way to silence false teachers is through the true, refreshing Word of God. That is the fragrance that will fill the house clearing out the stench of idolatry and the boredom of useless speech. Paul's message to Timothy and Ephesus was the same message he wrote to the church in Corinth:

> *¹⁵ For we are a fragrance of Christ to God among those who are being saved and among those who are perishing; ¹⁶ to the one an aroma from death to death, to the other an aroma from life to life. And who is adequate for these things? ¹⁷ For we are not like many, peddling the word of God, but as from sincerity, but as from God, we speak in Christ in the sight of God.* (2 Corinthians 2:15-17)

FALSE TEACHERS OFFER ONLY DIVISIONS AND MISERY.

The New Testament book of Jude gives illuminating descriptions about false teachers in the body of Christ:

- "¹² These are the ones who are hidden reefs in your love feasts when they feast with you without fear,
- like shepherds caring only for themselves;
- clouds without water, carried along by winds;
- autumn trees without fruit, doubly dead, uprooted;

- ^{13} wild waves of the sea, churning up their shameful deeds like dirty foam;
- wandering stars, for whom the gloom of darkness has been reserved forever.
- *These are grumblers, finding fault, following after their lusts*
- *they speak arrogantly, flattering people for the sake of gaining an advantage.*
- ^{19} *These are the ones who cause divisions,*
- *worldly-minded, devoid of the Spirit."*

  (Various descriptions are all taken from the book of Jude)

PRINCIPLES TO LIVE BY.

If we are not building up, it will break down. The problem with empty speech is that if we are not redeeming our time, we are wasting our time. You can't fill a glass with clean water to drink if it is filled with dirt. If our hearts are filled with pride, we will never carry water to one who is thirsty. Like Timothy, God is looking for pastors and leaders today who have pure hearts, not contaminated with the language and thinking of the lost world. We need a clear conscience, not even accusable of any offense. Our faith should be anchored to the rock of the Word of God, unshakable. We will never be the pastor God will use or the leader who attracts others to our Savior if we are not fully committed to Him. God is still seeking people like Timothy.

Let's be building what will last.

The Gospel, the Law, and the depraved conditions in the city of Ephesus. Standing for righteousness in a sinful world. (1:8-11)

⁸ But we know that the Law is good, if one uses it lawfully, ⁹ realizing the fact that law is not made for a righteous person, but for those who are lawless and rebellious, for the ungodly and sinners, for the unholy and profane, for those who kill their fathers or mothers, for murderers ¹⁰ and immoral men and homosexuals and kidnappers and liars and perjurers, and whatever else is contrary to sound teaching, ¹¹ according to the glorious gospel of the blessed God, with which I have been entrusted.

THE LAW WAS NOT UNDERSTOOD PROPERLY BY THE EPHESIANS.

Paul and Timothy were raised in different environments and towns but they had a common religious background. They were both Jewish, brought up to respect the Law of God and the teachings of Moses. The Law was given by God for a specific purpose but over the years the Law became neglected by the people. Priests became compromised during the split kingdoms after Solomon's reign. Idolatry became widespread; the Word of God was ignored. Prophets were raised by God to call the people back to Himself but their words were mostly rejected and many of them were killed by the disobedient nation. Israel became a lawless people abounding with social injustices.

The purpose of the moral Law that God gave man was to expose the sin of our hearts. It was a bright light illuminating our darkness. It was a mirror that revealed what we were really like on the inside. It was also a teacher that showed us the way back to God. The way back was faith. The Law was never given so we would follow it and that would make us fit for heaven. No one can keep it perfectly because we are sinful, broken people. We can never reform ourselves into good people. Only God can do that. The Law was given to expose our condition and drive us to God, Who alone can save us by faith.

Paul explained this to young Timothy when he said, *"we know that the Law is good if one uses it lawfully."* Use the Law the way it was meant to be used. Expose the sin of the people and lead them to the one who can save them. Jesus used it that way with the rich young ruler. Once the ruler understood what the Law meant he realized for the first time that he was lost (Mark 10:17-27).

Paul continued, *"⁹ realizing the fact that law is not made for a righteous person, but for those who are lawless and rebellious, for the ungodly and sinners, for the unholy and profane."* Jesus said the same thing, *"I have not come to call the righteous to repentance, but sinners"* (Luke 5:32). The problem is that no one is righteous in our natural state.

> *. . . for we have already charged that both Jews and Greeks are all under sin; 10 as it is written:*
> *"There is no righteous person, not even one;*
> *¹¹ There is no one who understands,*
> *There is no one who seeks out God;*
> *¹² They have all turned aside, together they have become corrupt;*
> *There is no one who does good,*
> *There is not even one.* (Romans 3:9-12)

The point of all this was to restore the message of the gospel to Ephesus. We are all sinners and the Law of God exposes that sin. We all fall short of the righteousness God demands. We need to see ourselves the way God sees us. We need to stop putting our trust in our works but in the finished work of Christ. That is using the Law lawfully, the way it was intended to be used.

The Law was a shadow of what was to come, the cross where Jesus died for the sins of the world.

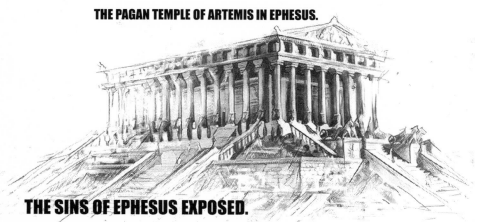

THE PAGAN TEMPLE OF ARTEMIS IN EPHESUS.

THE SINS OF EPHESUS EXPOSED.

Paul lists the sins of the people. They were well-known, evil practices found in the Roman Empire. The book of Romans provides an even more detailed list (Romans 1:18-32). Ephesus was one of the largest cities in the early Roman Empire. It was like Rome in many ways with its temple and immoral practices. Paul reminded Timothy of several of the abominations of Ephesus which influenced the Ephesian Church (1:9, 10):

- Lawlessness
- Rebellion
- Ungodliness
- Unholy and profane sinners
- Those who kill their fathers or mothers
- Immoral men
- Homosexuals
- Kidnappers
- Liars
- Perjurers
- Whatever else is contrary to sound teaching,

The small church at Ephesus was living in a powerful Roman city. Christians were persecuted, tortured, and killed. They had been labeled as enemies of the state since they did not bow the knee to Emperor Caesar. Christians spoke out against idolatry which caused the idol makers to riot in the city (see Acts 19 and 20). It is not necessary to explain all the sins listed by Paul in these verses but you can see that the pagan, immoral world of Ephesus was a constant temptation and pressure on the church. It was also a dangerous world where men lived for pleasure and life was cheap. Christians were a bright light in a very dark place that did not like having its sins exposed. Spiritual warfare was intense (Ephesians 6:10-19).

Timothy traveled with Paul and had been discipled by him. He had seen the evil of the Roman Empire first hand for years. Paul wrote two letters to his true son in the faith knowing that he had placed him in the heart of the beast. He knew Timothy would be the kind of Christian to stand strong and keep his heart pure. He had full confidence in his disciple.

PRINCIPLES TO LIVE BY.

Believers represent conviction and guilt to the lost, a message they don't want to hear. Satan has held captive the hearts of people for a long time. He hates Christians spoiling his plans. We are marked out as enemies of the kingdom of darkness. We will face strong opposition. If we don't, we aren't taking the Gospel to the lost. Mark deserted Paul. Demas deserted Paul. The call of the world was louder to these men than the call of God. Are we resolved to serve Christ no matter the cost? When a building catches fire, people run out to save their lives. Firemen run into a place of danger to rescue others. The world is on fire with sin, God needs a rescue squad to run into danger to rescue the perishing. Is that you?

Even in a sinful world, no one is beyond saving. Paul shares his testimony of the grace and mercy of God shown to him. (1:12-17)

¹² I thank Christ Jesus our Lord, who has strengthened me, because He considered me faithful, putting me into service, ¹³ even though I was formerly a blasphemer and a persecutor and a violent aggressor. Yet I was shown mercy because I acted ignorantly in unbelief; ¹⁴ and the grace of our Lord was more than abundant, with the faith and love which are found in Christ Jesus. ¹⁵ It is a trustworthy statement, deserving full acceptance, that Christ Jesus came into the world to save sinners, among whom I am foremost of all. ¹⁶ Yet for this reason I found mercy, so that in me as the foremost, Jesus Christ might demonstrate His perfect patience as an example for those who would believe in Him for eternal life. ¹⁷ Now to the King eternal, immortal, invisible, the only God, be honor and glory forever and ever. Amen.

PAUL PRESENTS HIS LIFE AS PROOF OF THE INDESCRIBABLE MERCY OF GOD.

After reading the list of sins in the previous verses, it would be natural to wonder if there is any hope for people who lived in depravity. Paul anticipated that response and addressed it. He used his experience of redemption as the primary example to teach that no one is beyond the reach of God.

Paul describes himself as the chief of sinners. He grew up in a conservative religious home, the son of a Pharisee. He knew the holy Scriptures since he was a child and he later became a Pharisee and a member of the northern Sanhedrin, a Jewish ruling council. He became an enforcer for the greater Sanhedrin in Jerusalem, given the task of eradicating the followers of Jesus. Paul was a prideful man and ruthless in his pursuit of making a name for himself. He was responsible for the stoning of Stephen, one of God's shining lights. Paul would have heard the convicting words of Stephen's powerful defense of Christ and condemnation of hypocritical Jewish self-righteousness. As Paul said it, he *"was formerly a blasphemer and a persecutor and a violent aggressor."* When God knocked him off his horse and flooded his lost soul with light, he became aware that all the evil he had done was ultimately against the spotless Lamb of God, the Messiah. He had the blood of God on his hands.

In that state, God showed mercy and grace to Saul of Tarsus and made him Paul the Apostle. In every letter he wrote he always referred to the grace, mercy, and peace of God. Paul was changed from a merciless blasphemer to an adopted child of God and joint-heir of the riches of Christ. His point to young Timothy was if God could do that for such a sinner, then no man is beyond the reach of God, even the pagan, depraved Romans. It was, after all, the very reason Christ came into the world, to seek and save the lost.

> [15] *It is a trustworthy statement, deserving full acceptance, that Christ Jesus came into the world to save sinners, among whom I am foremost of all.* [16] *Yet for this reason I found mercy, so that in me as the foremost, Jesus Christ might demonstrate His perfect patience as an example for those who would believe in Him for eternal life.*
> (1 Timothy 1:15, 16)

PAUL OFFERED ALL PRAISE TO GOD WHO ACCOMPLISHED ALL THESE THINGS.

Paul praised God with a doxology.

*¹⁷ Now to the King eternal, immortal, invisible, the only God,
be honor and glory forever and ever. Amen.*
(1 Timothy 1:17)

Paul gave all glory to the King of the ages. Only the true God of the Bible is eternal. He alone is the immortal One. There is no God other than God. All glory is for Him forever and forever. What wisdom and grace are found in the incarnation, God the Son who *"came into the world to save sinners"* has put on full display the invisible One. The mystery is so deep and wonderful that when the Gospel of John seeks words to describe the incarnation, we still find ourselves straining to understand it:

¹⁸ No one has seen God at any time; God the only Son, who is in the arms of the Father, He has explained Him. (John 1:18)

THE DOXOLOGY.

"King Eternal." It literally means the "King of the ages." God is infinite, having no beginning or ending—He exists outside of time.

"Immortal." It means God is perfect, everlasting without change, or wearing down. He is outside of and untouched by the corruption found in the physical creation. He is the same yesterday, today, and forever.

"Invisible." God told Moses, *"You cannot see My face, for man may not see Me and live"* (Exodus 33:20). In our present condition, we cannot see or experience God in His glory. Just as we cannot stare at the sun without destroying our eyes, so we cannot experience God in His fullness in our fallen state. We would be consumed. His glory is a billion-trillion times brighter than the sun. The incarnation of Jesus made the invisible God visible. He is *"the image of the invisible God, the firstborn of all creation"* (Colossians 1:15).

⁸ Philip said to Him, "Lord, show us the Father, and it is enough for us." ⁹ Jesus *said to him, "Have I been so long with you, and yet you have not come to know Me, Philip? He who has seen Me has seen the Father; how can you say, 'Show us the Father'? (John 14:8-9)

One day the veil will be lifted and we will see Him. John wrote, *"Beloved, now we are children of God, and it has not appeared as yet what we will be. We know that when He appears, we will be like Him, because we will see Him just as He is."* (1 John 3:2).

"Honor and glory." Only God is worthy of our highest praise. No pagan deity can compare to our great God.

"Forever and ever." It literally means, "into the ages of the ages." Our eternal God will receive eternal praise.

"Amen." It means "I agree; may it be so." We cannot understand everything about God but we can praise Him, giving Him the honor and glory He deserves.

THE SECOND DOXOLOGY IN 1 TIMOTHY, CHAPTER 6:15,16.

¹⁴ that you keep the commandment without fault or reproach until the appearing of our Lord Jesus Christ, ¹⁵ which He will bring about at the proper time—He who is the blessed and only Sovereign, the King of kings and Lord of lords, 16 who alone possesses immortality and dwells in unapproachable light, whom no one has seen or can see. To Him be honor and eternal dominion! Amen.
(1 Timothy 6:15, 16)

The encouragement of all this to Timothy was that our great God can save the vilest sinner. The greatest of all proof is that the eternal, infinite God the Son took on flesh to bear all of humanity's sins. He exhausted the wrath of God in our place. In essence, Paul is saying to young Timothy, "Go preach the gospel to even the worst of sinners in Ephesus because God can save any He chooses. Fear not, Timothy, the all-powerful, one and only God is with you."

Paul's charge to young timothy to press on in the fight. The opposition is great. (1:18-20)

[18] This command I entrust to you, Timothy, *my* son, in accordance with the prophecies previously made concerning you, that by them you fight the good fight, [19] keeping faith and a good conscience, which some have rejected and suffered shipwreck in regard to their faith. [20] Among these are Hymenaeus and Alexander, whom I have handed over to Satan, so that they will be taught not to blaspheme.

Paul reminded Timothy that there were prophecies made concerning him.

> *"Apparently, God had spoken to Timothy through others through the gift of prophecy and the words were an encouragement for Timothy to stay strong in the difficulty right in front of him. It may have been a description of Timothy's future ministry; it may have been a warning against being timid in his work for God. Whatever it was, God wanted Timothy to draw strength from it in his present difficulty."*
> (David Guzik, The Blue Letter Bible)

The Port of Ephesus was one of the greatest seaports of the ancient world. It helped make the city a hub of commerce for its 250,000 residents. It was a gateway into Asia Minor.

Because of the dangerous rocky coastline, the region was known for shipwrecks. The book of Acts describes the type of storms that pounded the seashore and the damage ships endured. Paul was shipwrecked in the same treacherous waters (Acts 27). He would later use the imagery of a shipwreck when describing those who gave up on their walk with God *"and suffered shipwreck in regard to their faith"* (1 Timothy 1:19).

Paul names two who turned away from God and cursed Him — Hymenaeus and Alexander. These two were known to Timothy even though today we know nothing about them. There is a good lesson here for all of us. These men had heard the gospel and were numbered with the believers in Ephesus, but the cares and temptations of the world lured them away from God. Their lives ended up shipwrecked on the spiritual rocks. They have their names forever etched in the Lamb's book of shame. They were the seed that grew at first, but the thorns choked them out. Finishing well is the the valuable lesson God wants us to learn.

Paul treated them the same way he told the Corinthians to handle a problem of immorality in the church:

> *¹ It is actually reported that there is immorality among you, and immorality of such a kind as does not exist even among the Gentiles, that someone has his father's wife. ² You have become arrogant and have not mourned instead, so that the one who had done this deed would be removed from your midst.*
> *³ For I, on my part, though absent in body but present in spirit, have already judged him who has so committed this, as though I were present. ⁴ In the name of our Lord Jesus, when you are assembled, and I with you in spirit, with the power of our Lord Jesus, ⁵ I have decided to deliver such a one to Satan for the destruction of his flesh, so that his spirit may be saved in the day of the Lord Jesus.*
> (1 Corinthians 5:1-5)

Paul in both cases was telling the church to remove the

offenders and let them come out from under the God-given protection of the church. They would be alone in a heartless world with no support system to face Satan. The hope was it would drive them back to their God as it did the Corinthian offender.

Paul uses these two as examples of casualties of the spiritual war all believers face. Just like the sower parable Jesus gave. Just as there are different types of soil, so there are different types of hearts. Some respond and grow and others fall away for different reasons. Paul encourages Timothy to keep his eyes on the goal of finishing the course well with a good fight, a strong faith, and a clear conscience.

PRINCIPLES TO LIVE BY.

We must not live our lives based on what others do, but according to the Word of God. Timothy was called to minister in a spiritual war zone. Some soldiers in a time of war become deserters. Others were severely wounded but fought on to become heroes. We are all engaged in that great war for the souls of men who have been captured by an enemy. We have received our commission to rescue those captives. It is a dangerous and difficult assignment. What kind of soldiers will we be?

1 Timothy 2

How to pray for the lost and the ones in authority. (2:1-7)

¹ First of all, then, I urge that entreaties *and* prayers, petitions *and* thanksgivings, be made on behalf of all men, ² for kings and all who are in authority, so that we may lead a tranquil and quiet life in all godliness and dignity. ³ This is good and acceptable in the sight of God our Savior, ⁴ who desires all men to be saved and to come to the knowledge of the truth. ⁵ For there is one God, *and* one mediator also between God and men, *the* man Christ Jesus, ⁶ who gave Himself as a ransom for all, the testimony *given* at the proper time. ⁷ For this I was appointed a preacher and an apostle (I am telling the truth, I am not lying) as a teacher of the Gentiles in faith and truth.

THE PASTOR, A MAN OF PEACE, AND HIS PRAYERS. (2:1-4)

Paul gave the church at Rome instructions on how the believers should try to keep peace with their Roman neighbors and leaders:

> ¹⁸ *If possible, so far as it depends on you, be at peace with all people.* (Romans 12:18)

Ephesus had the same government, culture, idolatries, and temples as Rome. Paul knew there was great hostility to the gospel and it was not wise to willfully antagonize the people. The more we can maintain peace with our neighbors, the greater the opportunities to influence them for Christ. Paul told Timothy to be in prayer for all those in authority, to not only seek their salvation, but also *"so that we may lead a tranquil and quiet life in all godliness and dignity. ³ This is good and acceptable in the sight of God our Savior"* (2:2).

45

Whether one is a pastor or a church planter, we will have a greater influence if we are men and women of peace. Jesus said, *"9 Blessed are the peacemakers, for they will be called sons of God"* (Matthew 5:9). Paul used the word "peace" in the greetings of his letters. The believers needed to enjoy what little peace they could get because the Roman Empire would soon declare them an illegal religion.

The primary prayer we pray for the lost, even those who persecute us, is for their salvation. Paul has already shown that no one is out of the reach of God. It is hard to explain that God desires all men to be saved when we know that all will not be saved. We have to conclude that the door is open to all, however each man must ultimately take responsibility for his decision to accept or reject Christ. They will never be able to say it was God's fault. The next verses tell what God has done to purchase salvation for all who would call on Him in faith.

JESUS FULLY MAN, FULLY GOD. (2:5-7)

The Greeks and Romans trusted in their wisdom and pagan sacrifices. They built numerous temples to their deaf and dumb deities. They had numerous paths to hopefully find favor with their gods. We have a very different message and hope:

> *⁵ For there is one God, and one mediator also between God and men, the man Christ Jesus, ⁶ who gave Himself as a ransom for all, the testimony given at the proper time. (2:5,6)*

There are not many gods nor priests to these gods as the Romans believed. There is one God Almighty and only one Great High Priest, the final Mediator between God and sinful man. Jesus said, "I am the way, and the truth, and the life; no one comes to the Father except through Me" (John 14:6). Jesus is not just our

Mediator, our bridge to a right relationship with the Father, but He is also the One who paid the ransom for our sins with His blood. Zeus, Mercury, and the others never did that. They were only fables of man.

The many false religions of man today are no different than the false beliefs of the Romans. Hinduism is based on human efforts to attain peace with the universe. The Buddhists live in monasteries and spin prayer wheels hoping their good efforts will outweigh their bad ones. False cults abound today which have some kind of human effort or good works required that they hope will swing the balance on judgment day and get them into Heaven. All of them are wrong. No man is saved by what we do. We can only be saved by what was done when He took our sin in His own body on the cros. He paid the price to redeem us, buy us back from the slave market of sin. He did all this by becoming a man. God became flesh and dwelt among us (John 1:14).

Today, we still have *"one mediator also between God and men, the man Christ Jesus."* The word "man" in this verse refers to not only Christ's incarnation, but reveals an immense thought. Paul is writing these things to Timothy after the resurrection of Christ. He ascended to the Father in His resurrected body. An angel present at Christ's ascension told the disciples that the "same Jesus" they saw ascend would one day return as they had seen Him ascend. We know the resurrected Jesus told Thomas to touch His nail holes which were in His resurrected body. They were the love wounds of His finished sacrifice. The blood had stopped flowing, the work was complete. But the scars remained and will forever.

In the book of Revelation, John sees a heavenly scene and, on the throne, next to the Father, is the Lamb as He had been slaughtered.

"¹ I saw in the right hand of Him who sat on the throne a scroll written inside and on the back, sealed up with seven seals. ² And I saw a strong angel proclaiming with a loud voice, "Who is worthy to open the scroll and to break its seals?" ³ And no one in heaven or on the earth or under the earth was able to open the scroll or to look into it. ⁴ Then I began to weep greatly because no one was found worthy to open the scroll or to look into it. ⁵ And one of the elders said to me, "Stop weeping; behold, the Lion that is from the tribe of Judah, the Root of David, has overcome so as to be able to open the scroll and its seven seals."
⁶ And I saw between the throne (with the four living creatures) and the elders a Lamb standing, as if slaughtered, having seven horns and seven eyes, which are the seven spirits of God sent out into all the earth. ⁷ And He came and took the scroll out of the right hand of Him who sat on the throne. ⁸ When He had taken the scroll, the four living
creatures and the twenty-four elders fell down before the Lamb, each one holding a harp and golden bowls full of incense, which are the prayers of the saints. ⁹ And they sang a new song, saying,
Worthy are You to take the scroll and to break its seals; for You were slaughtered, and You purchased people for God with Your blood from every tribe, language, people, and nation.
¹⁰ You have made them into a kingdom and priests to our God, and they will reign upon the earth."
(Revelation 5:1-10)

Someone once asked if there is anything manmade in Heaven. Yes, there is, the nail holes in our Savior's resurrected body! The wonderful truth for us is that Jesus was and still is truly God and truly man. "His humanity is glorified and resurrected. It is the pattern of the humanity that we will experience in heaven"(Blue Letter Bible).

⁵ For there is one God, and one mediator also between God and men, the man Christ Jesus, ⁶ who gave Himself as a

ransom for all, the testimony given at the proper time.
This is the message Paul was appointed to preach to
the Gentiles (2:7).

*[7] For this I was appointed a preacher and an apostle (I am
telling the truth, I am not lying) as a teacher of the Gentiles
in faith and truth.* (2:7)

*[1] And when I came to you, brothers and sisters, I did not
come as someone superior in speaking ability or wisdom,
as I proclaimed to you the testimony of God. [2] For I
determined to know nothing among you except Jesus
Christ, and Him crucified.* (1 Corinthians 2;1, 2)

Lifting up holy hands. (2: 8)

8 Therefore I want the men in every place to pray, lifting up
holy hands, without wrath and dissension. (2:8)

This is a further exhortation to pray. Paul just told Timothy to
pray for leaders that they would find eternal life. He
reminded his disciple about the great cost of the incarnation
and the redemption Christ purchased on the cross. He now
returns to the role Christians have in any society, even
repressive ones. We should pray for those in authority. The
point of this instruction seems to be the attitude of the one
praying. Whether in the first century or our times today,
Christians are not to pray with wrath in their hearts or
dissension. These words mean we are never to pray with anger
or vindictiveness in our hearts. Prayer is not a time to get even
with mistreatment or to call down judgment on our enemies,
but a time to intercede for those who treat us with contempt.
This is what he means when Paul says not to pray in wrath.

The word translated as "dissension" means to doubt or lack
faith. Believers should always pray in faith, not doubting God.

These two words indicate that an attitude of hostility along with a lack of faith had grown in the Ephesian church. When they lifted their hands to pray, it was for the wrong reasons. The lifting of hands is but one posture to pray which must have been common. The passage is not telling people to lift their hands when they pray, but it is saying when they lift their hands to make sure they are "holy" hands. It doesn't matter what posture a person uses in prayer but it does matter what attitude we have when communicating with our holy God. It also seems that the use of the word "men" who lift their hands indicates that public prayer in the first century was done by men.

The godly woman in an ungodly world. (2:9-10)

9 Likewise, *I want* women to adorn themselves with proper clothing, modestly and discreetly, not with braided hair and gold or pearls or costly garments, 10 but rather by means of good works, as is proper for women making a claim to godliness. 11 A woman must quietly receive instruction with entire submissiveness. 12 But I do not allow a woman to teach or exercise authority over a man, but to remain quiet. 13 For it was Adam who was first created, *and* then Eve. 14 And *it was* not Adam *who* was deceived, but the woman being deceived, fell into transgression. 15 But *women* will be preserved through the bearing of children if they continue in faith and love and sanctity with self-restraint.

THE MANNER AND GRACE OF A GODLY WOMAN. (2:9, 10)

Today we live in a world where the lines between men and women are blurred. There is even a growing movement to remove the lines altogether between the two genders clearly established by God. In the first century, the lines were clear and the roles of men and women were more clearly understood than in our society today. Paul knew that the temple prostitutes of Ephesus were not the perfect model of a woman. Christian women were not to look and act like the fallen world. That is the basis of his first comments, how a godly woman should look and act to set her apart from the cultural norms of a fallen society.

> *9 Likewise, I want women to adorn themselves with proper clothing, modestly and discreetly, not with braided hair and gold or pearls or costly garments, 10 but rather by means of good works, as is proper for women making a claim to godliness.* (2:9, 10)

By beginning with the word "likewise," Paul is continuing his presentation of a Christian's attitude and practices. He finished with men holding up holy hands. Now, "*likewise*," the women have roles and attitudes as well that honor God. The first thing he mentions is how a godly woman dresses and acts. Remember, the contrast in Ephesian society is the widespread, public practice of temple prostitution. Also, the wives of Roman leadership and military were esteemed and a wealthier class than the lower class of everyday citizens. Christians were in the lower class, not the wealthy ruling class. Even certain colors were designated for the upper class. The royal purple garments which Lydia sold were only used for the elite. She had a very successful business supplying the Roman elite with the exclusive purple fabrics (Acts 16:14, 40, 17:1).

> *A woman named Lydia, from the city of Thyatira, a seller of purple fabrics, a worshiper of God, was listening; and the Lord opened her heart to respond to the things spoken by Paul.* (Acts 16:14)

Paul, who had a great love and respect for godly Christian women, wanted to make sure the world system did not conform them into its patterns. Even today the principle remains. We are in the world, but not to become like the world.

NOTE: *Before we look at Paul's counsel to Timothy about women, it is important to note that some characterize Paul as one who hated women, a male chauvinist, who thought men were superior to women. This is a completely false view of Paul. He had a band of godly women who supported him. He gave the manuscript of Romans to an amazing woman he knew and respected in Cenchrea, the seaport of Corinth. That woman was the first one named in the greetings in Romans 16. Her name was Phoebe. She was a patron of the Christian movement. She supported Paul and others by her successful business. She was also the deaconess, the leader of a house church. She is one of ten women Paul addressed in Romans 16. In that chapter he listed 30 special people in his life and ten were women. No, Paul did not hate women. He knew they had a vital role in the growth of the church.*

Paul began with the principle that a godly woman emphasizes spiritual attributes above physical beauty. It is apparent, when reading verses 9 and 10, that the Roman culture in the first century placed importance on how people dressed. The people understood that certain styles of clothing and personal adornment indicated a person of low morals. The temple prostitutes dressed for their work just a soldier dressed for his work or a stone mason dressed for his occupation. The wives of rich military generals and political leaders also had their style of dress. They displayed their wealth and position. Paul reminded the ladies of the Christian fellowship that they should choose to dress with modesty and be discreet.

The particular items he mentions were the adornment of braided hair, displaying gold, pearls, and wearing expensive garments. In that time these were ways the women displayed their wealth or status. The women of the temples were alluring and immodest. It is no different today. Maybe the types of clothing, or particular styles have changed, but the heart condition has not. People dress to be seen or noticed. Paul was communicating that a discreet woman is trying to not draw attention to herself. A married woman should not be a distraction to other men. The appeal of Paul is for the women to display godliness, not worldliness. That is the big picture, the great principle. It is not a law about pearls, gold, or braided hair. It is about anything that gets in the way of a woman being single-minded about God. Styles change but a lady should always seek to dress appropriately for the occasion, not over-dressed or under-dressed. It is all a reflection of the heart.

People that live for the world system, dress for the occasion. Christians should focus on inward beauty.

The role of women in the church. (2:11-15)

[11] A woman must quietly receive instruction with entire submissiveness. [12] But I do not allow a woman to teach or exercise authority over a man, but to remain quiet. [13] For it was Adam who was first created, *and* then Eve. [14] And *it was* not Adam *who* was deceived, but the woman being deceived, fell into transgression. [15] But *women* will be preserved through the bearing of children if they continue in faith and love and sanctity with self-restraint.

THE CULTURE AND THE CONTROVERSY.

Women who would claim to be godly are exhorted to display good works as evidence. Verse 11 reveals how the attitude of the godly woman will result in a submissive spirit within the Church.

The role of women in the Church is a controversial topic with several conflicting viewpoints in the body of Christ. It is like getting directions to a location. One says the road is closed. Another says there is one road and it is very narrow, never leave it. Another says he gets lost every time so he never goes there.

The context of history and the Old Testament is the background for this section of Timothy. Men usually were the dominant leaders in both the Old Testament and New Testament. Men were numbered and mentioned in lists with little mention of women or children. Empires had dominant and powerful kings, like Assyria, Babylon, Greece, and Rome.

There were also Queens that had great importance as well. Judges in the Old Testament were normally men but Deborah was a judge. Queens sometimes were the dominant leader like the Queen of Sheba. They held important positions in the nation like Cleopatra in Egypt. God called men in the New Testament to become deacons (*diakonos*). The same Greek word is used for Phoebe in her leadership of a house church in Cenchrea. Sometimes a husband-and-wife team equally shared ministry like Priscilla and Aquila. Priscilla seemed to be most dominant.

The general conclusion from observation of history and Scripture is that both men and women held leadership roles in government. Men primarily dominated the landscape in the leadership roles in the church, especially the pastorate. In modern society, you find a larger number of women taking the top leadership roles in certain denominations. Cultures for the most part were male-dominated.

The history of the church can help us see how certain periods interpreted the Biblical passages but in the end, the most important thing is to look at the passages ourselves and analyze what the texts tell us. Let's do that with how Paul instructed Timothy concerning the role of women in the church.

THE ISSUES OF SUBMISSION AND AUTHORITY. (2:11)

New American Standard translation of verse 11

11 A woman must quietly receive instruction with entire submissiveness. 12 But I do not allow a woman to teach or exercise authority over a man, but to remain quiet. (NASB)

King James Bible translation of verse 11

11Let the woman learn in silence with all subjection. 12 But I suffer not a woman to teach, nor to usurp authority over the man, but to be in silence. (KJV)

The first issue is the matter of submission and the second is authority. In these two translations, we find two different perspectives on the concept of submission.

The King James Version tells women to be silent and subjective to men. The NASB tells women to receive instruction quietly with a submissive spirit to men in the church. Historically, the command that women remain silent is not supported in New Testament practice. In 1 Corinthians 11:1-16, Paul gives extensive instructions how men and women are to pray in the churches. Phoebe, a deacon, was the head of a church in her home. A deacon had to be able to teach. There is no hint that women were to be silent. There is an issue of headship and authority that will be addressed next. The matter of complete silence is not supported. The NASB translation is far better when it says *"A woman must quietly receive instruction with entire submissiveness."* The Greek word means the woman should not be contentious (combative, argumentative, quarrelsome) but respectful of her husband and those in authority.

Some historians feel that this was the reason in early house churches, that women did not sit with the men. This is still a practice in some denominations and cultures today. A woman would be disruptive of the service if she was argumentative and might be an embarrassment to her husband publicly. She was to learn quietly to respect the existing authority structure. She would discuss her views privately later.

WHAT DOES SUBMISSION MEAN?

The word submission indicates a person is under a rank. There is someone higher in authority. This is common every day in all we do. We work for a company and have bosses and directors over us. Governments are organized with different ranks and responsibilities. Schools have students, teachers, administrators. Without authority, the world would be in chaos. The military would be useless without authority structures and rankings. Submission is the acknowledgment that we are under another's rank or position. We are all under Christ, we are all submissive to Him as our authority. In this aspect men and women are all equal.

The submission has nothing to do with ability or personal importance. It is our position within the group, organization, and even marriage. We are all equally important to God. A submissive spirit validates the godly heart of the woman. She does not depend on clothing or physical adornment *"[10] but rather by means of good works, as is proper for women making a claim to godliness."*

AUTHORITY WITHIN THE CHURCH AND MARRIAGE. (2: 12-14)

> *[12] But I do not allow a woman to teach or exercise authority over a man, but to remain quiet. [13] For it was Adam who was first created, and then Eve. [14] And it was not Adam who was deceived, but the woman being deceived, fell into transgression.*

We need to begin with the meaning of the word that has caused some confusion in verse 12. It is the word translated "exercise" or "usurp" depending on the translation you use. The Greek word is αὐθεντέω (authentéō). Here is what a trusted Greek scholar has given us in Strong's Concordance:

αὐθεντέω (authentéō)

NEW TESTAMENT USAGE

- One who with his own hands kills another or himself .
- One who acts on his authority, autocratic.
- One who is an absolute master.
- One who governs, exercises dominion over another.

Paul is saying, "*12 But I do not allow a woman to teach*" with the attitude of taking or seizing control over a man to be his master. The Greek word reveals an attitude that Paul is warning against, one of grabbing power. The word "usurp" used in some versions is closer to the true meaning. The word "commandeer" or "take over" is also pictured in the word. It is a destructive attitude actually for either men or women, but Paul is directly talking to the ladies at this point. He will deal with the men later.

In 1 Corinthians 12, Paul discusses the head covering as a picture of submission. Women could pray and prophecy in the fellowship, but only if they had a head covering which was the way the woman acknowledged she was under submission to the leadership of the church. In Ephesians 5, Paul gives a similar instruction concerning submission within the marriage relationship:

> *22 Wives, be subject to your own husbands, as to the Lord.*
> *23 For the husband is the head of the wife, as Christ also is the head of the church, He Himself being the Savior of the body. 24 But as the church is subject to Christ, so also the*

wives ought to be to their husbands in everything.
(Ephesians 5:22-24)

When Jesus walked the earth, He was in submission to the will of the Father. Does this mean the Son was less important? Of course not! God has placed an order to everything in the universe. The commands of Scripture in regards to submission are concerning the church and the home. It is not given to society in general or the corporate world. It is only for the operations of the church and the Christian home. A husband may have a wife with strong administrative skills and in a leadership role in a business. But she should still maintain her submissive spirit and respect for the church and her husband's spiritual headship in the home.

Now, let us look at the reason given for this in verses 13 and 14.

THE CREATED ORDER AND THE FALL OF MAN. (2:13, 14)

13 For it was Adam who was first created, and then Eve.
14 And it was not Adam who was deceived, but the woman being deceived, fell into transgression.

The created order is listed and the reason. Adam was created first and then the woman. The woman was made for man since there was no companion for the man on earth suitable for him. The woman was made for the man, not the man for the woman. This is simply the stated purpose and order.

Both the man and the woman share responsibility for the fall. But the order is again mentioned. The woman was deceived by Satan and then later the man listened to the woman and disobeyed God.

The first reason given was that the man was created first. The second reason was that the woman was deceived. Adam received the commands directly from God. The woman, after she was formed from man, got her instructions from the man. There was order in the arrangement.

Eve sinned first, then the man. The man was the spiritual head and so assumed greater responsibility for the act. Adam is ultimately given the blame for the fall:

> *12 Therefore, just as through one man sin entered into the world, and death through sin, and so death spread to all men, because all sinned— 13 for until the Law sin was in the world, but sin is not imputed when there is no law. 14 Nevertheless death reigned from Adam until Moses, even over those who had not sinned in the likeness of the offense of Adam, who is a type of Him who was to come. (Romans 5:12-14)*

The fall is described as the result of Adam's sin. It is true that both share some responsibility because Adam's name means "mankind," the entire human race at that time. Mankind fell in the garden, All of the rest of mankind to come came from the original fallen "Adam" or mankind. We are all born in the likeness of the fallen Adam.

Eve was deceived or fooled. Adam entered into sin with full knowledge. The issue is that the woman, by being deceived, could pass on the deception. This makes her a less trustworthy candidate for spiritual authority.

The curse by God on all creation emphasized this headship arrangement:

> *16 To the woman He said,*
> *"I will greatly multiply*
> *Your pain in childbirth,*
> *In pain you will bring forth children;*
> *Yet your desire will be for your husband,*
> *And he will rule over you.* (Genesis 3:16)

THE CHRISTIAN WOMAN AND THE CURSE. (2:15)

This final verse of 1 Timothy Chapter 2 is considered by some as the most confusing verse in the Bible. At first reading, it seems to be an odd statement, in contradiction to what we know about salvation. We believe salvation is by faith. Some believe salvation is depending on works. But no one believes salvation is based on childbirth? Let's read the text:

> *15 Notwithstanding she shall be saved in childbearing, if they continue in faith and charity and holiness with sobriety.* (1 Timothy 2:15, KJV)

That was in the King James Version of the Bible (1611 A.D.). It was the only translation most people ever read until the 20th century. The word "saved" in English can mean several different things. It could refer to salvation. It could refer to putting something aside to keep it for later, like saving money in the bank. The dictionary gives several meanings for the English word. It uses words like protected, kept, hoarded, kept back, and set aside.

The important question is "What is the Greek word that the translators used?" Here is how the Greek concordance describes the Biblical usage of the word:

> *σώζω sốzō, sode'-zo; from a primary σῶς sōs (contraction for obsolete σάος sáos, "safe"); to save, i.e. deliver or protect (literally or figuratively):—heal, preserve, save (self), do well, be (make) whole.* (Strong's Concordance)

You can see that the primary usage is to deliver, protect and preserve. That is why modern translations rightfully translate the verse as follows:

> *15 But women will be preserved through the bearing of children if they continue in faith and love and sanctity with self-restraint.* (1 Timothy 2:15, NASB)

If we save something, we are not throwing it away, but hanging on to it, or keeping it, or preserving it. If you save money to buy something, you are keeping it for a future purpose. What Paul is telling us is that even though the woman was deceived and was cursed with pain in childbirth, God still showed grace to the woman by preserving her future generations and ultimately to be the channel of bringing the Savior into the world.

THERE IS A GREAT HOPE FOR WOMEN IN VERSE 15.

This is a very hopeful verse. We read in the previous verses describing the reason for the headship of the husband in the home and the spiritual headship of the male church leaders was because of the curse and the fall of mankind. Both men and women are equal in God's eyes, but there is a created order much like the military that has ranks. This does not indicate anyone is inferior, just in submission to others in a higher rank. Jesus Himself submitted to the Father's will, not His own.

Women being more prone to deception were placed under submission to their husbands. The greater responsibility lies with the husbands to fulfill their spiritual leadership in the home and in the church. So, what about the woman? is there any specific hope found in this text? Yes, there is wonderful hope.

After the fall of mankind, God cursed the serpent. Then the woman was told that her children would be brought forth in pain. But immediately after that, we have the very first promise of the Gospel, the hope of salvation and it will come through a child yet to be born.

> *14 Then the Lord God said to the serpent,*
> *"Because you have done this,*
> *Cursed are you more than all the livestock,*

And more than any animal of the field;
On your belly you shall go,
And dust you shall eat
All the days of your life;
¹⁵ And I will make enemies
Of you and the woman,
And of your offspring and her Descendant;
He shall bruise you on the head,
And you shall bruise Him on the heel. (Genesis 3:14, 15)

The curse on the serpent also contained a promise that the woman and the serpent would be at odds, or at war with each other. There would be strife between them until one day a woman would give birth to One who would crush the serpent. This One is simply referred to in verse 15 as her descendent, her offspring. The promise was that child would one day crush the head of the serpent, our enemy.

The curse on the woman was hard:

¹⁶ To the woman He said,
"I will greatly multiply
Your pain in childbirth,
In pain you shall deliver children;
Yet your desire will be for your husband,
And he shall rule over you." (Genesis 3:16)

Even though God decreed a curse on the woman, God also gave her an amazing promise and hope. The woman would be the source of the birth of the Savior of the world. It is this background that leads us to 1 Timothy 2:15. A very important definite article is used before the word "childbirth." It is saying is women will be preserved by "the childbirth." It is not just referring to having children, but it is a promise of a specific childbirth, the same childbirth we read in Genesis 3:15. Even after all the curses God gave the serpent, the woman, the man, and the earth, He still promised hope in the end. One day the Son of God would be born of a woman and crush the head of

Satan, deal a fatal wound. That would happen at the cross and resurrection. Paul is telling all Godly women that their role of submission is part of that great plan of God and will ultimately lead to the preserving of the Godly race. Redeemed from the curse and restored to a full, right relationship with our Creator on a new earth. And the very tree of life mankind lost in the garden will once again be on the earth.

God has given the woman an amazing role in the plan of Salvation

> *"Probably, the idea here is that even though the "woman race" did something bad in the garden by being deceived and falling into transgression, the "woman race" also did something far greater, in being used by God to bring the saving Messiah into the world. The summary is this: Don't blame women for the fall of the human race; the Bible doesn't. Instead, thank women for bringing the Messiah to us. Faith, love, and holiness, with self-control: Most of all, we should note these positives. They are all qualities God wants to be evident in women, and that women have effectively nurtured in their children through generations."* (Blue Letter Bible commentary)

There are times when we feel like the sun will not shine again. Just as Paul encouraged godly women, even when describing what could have been a discouraging subject, so we must never lose hope. When it seems like we are trapped in a circumstance, God is always seeing, always knowing, and always working for our best. Even the trials God sent to the Apostle Paul had an eternal purpose for him and the body of Christ. The curse and pain in childbirth which seemed like non-ending suffering had a great end in sight. Only God can turn ashes into beauty and suffering into joy. When Israel was unfaithful to God, God never forgot His people:

¹¹ For I know the plans that I have for you,' declares the Lord, 'plans for prosperity and not for disaster, to give you a future and a hope. (Jeremiah 29:11)

SUMMARY OF THE ROLE OF WOMEN IN THE CHURCH.

The Apostle Paul had great respect for godly women. From the beginning of creation, God intended women to be companions with men, one flesh, in life and ministry. In Christ there is no male or female, all are equal in the eyes of God. At the same time, the Bible is clear that the roles of men and women are not the same. Just as a military force has different ranks or orders, so the roles of men and women in the home and the church are different, prescribed by God.

Paul reminds us that the created order was the man was formed first and then the woman was formed for man. God instructed the man not to eat from *"tree of the knowledge of good and evil"* (Genesis 2:17). This was before the woman was created. The man later passed on the words of God to the woman. The woman was deceived by the serpent and then she enticed the man to disobey God. Both sinned, but there was a difference. The woman was fooled, the man decided to willfully go against God. Because the man listened to the woman instead of God, the responsibility for the fall was charged against the man:

¹² Therefore, just as through one man sin entered into the world, and death through sin, and so death spread to all men, because all sinned. (Romans 5:12)

God then cursed the serpent and promised that one day a man would come, born of a woman, who would crush the serpent's head (Genesis 3:15). Then God cursed the woman for her weakness in listening to the evil one. She was assigned under the rank of the man in spiritual authority from then on. All children that would be born would be birthed in great pain. Her submission to the man is not a statement of inferiority, but an agreement with the assigned ranking of God. Paul then reminded both men and women in the church that the promise made in Genesis 3 was fulfilled in Christ. *"⁴ But when the fullness of the time came, God sent His Son, born of a woman, born under the Law"* (Galatians 4:4). The first woman was the first to sin and later a woman would be the one who brought the Saviour into the world. Godly women would be preserved because of that birth. What began in sin and shame was turned to salvation and hope.

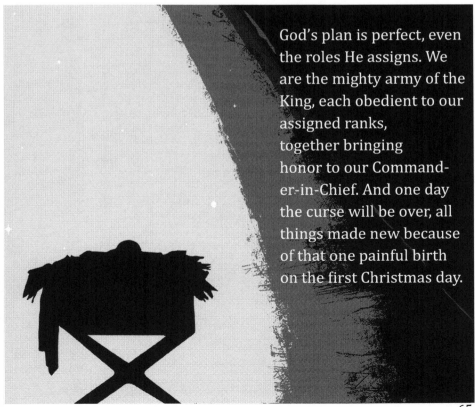

God's plan is perfect, even the roles He assigns. We are the mighty army of the King, each obedient to our assigned ranks, together bringing honor to our Commander-in-Chief. And one day the curse will be over, all things made new because of that one painful birth on the first Christmas day.

1 Timothy 3

RECOGNIZING AND APPOINTING CHURCH LEADERSHIP.

When Paul preached in cities, he saw many come to faith in Christ, both Jew and Gentile. He then invested time to disciple the new believers. He discerned those who showed great dedication and growth. He appointed them to church leadership in the house churches that sprang up all over the region. There were two groups of appointed leaders, elders, and deacons. The previous chapter specified how women should conduct themselves in the home and the church. Chapter 3 sets high standards for men who would become leaders in the church.

Appointing elders. (3:1-7)

[1] It is a trustworthy statement: if any man aspires to the office of overseer, *it is* a fine work he desires *to do*. [2] An overseer, then, must be above reproach, the husband of one wife, temperate, self-controlled, respectable, hospitable, skillful in teaching, [3] not overindulging in wine, not a bully, but gentle, not contentious, free from the love of money. [4] *He must be* one who manages his own household well, keeping his children under control with all dignity [5] (but if a man does not know how to manage his own household, how will he take care of the church of God?), [6] *and* not a new convert, so that he will not become conceited and fall into condemnation incurred by the devil. [7] And he must have a good reputation with those outside *the church*, so that he will not fall into disgrace and the snare of the devil.

The list of qualifications Paul wrote to Timothy and the list he sent to Titus are the two core passages concerning the kind of man God wants to shepherd His church. To be clear, only men are given this role in the Scriptures. Male leadership is undisputed. Even if the trends in society may change, the standards of God never move. There are situations where there are no men and everyone does the best they can, but the goal is to establish leadership according to the Biblical pattern as soon as possible. The Elder is the chief shepherd. Different denominations give this position different titles. The Greek term episkapos means "over, overseer." It has also been translated as "episcopal," "elder," "overseer," or "pastor." All refer to the same office and are therefore synonyms. The most common term in the early church was "elder."

Biblical usage of "overseer." (Strong's Concordance)

> 1. A man charged with the duty of seeing that things to be done by others are done rightly, any curator, guardian, or superintendent.
> 2. The superintendent, elder, or overseer of a Christian church.

When Paul completed his third missionary journey he arrived at Miletus and because of the riot that happened in Ephesus, he called for all the "elders" from the house churches in Ephesus to come out and meet with him, *"From Miletus he sent to Ephesus and called for the elders of the church"* (Acts 20:17). He told them to be faithful in their calling of being overseers, *"Therefore take heed to yourselves and to all the flock, among which the Holy Spirit has made you overseers* (episkapos), *to shepherd the church of God which He purchased with His own blood"* (Acts 20:28).

Over the centuries the church grew and became more ecclesiastical and the word "Bishop" became associated with regional leaders. But whatever they may be called, the *"**episkapos**"* has qualifications that never change; they are God's description of the ideal leader. For the one who wishes to fill the calling, God says *"it is a fine work he desires to do."* Keep in mind that these job descriptions are not optional. We are not encouraged to have some of them, but all of them. God says that the one who seeks the appointment "**must be _____**." Must, not might be, or hopefully be. No, he **must be** . . .

- He must be above reproach.
- He must be the husband of one wife.
- He must be temperate.
- He must be self-controlled.
- He must be respectable.
- He must be hospitable.
- He must be skillful in teaching.
- He must not be overindulging in wine.
- He must not be a bully.
- He must be gentle.
- He must not be contentious.
- He must be free from the love of money.
- He must be one who manages his own household well.
- He must be keeping his children under control with all dignity. If a man does not know how to manage his own household, how will he take care of the church of God?
- He must not be a new convert, so that he will not become conceited and fall into condemnation incurred by the devil.
- He must have a good reputation with those outside the church, so that he will not fall into disgrace and the snare of the devil.

That is quite a list, almost terrifying. Who can measure up to these standards? You will if you dedicate yourself to being God's elder to shepherd His people. The Holy Spirit will be your guide, teacher, sanctifier, corrector, and strengthener to follow your conviction. Trust Him. Don't get discouraged.

Now let's look at each of the requirements.

He must be above reproach. This quality has been described as if something improper or wrong happens, you will be the last person anyone would think of us as the one responsible. There is nothing in your life that can be a source of any accusation.

He must be the husband of one wife. The question always arises, "Can a divorced person pastor a church? The words in the original language describe a man who is a one-woman-man. He is single-minded, his wife is his only passion when it comes to human relationships. In its purest form that rules out divorce and it rules out polygamy. It also rules out women as elders since the word is not "spouse" but "wife." And homosexual marriage is not a biblical arrangement. The ideal may not always be possible and we never want to rule out the grace and forgiveness of God. There are formerly divorced men who pastor churches. The question is, what do we want? God's best or someone that does not meet the Biblical qualification. Marriage in Ephesians 5 is described as a picture of the church with Christ as the bridegroom and the church as the bride. Jesus is faithful and the only husband in the illustration. The Church, like a faithful wife, in a singleminded way, seeks no other. She honors God. That is God's ideal when he says, "He must be the husband of one wife."

He must be temperate, vigilant. The Greek word here is more accurately rendered sober. *"The presbyter or elder should be sober-minded, self-restrained, temperate (not merely in wine, but all things)"* (Ellicott's commentary) *"Intent upon his duty, ready to resist temptation, and careful to preserve his flock from seduction"* (Benson Commentary). This describes a person who is sober and alert to the dangers around and the needs of the flock. He is ever "alert," "watchful," "vigilant," or "clear-headed." Elders must be able to think clearly.

He must be self-controlled, disciplined. Better rendered, discreet. Greek, σωφρονα, prudent; or, as the word also implies one who governs well his passions, and whose mind is well regulated. *"He must be lively and zealous, yet calm and wise"* (Benson Commentary).

He is intentionally disciplined, knows how to properly order his priorities, and is serious about spiritual matters

He must be respectable. Good behavior. Elders must not be chaotic in decisions otherwise how can they bring order to the ministry? This was the same word used previously of women who were careful not to dress in excess or immoral fashion. This means the elder is not extreme in his appearance but has a modest appearance. In regards to customs and trends in society, the respectable elder would neither be the first one to get into a new trend or the last one to get out of an old style. He is not interested in shocking or making a scene. His life is dignified and orderly. His life is characterized by a high moral character.

He must be hospitable. A lover of strangers. He is open and generous to guests. He is a people person. A leader loves people and serves them. Sometimes we think of Paul as a driven man, unyielding. We remember John Mark being rejected by Paul on his second journey because he deserted Paul on the first journey. But Paul had an open door and worked tirelessly with people even preaching and teaching late into the night. When he was under house arrest awaiting his hearing, we read this: *"Now Paul stayed two full years in his own rented lodging and welcomed all who came to him"* (Acts 28:30). Paul was busy writing four books of the New Testament, but he welcomed all who came. Hospitality puts the focus on the importance of people. Paul later forgave John Mark and had good things to say about him.

He must be skillful in teaching. In Ephesians 4, Paul lists four gifted people God has provided for the church to help establish it, disciple it, and train it in God's path. *"[11] And He gave some as apostles, some as prophets, some as evangelists, some as pastors and teachers, [12] for the equipping of the saints for the work of ministry, for the building up of the body of Christ"* (Ephesians 4:11, 12). The fourth gifted person is the pastor/teacher. The Greek word used for a pastor is a shepherd. A shepherd watches over and protects his flock. He leads the sheep to food and drink. As a spiritual shepherd, one of your tasks is to provide nourishing spiritual food. You need to be skilled in teaching to be a good shepherd. Skills are things you develop with work and a heart to communicate the best way possible. That is teaching. Knowledge of God's Word is very important, but that alone does not make one a good teacher.

He must not overindulge in wine. Literally, not a drunken person. He should not be a quarrelsome person or belligerent like a drunk. This is not a prohibition from drinking wine, but a warning that an elder should not spend his time sitting around with those who overindulge.

He must not be a bully. An elder should not be "a striker." He should not be known as an argumentative or violent person or one who uses his authority to overcome another. He should be a man of peace, a peacemaker. John the Apostle wrote about a church leader who abused his position and damaged his fellowship.

> *⁹ I wrote something to the church; but Diotrephes, who loves to be first among them, does not accept what we say. ¹⁰ For this reason, if I come, I will call attention to his deeds which he does, unjustly accusing us with malicious words; and not satisfied with this, he himself does not receive the brothers either, and he forbids those who want to do so and puts them out of the church.* (3 John verses 8 and 19)

He must be gentle. It is a fruit of the spirit. A good Christian leader provides a calming influence. It is not possible to picture Jesus as loud, boisterous, arrogant, or domineering. He treated others with compassion and mercy. When Jesus spoke to the woman caught in adultery, do you hear an angry, judgmental tone in His voice or do you hear a man with a gentle voice helping a woman filled with shame?

He must not be contentious. Not easily provoked, or one who provokes others to conflict. A leader should seek conversation, not confrontation. When a disagreement occurs in the body of Christ, the leader should encourage calm, not add fuel to the fire.

He must be free from the love of money. The things of this world should have no grip on the godly leader. Wealth, position, and titles are seen as passing away without eternal value. The elder needs to have an eternal perspective. Paul would later remind Timothy of the dangerous temptation of wealth. The cure for materialism is contentment.

> *[8] If we have food and covering, with these we shall be content. [9] But those who want to get rich fall into temptation and a trap, and many foolish and harmful desires which plunge people into ruin and destruction. [10] For the love of money is a root of all sorts of evil, and some by longing for it have wandered away from the faith and pierced themselves with many griefs.*
> /(1 Timothy 6:8-10)

He must be one who manages his own household well. The home life of a pastor is the foundation for his public life. How can a pastor teach on loving his wife, or being a spiritual leader when his own home life is not right? Can two walk together and not agree? We become one flesh with our spouse and if that is not a healthy relationship then we are a fractured person. If you are still single, then be careful if you decide to marry to choose wisely. Image if one member of an ice skating pairs competition didn't show up. What if the final runner of a relay race decided to stay home. Becoming one flesh means in every aspect, emotionally and spiritually. If we are not pulling together, then we are pulling apart. Marriage failure means ministry failure.

He must keep his children under control with all dignity. If a man does not know how to manage his own household, how will he take care of the church of God? Loving the church begins with loving our spouse. True church leadership is parallel to leadership in the home. The pastorate is very demanding and can consume much of a leader's time. There is a danger in neglecting the training and discipling of our children. A parent that takes time to lovingly nurture his children will be respected by his flock. Children who are disciplined in love will be a crown, not a curse. Married pastors need to be wise and self-controlled, to balance the variety of needs and crises that come to a family and a church. The point of this command is that godly, well-disciplined children are evidence of a pastor's ability to lead.

He must not be a new convert. A new believer is apt to become proud and fall into condemnation incurred by the devil. Spiritual maturity is not something we are born with or born-again with. It comes with time. A new believer is not equipped for the challenges faced by a spiritual leader of a church. This elder qualification includes a warning that a new believer not only lacks spiritual maturity, but also is a target of the enemy of our souls. Satan always looks for weaknesses. The new believer has not yet developed his spiritual immune system so to speak. As we mature we become aware of Satan's strategies and we have learned how to protect our hearts and minds against his attacks.   A new believer plunged into the battles of the unseen world is like a newborn child being abandoned on an active battlefield. The church is the primary target of Satan. It needs a field commander who has the proper armor and knows how to use his sword, the Word of God (Ephesians 6:10-19). A new believer is not yet battle-proven. He is an easy target.

He must have a good reputation with those outside the church. He must not not fall disgrace and the snare of the devil. Character is what you are. Reputation is what people think you are. The two things should be the same. An elder or pastor must be an honorable person and live in such a way that others see you the way you are, inside the church and outside.

> *A good name is to be more desired than great wealth,*
> *Favor is better than silver and gold.* (Proverbs 22:1)

PRINCIPLES TO LIVE BY.

Christian leadership is about character, not popularity or a seminary degree. Timothy was a young man who walked in the shoes of the Apostle Paul. He went through the fire and came out like pure gold. Paul continually reminded him to keep his eye on the prize of the high calling in Christ. Timothy was tested and approved in the heat of the furnace of ministry where men of God are purged and formed into vessels that God can use. Knowing the Word of God is necessary, but living it is where effective leadership begins.

Appointing deacons. (3:8-13)

[8] Deacons likewise *must be* men of dignity, not insincere, not prone to *drink* much wine, not greedy for money, [9] *but* holding to the mystery of the faith with a clear conscience. [10] These men must also first be tested; then have them serve as deacons if they are beyond reproach. [11] Women *must* likewise *be* dignified, not malicious gossips, but temperate, faithful in all things. [12] Deacons must be husbands of one wife, *and* good managers of *their* children and their own households. [13] For those who have served well as deacons obtain for themselves a high standing and great confidence in the faith that is in Christ Jesus.

One of the best examples of deacons is found in Acts 6. We can see many good principles from this passage about what they did, how they were appointed, and what kind of people they were.

[1] Now at this time, as the disciples were increasing in number, a complaint developed on the part of the Hellenistic Jews against the native Hebrews, because their widows were being overlooked in the daily serving of food. [2] So the twelve summoned the congregation of the disciples and said, "It is not desirable for us to neglect the word of God in order to serve tables. [3] Instead, brothers and sisters, select from among you seven men of good reputation, full of the Spirit and of wisdom, whom we may put in charge of this task. [4] But we will devote ourselves to prayer and to the ministry of the word." [5] The announcement found approval

with the whole congregation; and they chose Stephen, a man full of faith and of the Holy Spirit, and Philip, Prochorus, Nicanor, Timon, Parmenas, and Nicolas, a proselyte from Antioch. ⁶ And they brought these men before the apostles; and after praying, they laid their hands on them. (Acts 6:1-6)

Using Acts 6 and 1 Timothy 3, we have a complete training manual on deacons. Before we look at the qualification list in 1 Timothy 3:8-13, let us first list what we learn about deacons from Acts 6.

- As the church grew in size there was too much for one person to do. Spiritually qualified men were needed to assist the elders in the ministry.
- This need was brought about because of a dispute. The Greek Jewish widows were being overlooked in favor of the Hebrew Jewish widows. It was a problem of prejudice. The Apostles had their hands full sharing the Gospel and discipling the people. They needed help to sort out the everyday issues and free them to focus on the Word of God.
- The Apostles challenged the church to find special servants from among themselves who could take care of the everyday matters that come up so the Apostles could be effective in their calling.
- The Church picked their representative servants. They had to be the best from among them, with good reputations, filled with the Holy Spirit, wise men who could serve with honor and be part of the ministry team. Deacons should be chosen by the flock since they represent the flock. They are then confirmed by the Elders.
- The choices were brought before the Apostles and the church for a prayer of dedication and they laid hands on them, a sign of singularity of purpose and committing the

new appointees to be servants of the church. The word "deacon," means "servant."

- The very first deacon appointed was Stephen. He was a man who filled all the qualifications. He was humble enough to be a table waiter for the Greek and Hebrew Jewish widows while at the same time, a mighty man of the Word of God and great resolve and courage. This was evidenced by his defense of the Gospel to a hostile Jewish mob who later stoned him to death. He was the first martyr of the Christian church (Acts chapters 6 and 7). His death was supervised by Paul, the man who would one day write one half of the New Testament. That same Paul would one day write the qualifications for deacons and challenge them to boldly stand for Christ. He surely remembered the triumphant way Stephen died.

The qualifications for the deacon are very similar to that of the elder. There is no lesser position or calling with God. A deacon is not a less spiritual man than an elder. Elders and deacons are called to the very highest station. The toughest test calls for the best. Let's look at the list of qualifications given to Timothy:

QUALIFICATIONS OF DEACONS.

Deacons must be men of dignity, Deacons are respectful people to both man and God. They serve both. They must have a proper reverent attitude. They must take their role in the church seriously.

Deacons must be sincere. The body of Christ needs the genuine article. When he speaks he means what he says and says what he means. There is no question about what he believes. He is not double-tongued.

Deacons must not drink much wine. As with the Elder, a Christian leader must not be known as a drunkard or being around drunkards. Any kind of addiction indicates a person is under the influence or control of something other than God. This is not a prohibition from drinking wine at a meal, but is simply a warning of the dangers of excess. Ephesians 5 describes a person who is saturated with wine when they should be saturated with the Holy Spirit. In the case of leaders of the church, it is always best to choose to live lives of caution in our decisions and even our freedoms. We always want to avoid offenses or even the appearance of evil. We never want to be a stumbling block to weaker brothers.

Deacons must not be greedy for money. Where our treasure is, our hearts will be found. When the body of Christ is our treasure, that is where we will invest our time and talents.

> *"⁸ If we have food and covering, with these we shall be content. ⁹ But those who want to get rich fall into temptation and a trap, and many foolish and harmful desires which plunge people into ruin and destruction. ¹⁰ For the love of money is a root of all sorts of evil, and some by longing for it have wandered away from the faith and pierced themselves with many griefs."*
> (1 Timothy 6:8-10)

Deacons must hold to the mystery of the faith with a clear conscience. The deacon believes in the doctrines of the word of God without any hesitation or compromise. He never agrees to something because others do, but knows what he believes and stands firm on truth, his conscience is clear on all matters of faith.

Deacons must be tested; then have them serve as deacons if they are beyond reproach. Neither elders nor deacons should be appointed too quickly. Sometimes, a position is vacated or a need arises for an additional deacon to assist that need. A Church may feel pressured to quickly appoint someone. This is not a wise decision. They need to first be observed and tested with a simple assignment to see how they respond. They need to handle the tests without hesitation or in any way which could bring accusation to the church. The church needs to be sure the candidate is without reproach in all matters before permanent assignment. The Church is not so much appointing someone but recognizing someone that God has His hand upon.

Women *must* likewise *be* dignified, not malicious gossips, but temperate, faithful in all things. The Greek word translated "woman" in English has two possible meanings:

> *"1. universally, a woman of any age, whether a virgin, or married, or a widow:*
> *2. A wife, or betrothed woman."* (Thayer's Greek Lexicon)

Because there is no way to know which meaning Paul was using, we will consider both, and they both may be correct. The immediate context would be the wife of a deacon since that is what Paul was referring to when addressing the qualifications of the elder. The deacon's wife would be expected to have the same spiritual qualities as the elder's wife. This would be true even if Paul was not specifically addressing the wives in this verse.

The second way it is understood and not everyone takes this view is that Paul was addressing women as servants in the church the same way a man was addressed. Phoebe would be an example of such a woman.

> *I commend unto you Phoebe our sister, which is a servant of the church which is at Cenchrea.* (Romans 16:1)

The Greek word translated "servant" of the church is ***diakonos***, which is the same word for the male deacons in this section. Verse 8 begins ***"Deacons likewise must be . . ."*** The word in Greek is the very same, "***diakonos."*** *Some people refer to Phoebe as a deaconess, or female deacon*. But the Greek lexicon simply describes the word as a "masculine/feminine noun." It is used for both males and females. One distinction between elder and deacon is that the word for elder when it is used as the holder of the office of elder or bishop is described as a man. The men and women that serve the church have the same standards, which are temperate in all matters, dignified, not gossips but controlled in their speech, never speaking poorly of others, and are faithful in their relationships and service to the Lord.

Deacons must be husbands of one wife, *and* good managers of *their* children and their own households. This would specifically apply to men, whereas the previous point talks to women. Just as the elder needed to be single-eyed, a one-woman-man, so the deacon has the same standards. **See the discussion in verse 2** for more information about this point.

A promise for the deacons. (3:13)

¹³ For those who have served well as deacons obtain for themselves a good standing and great boldness in the faith which is in Christ Jesus.

The requirements to become an elder or a deacon are high. Paul wants Timothy to tell his deacons not to become discouraged with the high standards because it is worth the challenge. A deacon obtains an honor before God that the world cannot offer. Besides the joy of doing the honorable thing, the role of deacon gives additional opportunity to trust God which in turn produces a boldness of faith that only comes from walking with God and doing His will. It is worth it all to be a servant of Christ. The rewards far exceed the sacrifices.

> *"¹⁰ And do not be called leaders; for only One is your Leader, that is, Christ. 11 But the greatest of you shall be your servant. 12 Whoever exalts himself shall be humbled, and whoever humbles himself shall be exalted."*
>
> (Matthew 23:11)

The mystery of what god has done in the church through christ. (3:14-16)

¹⁴ I am writing these things to you, hoping to come to you before long; ¹⁵ but in case I am delayed, *I write* so that you will know how one should act in the household of God, which is the church of the living God, the pillar and support

of the truth. [16] Beyond question, great is the mystery of godliness:

> He who was revealed in the flesh,
> Was vindicated in the Spirit,
> Seen by angels,
> Proclaimed among the nations,
> Believed on in the world,
> Taken up in glory.

Paul tells Timothy why he is writing this letter to him. We already know that Paul considered Timothy to be like a son. He desired to travel and see his son in the faith. In chapter one we learned that Paul had visited the church at Ephesus with Timothy and realized there were serious problems needing attention, mostly concerning false teaching that had infiltrated the church. Paul had a great burden for the church where he had spent three years planting and discipling. He left Timothy behind in Ephesus as the main teaching elder or shepherd. Paul needed to take care of the churches in Macedonia. While he was there he had a burden to write his true son in the faith and give specific counsel and encouragement to Timothy. That is why he is writing and telling Timothy he hopes to come as soon as he can, but he might be delayed. History is not clear whether he was able to see Timothy again in the flesh.

Paul communicated with Timothy like a father to his son. He knew Timothy would face great opposition and temptation in the pagan city of Ephesus. That is why he reminded him *"how one should act in the household of God, which is the church of the living God, the pillar and support of the truth"* (3:15). His writing was also refreshing Timothy's calling to the church. That would have been enough to encourage Timothy to know that his spiritual father was hoping to visit him and that Timothy's work was the noblest of all callings.

A SONG OF THE EARLY CHURCH.

However, Paul did not stop there. He included in that letter what has been called "an early hymn of the first-century church which expressed the foundations of the faith" (Blue Letter Bible). It was like getting a basic doctrinal statement of the church in a song. He introduces it as a great mystery:

> *16 Beyond question, great is the mystery of godliness*

The letter Paul wrote to the Ephesian church described that mystery:

> *"3 that by revelation there was made known to me the mystery, as I wrote before briefly. 4 By referring to this, when you read you can understand my insight into the mystery of Christ, 5 which in other generations was not made known to mankind, as it has now been revealed to His holy apostles and prophets in the Spirit; 6 to be specific, that the Gentiles are fellow heirs and fellow members of the body, and fellow partakers of the promise in Christ Jesus through the gospel, 7 of which I was made a minister, according to the gift of God's grace which was given to me according to the working of His power."*
> (Ephesians 3:3-7)

The entire third chapter of Ephesians needs to be read. What was hidden in the past has now been revealed and it was wondrous. Paul said it was "beyond question." There was no contention. There are certain great truths where Christians should agree. These are some of those primary beliefs. They were something to sing about. As believers, we should have what are sometimes called the "non-negotiables." Certain beliefs need to be convictions, things worth dying for. Non-negotiables mean no compromise, no changing course. The basic doctrines of the Christian faith are set in eternity. Jesus is the same yesterday, today, and forever. We are saved by grace alone, by faith alone in Christ alone. It is "beyond question."

How is it possible that a sinner cut off from God can be forgiven? How can we who have violated the holy God of the universe be accepted into His forever family and become heirs of His kingdom? How can any of this happen? One can almost hear the early church singing with joyful hearts this early hymn of praise:

> *"He who was revealed in the flesh,*
> *Was vindicated in the Spirit,*
> *Seen by angels,*
> *Proclaimed among the nations,*
> *Believed on in the world,*
> *Taken up in glory."*

The grace of God has opened the door to all peoples. The eternal Son of God was revealed in the flesh. The Holy Spirit testified of that wonder. The angels witnessed it. The blood of Christ shed on the cross was for all nations, Jew and Gentile. The resurrected Christ ascended to Heaven. Today we have that matchless message which brings life to all who will listen.

Paul wanted to remind Timothy of the amazing heritage he had as a believer. Many of the residents of Ephesus needed to find that Savior and one day be able to sing that hymn.

1 Timothy 4

Some will fall from the faith, and some will add to the gospel. (4:1-5)

¹ But the Spirit explicitly says that in later times some will fall away from the faith, paying attention to deceitful spirits and teachings of demons, ² by means of the hypocrisy of liars seared in their own conscience as with a branding iron, ³ who forbid marriage *and advocate* abstaining from foods which God has created to be gratefully shared in by those who believe and know the truth. ⁴ For everything created by God is good, and nothing is to be rejected if it is received with gratitude; ⁵ for it is sanctified by means of the word of God and prayer.

Chapter 4 lifts the veil into the dark world of the Roman culture in Ephesus. It should not be surprising that the pagan culture of the times would follow new believers into the churches. The church was a new concept to the people. The Ephesians followed Zeus and numerous other pagan deities. They worshipped their demonic gods with sacrifices and immoral temple activities. New believers would often carry a lot of evil practices and destructive philosophies into the churches. If you have ever visited a pig farm you know that the smell of the pigs stays on your body for a long time. You may not notice it since you got used to it, but others know where you have been. The stench of evil often came with those who had participated in the depravity of the city.

Paul Addressed some of these matters and warned Timothy what to expect. He began with the deep attraction to evil found in the human heart. The allure of sin, the pleasures of sin for a season are strong temptations. We are reminded of Moses who, *25 choosing rather to endure ill-treatment with the people of God than to enjoy the temporary pleasures of sin, 26 considering the reproach of Christ greater riches than the treasures of Egypt; for he was looking to the reward"* (Hebrews 11:25, 26). Temptation was strong, and for some, it would overcome them and draw them back into the darkness, *"some will fall away from the faith, paying attention to deceitful spirits and teachings of demons"* (4:1). It happens today as well. Jesus warned that there would be some seeds that would fall among thorny ground; the cares of the world would choke out the life of the plant (Matthew 13:7).

PRINCIPLES TO LIVE BY

As sure as some seeds grow when planted, some will not survive. Every pastor and church planter has some vision of their future work. They hope their church will be special, be without the strife that happens in churches. It is more probable that you will face what Timothy faced and Paul dealt with each day. Yes, there will be great moments of victory, but there are long times of struggle in the trenches of the war. Every battle has casualties and losses. People will disappoint us and some will walk away and go back to the old way. Just as Paul was being realistic and telling Timothy what to expect, he also encouraged his son in the faith to be a good soldier, a faithful worker who honored God. You will face great trials and at times discouragement, but never give up. The words of Paul are meant for you, as well as they were for Timothy. He told the church in Corinth the same thing, *"16 Therefore we do not lose heart, but though our outer man is decaying, yet our inner man is being renewed day by day."* Hang in there!

Look at the list of challenges Timothy was told to expect from the Ephesians:

- They were saturated in wrong thinking, their minds deceived by the enemy of our souls. Their lives were filled with demonic teachings (4:1).
- They had followed false, lying teachers to the extent that their minds were branded like with a hot iron with the ownership marks of evil (4:2).
- They had damaged, seared consciences, lacking empathy, compassion, or wisdom in matters of truth (4:2).
- Their false teachers had enslaved their freedoms and demanded they follow strict prohibitions against marriage and even eating certain foods (4:3). This legalism strangles the joy out of people.
- Their false teachers called good things evil (4:4).

Timothy had a big challenge in front of him. He was to bring hope to those bound in destructive traditions. He was to model joy and freedom in Christ to those enslaved by false religion. *"36 So if the Son sets you free, you will be free indeed"* (John 8:36).

Paul reminded Timothy that his message was one of liberation:

> *4 For everything created by God is good, and nothing is to be rejected if it is received with gratitude; 5 for it is sanctified by means of the word of God and prayer.* (4:4)

As a pastor or church planter, you have the wonderful privilege of freeing slaves.

Disciplines of a godly leader. (4:6-10)

6 In pointing out these things to the brothers *and sisters*, you will be a good servant of Christ Jesus, *constantly*

nourished on the words of the faith and of the good doctrine which you have been following. ⁷ But stay away from worthless stories that are typical of old women. Rather, discipline yourself for godliness; ⁸ for bodily training is *just* slightly beneficial, but godliness is beneficial for all things, since it holds promise for the present life and *also* for the *life* to come. ⁹ It is a trustworthy statement deserving full acceptance. ¹⁰ For it is for this we labor and strive, because we have set our hope on the living God, who is the Savior of all mankind, especially of believers. ¹¹ Prescribe and teach these things. ¹² Let no one look down on your youthfulness, but *rather* in speech, conduct, love, faith, *and* purity, show yourself an example of those who believe. ¹³ Until I come, give your attention to the *public* reading, to exhortation, *and* teaching. ¹⁴ Do not neglect the spiritual gift within you, which was granted to you through *words of* prophecy with the laying on of hands by the council of elders. ¹⁵ Take pains with these things; be *absorbed* in them, so that your progress will be evident to all. ¹⁶ Pay close attention to yourself and to the teaching; persevere in these things, for as you do this you will save both yourself and those who hear you.

THE DISCIPLINE OF CORRECTION. (4:6)

Confrontation is difficult. It is usually easier to remain silent. No one likes to tell someone they are wrong. In Scripture we read *"Faithful are the wounds of a friend"* (Proverbs 27:6). If we are true friends, we will warn others of danger. Paul had just listed various abuses of false teachers. He wanted Timothy to be a good servant of Jesus and warning the body of Christ was part of that assignment. He had to confront the evil directly and warn the flock about what was happening. Timothy was to faithfully keep the church on track by exposing false teaching and establishing true doctrines. This is still a primary duty of a pastor today. Pastors protect the flocks from predators and lead them to food and drink.

THE DISCIPLINE OF SPIRITUAL FOCUS. (4:7)

It has been said of leaders and teachers that the "main thing is to keep the main thing the main thing. In other words, don't get distracted; stay focused on that which matters most. The first discipline was to get others on track. Now, Paul is telling Timothy, not to get distracted by "worthless stories" which seemed to be associated with some of the older women in the churches. It is not saying all "small talk" is of no value. Sometimes we discuss everyday matters. This passage seems to be talking about older people who have nothing to do so they spend most if not all their time discussing empty topics or gossiping about others. The conversations must have been ungodly since Timothy is urged to keep away from those conversations and remain clear-eyed, strongly focused on the assignment God had given him.

THE DISCIPLINE OF KEEPING BALANCED. (4:8-11)

"The hardest thing in life is to keep balanced!" (L.E. Maxwell, Bible college founder). Luke describes the early life of Jesus this way, *"52 And Jesus grew in wisdom and stature, and in favor with God and man"* (Luke 2:52). Jesus was truly God and He was truly man. This verse shows us His manhood. He learned and applied human qualities and kept them in balance. He grew intellectually (*"wisdom"*). He learned the important lessons concerning living, and making wise decisions. He grew physically and healthy (*"stature"*). By keeping the dietary laws of His ancestors and honoring His parents He had a balanced, healthy diet. He took care of His physical body. He also grew spiritually (*"God"*) and finally He grew socially, emotionally (*"man"*). He was comfortably connected to others. All of these disciplines were necessary for Him as He worked with His disciples and met strangers. He taught the crowds, answered hard questions, prayed to the Father for guidance, and walked the long roads between towns. Jesus was complete in all aspects of His life. He was well balanced.

This is what Paul is instructing Timothy when he tells him, *"Bodily training is just slightly beneficial, but godliness is beneficial for all things."* It is not saying to neglect our bodies, we just don't need to spend all our time building our physical body. Men seem to be often consumed with physical strength and women sometimes emphasize physical beauty too much. It is one thing to be clean, neat, and not abuse our God-given bodies, but it is another to worship them. A spiritually developed person is most important because the spiritual endures forever while the physical is for a short season. *"Godliness is beneficial for all things, since it holds promise for the present life and also for the life to come"* (4:8).

In the Greek and Roman culture much emphasis was on appearance and fitness, and physical pleasures. The stories and statues of the gods emphasize beauty and physical strength. They had bathhouses, sports events, and contests of strength and survival. They built colosseums for these things. They also had libraries to learn new things. What was missing? Godliness was missing. The society of Ephesus neglected the weightiest of matters, the things that had to do with God. That is why Paul tells Timothy to not only develop personal balance, but to also teach and train the church to develop the neglected discipline of godliness.

> ¹⁰ **For it is for this we labor and strive, because we have set our hope on the living God, who is the Savior of all**

mankind, especially of believers. [11] *Prescribe and teach these things.* (4:10, 11)

THE DISCIPLINE OF PERSEVERANCE, STEADFASTNESS. (4:12-16)

Timothy was a young man, around 30 years of age when he was left in charge of all the house churches in the city of Ephesus. In a society where age was equated with wisdom, he would have been considered a schoolboy, not a seasoned teacher or philosopher. He would have been the source of ridicule. Paul was aware of the society and the challenges a young man would have, so he told Timothy, *"[12] Let no one look down on your youthfulness, but rather in speech, conduct, love, faith, and purity, show yourself an example of those who believe"* (4:12). Paul told Timothy to live the godly life in front of them. They had been listening to false teachers and living worldly lives. It was time for them to see the real thing.

Timothy had Paul's full confidence that he could do that. Paul said he hoped to return one day, but until then, Timothy needed to be steadfast in public reading, exhortation, and teaching (4:13). He reminded Timothy of his godly heritage, his spiritual journey, his prophesied ministry, and his commissioned work from true spiritual leaders (4:14). It was time for Timothy to step up to his calling and his life would be evident to all when he lived it out in their presence (4:15).

Paul had full confidence in his son in the faith. He had discipled him and trusted him for many years before this final assignment in Ephesus. History teaches us that Timothy did just that and continued as a strong spiritual leader of the Ephesian churches until later in life when he died a martyr's death in the city.

Pay close attention to yourself and to the teaching; persevere in these things, for as you do this you will save both yourself and those who hear you. (4:16)

This final blessing of perseverance is that by remaining faithful, Timothy will not only save (preserve, protect, keep) himself from the wickedness of the city, but he would be the source of many coming out of bondage into the joy of life in Christ.

PRINCIPLES TO LIVE BY.

Are you a disciplined person? Everything we know about Timothy is positive. He began well with a godly upbringing. Shortly after his conversion, he was known in his hometown and the local region as a dedicated follower of Christ. He then traveled with Paul as his mentor for many years and was put in charge of helping new church plants become strong churches. When Paul put him in charge of the church in Ephesus, Timothy was a mature, seasoned leader. Even with that strong Christian discipleship and history of leadership, Paul still felt he needed to challenge his young disciple to live a disciplined life. Timothy was in the war of the ages for the souls of men and called to work in one of the spiritually hostile places on earth. He needed to continually keep a strong spiritual focus and not be sidetracked with unimportant pursuits. He needed to stay strong in God's Word, courageous in dealing with sin and disciplining those who failed. We too need the reminders of personal discipline and continually staying focused on the task God has given us.

1 Timothy 5

Treat older men and widows with honor. (5:1-10)

[1] Do not sharply rebuke an older man, but *rather* appeal to *him* as a father, *and to* the younger men as brothers, [2] to the older women as mothers, *and* to the younger women as sisters, in all purity.

[3] Honor widows who are actually widows; [4] but if any widow has children or grandchildren, they must first learn to show proper respect for their own family and to give back compensation to their parents; for this is acceptable in the sight of God. [5] Now she who is actually a widow and has been left alone has set her hope on God, and she continues in requests and prayers night and day. [6] But she who indulges herself in luxury is dead, *even* while she lives. [7] Give these instructions as well, so that they may be above reproach. [8] But if anyone does not provide for his own, and especially for those of his household, he has denied the faith and is worse than an unbeliever. [9] A widow is to be put on the list only if she is not less than sixty years old, *having been* the wife of one man, [10] having a reputation for good works; *and* if she has brought up children, if she has shown hospitality to strangers, if she has washed the saints' feet, if she has assisted those in distress, *and* if she has devoted herself to every good work.

RESPECTING THE ELDERLY. (5:1, 2)

The first two verses concern respect for the elderly and care for widows. In the Law of Moses, it was equated with honoring our father and mother. Paul begins with the elderly in society. He tells us we need to treat them the same way we honor our family. *"¹ Do not sharply rebuke an older man, but rather appeal to him as a father, and to the younger men as brothers, ² to the older women as mothers, and to the younger women as sisters, in all purity"* (5:1). If we are to treat them as a father and mother then it is expected that we are to honor them. The Fifth Commandment tells us *"¹² Honor your father and your mother, so that your days may be prolonged on the land which the Lord your God gives you"* (Exodus 20:12). This command was also restated in Leviticus:

> ³² **'You shall rise up before the grayheaded and honor the aged, and you shall revere your God; I am the Lord.'**
> (Leviticus 19:32)

One of the sad trends in today's youth in some cultures is the abuse of the elderly. God's judgment will be strong against such attitudes and activities. Within the Church, the godly elderly have much to teach the younger. They should be respected and given a voice and even taken care of by the body when they need help. When the text tells us to not *"sharply rebuke an older man"* (5:1), it is not saying we should never rebuke an elderly person if they are sinning. That is stated in verse 20:

> ²⁰ **Those who continue in sin, rebuke in the presence of all, so that the rest also will be fearful of sinning.** (5:20)

What we are told in verse one is the tone of the correction:

> *"Timothy was told there are times when not only an elder should be rebuked, but times when he should be rebuked publicly. Therefore, in this verse*

Timothy was not told to never rebuke, rather he was
told to never rebuke in a harsh, attacking manner."
(Blue Letter Bible Commentary)

The older women in the church were to be treated like we would honor our mother. The younger women were to be treated as we would love and protect our sisters (5:2). The church is the family of God. We should treat the body of Christ as our own family. All, young and old, are to be treated with dignity. These words of correction must have come from Paul's three years teaching the believers in Ephesus and his observation of the problems in the church he found when he returned there after his first Roman imprisonment. The problem of elder abuse and neglect of widows must have been severe enough for Paul to write at length about it.

HONORING GODLY WIDOWS. (5:3)

Godly widows were to receive special care. The early church neglected them at first according to the book of Acts, so the Apostles corrected the problem:

> *¹ Now at this time, as the disciples were increasing in number, a complaint developed on the part of the Hellenistic Jews against the native Hebrews, because their widows were being overlooked in the daily serving of food. ² So the twelve summoned the congregation of the disciples and said, "It is not desirable for us to neglect the word of God in order to serve tables. ³ Instead, brothers and sisters, select from among you seven men of good reputation, full of the Spirit and of wisdom, whom we may put in charge of this task. ⁴ But we will devote ourselves to prayer and to the ministry of the word." ⁵ The announcement found approval with the whole congregation; and they chose Stephen, a man full of faith and of the Holy Spirit, and Philip,*

Prochorus, Nicanor, Timon, Parmenas, and Nicolas, a proselyte from Antioch. ⁶ And they brought these men before the apostles; and after praying, they laid their hands on them. (Acts 6:1-6)

Notice that the task of caring for widows was taken very seriously and those chosen for the task were the godliest. They were of high reputation and filled with the Holy Spirit for the task. Caring for the widows in the church was a priority ministry. Paul is reminding the church at Ephesus of this established practice. In the first century, there was no system of government assistance available. The church accepted that role. Widows were the neediest, most had no financial support after their husbands were gone. Remember, we are family and family takes care of each other. The question arises, "Are all widows deserving of this special care?" That question is answered in the next seven verses.

WHO IS A TRUE WIDOW? (5:4-10)

⁴ but if any widow has children or grandchildren, they must first learn to show proper respect for their own family and to give back compensation to their parents; for this is acceptable in the sight of God. ⁵ Now she who is actually a widow and has been left alone has set her hope on God, and she continues in requests and prayers night and day. ⁶ But she who indulges herself in luxury is dead, even while she lives. (5:4-6)

The definition of a true widow contained several requirements. The church was not responsible to assist every elderly man or woman. Some were capable to take care of their own physical needs. Women were the most vulnerable in society and most likely to become an outcast when their family was gone.

- She had no children who could help her. If she had children who assisted her, then she was not considered a needy widow. The widow's children and family are first responsible to help. When they are not around, then the church takes the place of the family to help her. (5:4)
- She was a woman who had been left alone, abandoned. (5:5)
- She was a godly woman known for her consistent prayer life. She did not join a fellowship to get financial help, but she was a woman who followed God. She had come to a time of need in her life. (5:5)
- She was considered impoverished. A woman with assets and wealth was disqualified, even if a widow. The true widow was a description of a truly needy widow that had been left alone, abandoned. (5:6)
- She should be at least 60 years old. She is past her ability to work hard and provide for her own needs. (5:9)
- She had only been the wife of one man. (5:9)
- She must have a reputation as a woman who does good works and shows hospitality to strangers. She was a generous woman to others, but now she has no means to help others in distress. (5:10)

The church was never meant to be a social welfare agency taking care of every person walking through the door. Many people today who have become debilitated from a life of sin turn to local government welfare systems. When those are exhausted, they approach the church for free food or assistance with no interest in God. The true widow is active in the church and faithfully praying for the body of Christ. That is the only one we are commanded to help. Even the church has limited resources and they should be used for helping the truly needy in the family of God, not ones who can still work and support themselves. The next verses are instructions for a class of widows that can still take care of their own needs.

Instructions for younger widows. (5:11-16)

¹¹ But refuse *to register* younger widows, for when they feel physical desires alienating them from Christ, they want to get married, ¹² *thereby* incurring condemnation, because they have ignored their previous pledge. ¹³ At the same time they also learn *to be* idle, as they go around from house to house; and not merely idle, but also *they become* gossips and busybodies, talking about things not proper *to mention*. ¹⁴ Therefore, I want younger *widows* to get married, have children, manage their households, *and* give the enemy no opportunity for reproach; ¹⁵ for some have already turned away to follow Satan. ¹⁶ If any woman who is a believer has *dependent* widows, she must assist them and the church must not be burdened, so that it may assist those who are actually widows.

Not all widows were older women. The first-century church in Ephesus had a problem with younger widows. Life expectancy for men in that culture was lower than in today's society. Women who are left without a husband and were still young were admonished by Paul to remarry for several reasons. There is an indication that when women married they took a vow of some type to never marry again (5:12). This was a vow of faithfulness and devotion. Even when the husband died and the young woman still had desires for the married life (5:11). Paul's instructions to Timothy included freeing the women in this state from guilt if they remarry and even encouraging them to find another husband to fulfill their desires (5:11).

Women in the early centuries of the church rarely worked outside the home. Some Christian women were business women like Phoebe and Lydia, but they were not the norm. Women who were widowed while young were lonely and had little to do each day, so they either became lazy or they went around from house to house participating in local gossip (5:13). Timothy was instructed what to do with these situations:

> *Therefore, I want younger widows to get married, have children, manage their households, and give the enemy no opportunity for reproach.* (5:14)

Paul gave the Corinthian church a similar instruction. After he told the church that it is best for the work of the kingdom if a married person finds himself single again, the person should remain in that condition (I Corinthians 7). Then he told those who could not do that because of strong desires, that it was not wrong for them to marry:

> *8 But I say to the unmarried and to widows that it is good for them if they remain even as I. 9 But if they do not have self-control, let them marry; for it is better to marry than to burn with passion.* (1 Corinthians 7:8, 9)

In Ephesus, some of the young widows had even left the faith to follow the local false religions. *"15 for some have already turned away to follow Satan"* (5:15). The ideal for younger widows was to find a godly man and remarry, have a family, and have strong Christian leadership in the home.

One final instruction was to the mothers of the young widows. If they had the means to support their daughters, then they should do that until they remarry. That way the church was not financially responsible to help them and could use their resources on the truly needy widows (5:16).

The last section of Chapter 5 concerns the selection and

treatment of the elders of the church. A quick review of the church in Ephesus will be helpful.

PRINCIPLES TO LIVE BY.

We can become so busy with small details that we overlook more important matters? We have learned from this letter to Timothy that the church in Ephesus had a large number of problems such as false teachers, gossip, and some falling away from the faith. The church had become sidetracked from the true teachings of God's word. This resulted in the godly widows in the church being neglected. Widows, both young and old had special needs that needed to be addressed. How can a pastor balance the needs of his church and deal with every matter that arises? We need to continually seek God's priorities and discipline ourselves to stay on that track. The challenge is great, but God provides the Holy Spirit to guide us and leads us through the complicated challenges of ministry.

HISTORICAL INSIGHT — The church of Ephesus in the first century.

When we read about the church in Ephesus, what comes to your mind? Timothy was given the task to help the church get back on track. How did the church look in the first century? Where did the church meet? We tend to think of the word "church" as a group of believers meeting in some type of building with a pastor and staff. That is not what the church looked like in the first century. The early church during the first three centuries did not resemble what we see today. Let's look at some New Testament passages which lift the veil and give us a glimpse into the church in the time of Paul and Timothy.

When Paul first visited Ephesus at the end of his second missionary journey, he saw a large city with an estimated population of over 200,000, probably the third-largest city in the Roman Empire. It was a pagan city that was proud of its worship of Diana (Artemis) at the great temple of Artemis. There was a Jewish synagogue and Paul reasoned with the Jews there. *"19 They came to Ephesus, and he left them there. Now he entered the synagogue and reasoned with the Jews"* (Acts 18:19). On his next trip to Ephesus, Paul lived there three years. He found a small number of believers there on that trip. *"Now it happened that while Apollos was in Corinth, Paul passed through the upper country and came to Ephesus, and found some disciples"* (Acts 19:1). There was no actual assembly of believers in the city at that time.

Paul began to minister to the believers he found. Eventually he was able to use a local lecture hall to do more extensive teaching and discipling of the growing number of believers. This growing and gathering of disciples continued for two years.

> *8 And he entered the synagogue and continued speaking out boldly for three months, having discussions and persuading them about the kingdom of God. 9 But when some were becoming hardened and disobedient, speaking evil of the Way before the people, he withdrew from them and took the disciples away with him, and had discussions daily in the school of Tyrannus. 10 This took place for two years, so that all who lived in Asia heard the word of the Lord, both Jews and Greeks.* (Acts 19:8-10)

What was formerly a Greek lecture hall became the center of Biblical discussions and was in some ways the first church gathering in Ephesus. Believers grew, worshipped God, and evangelized the lost in the city. History also adds some general details to this story. Church historians note that no specific building was ever built to house the church, the body of believers, until 323 A.D. The body of Christ met for 300 years in existing facilities and in homes. In most cases, it was just in homes. Knowing this we can only assume that the Ephesian church did the same. They met in a gathered format at the lecture hall and then house to house where they fellowshipped and spread the Gospel to their neighbors.

When the church began at Pentecost we get a view of the dynamic activities of the early church in Acts chapter 2:

> *41 So then, those who had received his word were baptized; and that day there were added about three thousand souls. 42 They were continually devoting themselves to the apostles' teaching and to fellowship, to the breaking of bread and to prayer. 43 Everyone kept feeling a sense of awe; and many wonders and signs were taking place through the apostles. 44 And all the believers were together and had all things in common; 45 and they would sell their property and possessions and share them with all, to the extent that anyone had need. 46 Day by day continuing with one mind in the temple, and breaking bread from house to house, they were taking their meals together with gladness and sincerity of heart, 47 praising God and having favor with all the people. And the Lord was adding to their number day by day those who were being saved.*
> (Acts 2:41-47)

The believers were together continually. They met in the Temple in Jerusalem and then house to house. Some historians estimate that there were likely 200 house churches in Jerusalem in the first century. That same pattern would be seen throughout the known world wherever the Gospel went forth. Many passages in the New Testament refer to churches (gatherings of believers) in homes. The New Testament church was primarily a house church movement.

- *"And Apphia our sister and Archippus our fellow soldier, and the church in your house."* (Philemon 1:2)
- *"How I did not shrink from declaring to you anything that was profitable and teaching you in public and from house to house."* (Acts 20:20)

- *"And day by day, attending the temple together and breaking bread in their homes, they received their food with glad and generous hearts."* (Acts 2:46)
- *"And every day, in the temple and from house to house, they did not cease teaching and preaching Jesus as the Christ."* (Acts 5:42)
- *"The churches of Asia send you greetings. Aquila and Prisca, together with the church in their house, send you hearty greetings in the Lord."* (1 Corinthians 16:19)
- *"Greet also the church in their house. Greet my beloved Epaenetus, who was the first convert to Christ in Asia."* (Romans 16:5)
- *"Give my greetings to the brothers at Laodicea, and to Nympha and the church in her house."* (Colossians 4:15)
- *"I commend to you our sister Phoebe, a servant of the church at Cenchreae, that you may welcome her in the Lord in a way worthy of the saints, and help her in whatever she may need from you, for she has been a patron of many and of myself as well. Greet Prisca and Aquila, my fellow workers in Christ Jesus, who risked their necks for my life, to whom not only I give thanks but all the churches of the Gentiles give thanks as well. Greet also the church in their house. Greet my beloved Epaenetus, who was the first convert to Christ in Asia."* (Romans 16:1-27)
- *"What then, brothers? When you come together, each one has a hymn, a lesson, a revelation, a tongue, or an interpretation. Let all things be done for building up."* (1 Corinthians 14:26) These were house church functions.
- *"And suddenly there came from heaven a sound like a mighty rushing wind, and it filled the entire house where they were sitting."* (Acts 2:2)

So, what was the church in Ephesus like? Where did the believers gather? They were meeting like all the other bodies of believers in other cities and regions. They met in the Hall of Tyrannus for training and discussions and also in homes throughout the city where they used their spiritual gifts, built each other up, prayed, and worshipped. If Jerusalem is any example, there may have been 100 or more house churches throughout the city of Ephesus. When Paul refers to the Church of Ephesus or the Church in Rome or the church in Corinth, he is not talking about a building where the people gathered, but he was talking about the people, the believers scattered about the city in a network of house fellowships. Leaders would emerge in the house groups and some would be recognized to be over the general area, like Timothy, who Paul left behind to work with the house churches to confront false teachers and appoint godly, qualified, and gifted leaders to strengthen the body of Christ. Timothy shepherded the flocks in Ephesus just as Titus was given that assignment on Crete. Priscilla and Aquila had that role in Corinth.

PRINCIPLES TO LIVE BY.

Bigger is not better. The greatest movement of the church in history happened in the first three centuries. The church spread throughout the known world and survived ten major persecutions. It all happened by house churches. The first known buildings that were constructed for the body of Christ to meet began in the fourth century A.D. It became the beginning of a significant shift. The church for three hundred years had spread from house to house and was people-centered. When great cathedrals were built the church shifted from dynamic evangelism to stagnant ecclesiastical existence. It went from the warmth of homes to people sitting in rows, from participant to an audience. Pastor, as you plant a church or disciple your people, never lose the value of the small by focusing on the big.

Selection and treatment of elders. (5:17-22)

¹⁷ The elders who lead well are to be considered worthy of double honor, especially those who work hard at preaching and teaching. ¹⁸ For the Scripture says, "YOU SHALL NOT MUZZLE THE OX WHILE IT IS THRESHING," and "THE LABORER IS WORTHY OF HIS WAGES." ¹⁹ Do not accept an accusation against an elder except on the basis of two or three witnesses. ²⁰ Those who continue in sin, rebuke in the presence of all, so that the rest also will be fearful *of sinning*. ²¹ I solemnly exhort you in the presence of God and of Christ Jesus and of *His* chosen angels, to maintain these *principles* without bias, doing nothing in a *spirit of* partiality. ²² Do not lay hands upon anyone too quickly and thereby share *responsibility for* the sins of others; keep yourself free from sin.

ELDER ROLES.

Presbyteros is the Greek word that is translated as "Elder." It is used in three different ways.

- The first is a general designation of an elderly person. We think of respecting older people, our elders.
- The second is the way the Jewish world used it. They referred to the leaders of the ruling council, the Sanhedrin, as the elders. They knew the judges of old were older people who had attained wisdom in life and they had earned the right to judge the people. The wisdom that comes with age was part of the Jewish use.
- The third usage was by the Christian church. Similar to the Jewish use, they saw that certain men had attained knowledge in the ways of God and recognized certain people as leaders over the assemblies of believers. The Church over the centuries described various words or

positions of leadership with names like bishop, elders, and presbyters. The titles were used interchangeably.

Presbyteros describes leadership that includes teaching, preaching, ruling, and judging. It is usually reserved for men who are mature and older, not novices. Timothy was around 30 years old when Paul left him with the charge of being an elder to the Ephesian believers. Paul encouraged Timothy not to be discouraged when the Ephesians would challenge his leadership because he was young in years. Paul had discipled Timothy since he was a teen and left him in charge of other church problems. He was young in years, but mature in life. An elder has the gifts of eldership, teaching, preaching, or leading and has been diligent to utilize and develop his gifting for the body of Christ. Not all elders may be teachers, preachers, and leaders, but they will show maturity in their specific gifting.

ELDER DOUBLE HONOR, FINANCIAL SUPPORT. (5:17, 18)

Honor is not something that can be demanded, it must be earned. Paul told Timothy godly widows were worthy of honor (5:3). Godly leaders, Paul states, are worthy of honor, but even more, double honor (5:17). The verse that follows explains the meaning, *18 For the Scripture says, "YOU SHALL NOT MUZZLE THE OX WHILE IT IS THRESHING," and "THE LABORER IS WORTHY OF HIS WAGES."*

The point is that there is a special honor for the faithful church shepherd. He is eligible to receive financial support for his life of service. In the Old Testament, the Levite priests were supported by the people they served. The tithes taken in from the tribes of Israel supported the sacrificial system, priests, and the Temple operations. Priests even partook in some of the sacrifices for their food. Pastors today are no less worthy of support from church offerings since they have a similar function to the church, like the Levites, who were called to full-time ministry.

> *⁹ For it is written in the Law of Moses: "You shall not muzzle the ox while it is threshing." God is not concerned about oxen, is He? ¹⁰ Or is He speaking entirely for our sake? Yes, it was written for our sake, because the plowman ought to plow in hope, and the thresher to thresh in hope of sharing in the crops. ¹¹ If we sowed spiritual things in you, is it too much if we reap material things from you? ¹² If others share the right over you, do we not more? Nevertheless, we did not use this right, but we endure all things so that we will cause no hindrance to the gospel of Christ. ¹³ Do you not know that those who perform sacred services eat the food of the temple, and those who attend regularly to the altar have their share from the altar? ¹⁴ So also the Lord directed those who proclaim the gospel to get their living from the gospel.* (1 Corinthians 9:9-14)

If the church is too poor to supply support for the pastor. You will notice in the previous verses from 1 Corinthians 9 that Paul made a strong case for a church supporting its pastor, however he also chose to not receive that help. *"Nevertheless, we did not use this right, but we endure all things so that we will cause no hindrance to the gospel of Christ"* (1 Corinthians 9:12). Paul chose to support himself by the works of his hands as a maker of tents along with Priscila and Aquila while in Corinth. *"After these events Paul left Athens and went to Corinth. ² And he found a Jew named Aquila, a native of Pontus having recently come from Italy with his wife Priscilla, because Claudius had commanded all the Jews to leave Rome. He came to them, ³ and because he was of the same trade he stayed with them, and they worked together, for they were tent-makers by trade"* (Acts 18:1-3). Later Paul would tell the Ephesian elders how he never received wages for his ministry even though he was deserving of them:

> *[33] I have coveted no one's silver or gold or clothes. [34] You yourselves know that these hands served my own needs and the men who were with me. [35] In everything I showed you that by working hard in this way you must help the weak and remember the words of the Lord Jesus, that He Himself said, 'It is more blessed to give than to receive."*
> (Acts 20:33-35)

Not every church can afford to pay their pastor, especially in the early years of a church plant. Pastors sometimes need to be resourceful to provide or supplement their income. They can have jobs, or an occupation, or do part-time work. Pastors may able to be a missionary church planter or a supported pastor of an satellite church from a mother church. Paul chose to be a businessman, a self-supporting pastor, because he did not want to be accused of coveting silver and gold by taking a salary.

ELDER DISCIPLINE. (5:19-21)

Confronting sin in the church may be hard but necessary. It is especially difficult when the one needing discipline is a church leader.

> *[19] Do not accept an accusation against an elder except on the basis of two or three witnesses. [20] Those who continue in sin, rebuke in the presence of all, so that the rest also will be fearful of sinning. [21] I solemnly exhort you in the presence of God and of Christ Jesus and of His chosen angels, to maintain these principles without bias, doing nothing in a spirit of partiality. (5:19-21)*

Paul appointed Timothy to be the over shepherd of the believers in Ephesus. He took the role of an elder or pastor. The message given to Timothy in 5:19-21 was a reminder that no one is exempt when it comes to dealing with sin in the church. Pastors, as we have seen in Chapter 3, had a very high standard to maintain and were to be disciplined if they fell in sin the same as anyone else. There were to be no exemptions for the leaders. Discipline must be carried out without bias (5:21). The principle of having two or three witnesses to convict a person of a crime was to be applied to the elders who failed in ministry. This Biblical rule is found in Deuteronomy 19:15, John 8:17, and Matthew 18:15–20. A single accuser could not automatically get a leader removed. All accusations need to have witnesses and evidence to be considered. Elders could sin like any other person, but the concern is that a church would be disrupted because one person is angry with the leader or gossiping about him. The Biblical method of dealing with sin was to be applied evenly to everyone in the body of Christ, even the leaders.

CAREFUL ELDER SELECTION. (5:22)

²² Do not lay hands upon anyone too quickly and thereby share responsibility for the sins of others; keep yourself free from sin.

The decision to appoint someone as an elder is a serious decision. It should not be made quickly or carelessly. If an unqualified person is appointed just to fill a vacancy in leadership, the church will be held responsible for its faulty decision.

> *"He adds to Christ the angels (5:21), not that they are judges, but as future witnesses of carelessness or rashness or self-seeking or bad faith. They are present as spectators, for they have been given charge to care for the Church."*
> (John Calvin)

PRINCIPLES TO LIVE BY.

Choose leadership wisely. There is an old saying for those rushing into marriage. "It is better to be single than wish you were." When a church loses a pastor or deacon there is a tendency to quickly fill the vacancy. When you read the words of Paul about choosing and dealing with leaders it is clear that these decisions must be done carefully, not quickly. Israel regretted the choice of Saul as their king. He was chosen by the people for the wrong reason, his outward appearance not his character (1 Samuel 10). David, his replacement, was a man after God's heart and even with his flaws, he led the nation to greatness. The proper caution can lead to blessing but rushing will bring regret.

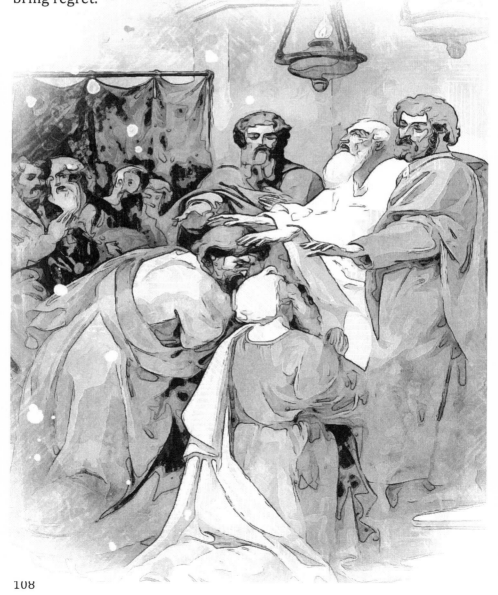

1 Timothy 6

Believing slaves should be respectful of those over them. (6:1-2)

¹ All who are under the yoke as slaves are to regard their own masters as worthy of all honor so that the name of God and *our* doctrine will not be spoken against. ² Those who have believers as their masters must not be disrespectful to them because they are brothers *or sisters*, but must serve them all the more, because those who partake of the benefit are believers and beloved. Teach and preach these *principles*.

- All believers, whether slave or free, need to develop an attitude of thankfulness. Thankful for grace, mercy, and salvation. They need to be thankful for each member of the church.
- All believers should be thankful for the shepherd God has given them.
- All pastors should be thankful for the flocks they are responsible to protect and teach. Mutual respect is the basis of a church building each other up in Christ.
- All believers are under some authority. Ultimately, we are under God's authority. There are authority structures in society, in the home, in our church, and in the Kingdom of God. Each of us needs to be respectful of authority.

In today's world, most of us will never see slavery as it

existed in the first century. These verses may not seem relevant. We don't own slaves and we are not slaves. Paul gave Timothy instructions about slaves and their masters in the church of Ephesus. Paul was not giving his approval to the system of slavery. It is estimated that slaves in the Roman Empire may have numbered as high as 60 million. It was the world where Paul and Timothy lived and ministered.

One additional note about most slavery in the Bible. It was very different from what the world saw when African slave traders sold their people to buyers from Europe and the Americas in the 18th and 19th centuries. Slavery in the 1st century did have forced labor from conquered peoples, but it also had a system of servants who worked off their debts. Indentured servants were able to buy their freedom after their debts were paid. The Bible listed ways this type of servant was to be humanely treated. It provided a pathway to freedom for those shackled with debts.

Paul was discussing this type of slavery or indentured servants. His counsel was for slaves to honor their earthly masters like an employee respects his employer. A Christian who was a slave could show the love of Christ with a proper submissive attitude towards his master. Paul was interested in the testimony of Christ in all situations. He wanted God to be glorified in the lives of both slaves and their masters. The book of Philemon was written by Paul to counsel a slave master to receive back a runaway slave as a brother in Christ.

Note: Centuries later in England, it was the Christian message and a few very brave believers in the Western world that eventually brought down the evil slave trade. Believers like John Newton and William Wilberforce helped abolish the wicked slave system that kidnapped Africans, separated families, and forced the slaves into a lifetime of abusive subjection.

A parallel passage to 1 Timothy 6 is Colossians 3:

> *22 Slaves, in all things obey those who are your masters on earth, not with external service, as those who merely please men, but with sincerity of heart, fearing the Lord.*
> *23 Whatever you do, do your work heartily, as for the Lord rather than for men, 24 knowing that from the Lord you will receive the reward of the inheritance. It is the Lord Christ whom you serve.* (Colossians 3:22-24)

Whether we are an employee or a Christian leader, we still should show honor and respect to one another. When we do that we do as unto the Lord. When we don't do that, it allows the name of God to be dishonored (6:1).

> *"We can almost imagine a slave saying, "My master is my brother! We are equal before the Lord. He has no right to tell me what to do." This attitude ignores the fact that God calls us into many relationships where submission is commanded – in the home, in the church, in the workplace. Our equality in Jesus doesn't eliminate God's order of authority."* (David Guzik)

PRINCIPLES TO LIVE BY.

There are different types of slavery. We may never encounter the type of slavery we find in the Bible times or was experienced in the horrible slave trade in England and the Americas in the 18th and 19th centuries. There are other ways we may be held captive. There are many addictions today, some lists have over 60 different types of addictions which have enslaved people. Any addiction is slavery whether it is alcohol, drugs, pornography, smoking, gambling, pleasure, vanity, or many others. When we no longer have control over our mind and body, we are under control by someone or something other than God. Our minds are the main battlefield. When our thought life is not focused on God and good, we will wander into the dark zones of sin. Paul told the Philippian believers how important it was to keep their minds on that which is good.

> *8 Finally, brothers and sisters, whatever is true, whatever is honorable, whatever is right, whatever is pure, whatever is lovely, whatever is commendable, if there is any excellence and if anything worthy of praise, think about these things. 9 As for the things you have learned and received and heard and seen in me, practice these things, and the God of peace will be with you.* (Philippians 4:8)

The greatest freedom is that of the heart. Jesus said *"if the Son sets you free, you really will be free"* (John 8:36).

The basis of true doctrine. (6:3-5)

3 If anyone advocates a different doctrine and does not agree with sound words, those of our Lord Jesus Christ, and with the doctrine conforming to godliness, 4 he is conceited *and* understands nothing; but he has a sick craving for controversial questions and disputes about words, from which come envy, strife, abusive language, evil suspicions, 5 and constant friction between people of depraved mind and deprived of the truth, who suppose that godliness is a means of gain.

Paul lived in Ephesus for three years evangelizing and discipling the believers. It must have been difficult to return and see the condition of the church. He had warned the elders of the church that after he left there would be false teachers and divisive people that would surface:

> *28 Be on guard for yourselves and for all the flock, among which the Holy Spirit has made you overseers, to shepherd the church of God which He purchased with His own blood. 29 I know that after my departure savage wolves will come in among you, not sparing the flock; 30 and from among*

your own selves men will arise, speaking perverse things to draw away the disciples after them. ³¹ Therefore, be on the alert, remembering that night and day for a period of three years I did not cease to admonish each one with tears. (Acts 20:28-31)

The very things Paul warned about did indeed come to pass. The "*savage wolves*" crept into the church. They caused disputes and doctrinal confusion. Their false teachings caused arguments and suspicions in the body (6:3-5). Paul reminded Timothy that whenever anyone leaves the pure teachings of the Lord Jesus, spiritual disaster will follow. Paul knew Timothy very well and knew he was strong in the faith and could confront these conceited, false teachers. The false teachers were using their positions to become wealthy (6:5). Paul will deal with that issue in the next verses but first, let's examine the lessons we learn about false teachers in the church.

- False teachers depart from the clear teaching of Scripture and present their ideas as doctrines. They are not just discussing matters foreign to the Word of God, we are told they "*advocate*" them (6:3). They strongly present their ideas as doctrines. False teachers can often be strong, charismatic-type people. We must always base our evaluation of any teaching on the Word of God, not persuasive speech.
- False teachers are almost fanatical about their divisive teachings. One description of a fanatic is a person who can't change his mind and won't change the subject. Paul describes him as having a "sick craving" for controversy (6:4).
- Paul's primary test of truth was Jesus Christ, His teachings. The false teachers in Ephesus did not agree with the teachings of Jesus (6:3). One of the

disagreements was that of wealth and prosperity. Jesus warned of the dangers of seeking wealth. The false teachers in Ephesus equated godliness with financial gain (6:5). Today, the Christian world is overrun with prosperity gospel teachers. This teaching has always been false, yet thousands still follow them.

- One of the danger signs of false teachers is they often have new spiritual information, teachings that were not known before. They have new terms and vocabulary to impress their audience. Beware of those who profess secret knowledge.
- Like a tsunami that floods the landscape and destroys homes, false teachers leave a trail of wreckage in the church including *"envy, strife, abusive language, and evil suspicions"* (6:4). This is what happens to the church when there are those in the body of Christ who deny, ignore, pervert, and change the meaning of God's Word.
- In the end, those who profess and teach false messages are arrogant and boastful, but God exposes them as conceited and knowing nothing (6:4). All the praise of men means nothing. Only honoring God is of value.

Paul warned the church in Rome about those who promote controversies:

> *17 Now I urge you, brethren, keep your eye on those who cause dissensions and hindrances contrary to the teaching which you learned, and turn away from them. 18 For such men are slaves, not of our Lord Christ but of their own appetites; and by their smooth and flattering speech they deceive the hearts of the unsuspecting. 19 For the report of your obedience has reached to all; therefore I am rejoicing over you, but I want you to be wise in what is good and innocent in what is evil.* (Romans 16:17-19)

Paul was preparing Timothy, and all pastors that follow, for an intense battle. Counterfeits will come. Temptations will arise to be wealthy. This is a warning that we cannot ever let our guard down. Danger lurks around every corner for the servant of God. Paul had written an earlier epistle to Ephesus. He warned the church about the dangers of these things:

> *⁶ See that no one deceives you with empty words, for because of these things the wrath of God comes upon the sons of disobedience. ⁷ Therefore do not become partners with them; ⁸ for you were once darkness, but now you are light in the Lord; walk as children of light ⁹ (for the fruit of the light consists in all goodness, righteousness, and truth), ¹⁰ as you try to learn what is pleasing to the Lord. ¹¹ Do not participate in the useless deeds of darkness, but instead even expose them; ¹² for it is disgraceful even to speak of the things which are done by them in secret. ¹³ But all things become visible when they are exposed by the light, for everything that becomes visible is light. ¹⁴ For this reason it says,*
>
> > *"Awake, sleeper,*
> > *And arise from the dead,*
> > *And Christ will shine on you."*
>
> *¹⁵ So then, be careful how you walk, not as unwise people but as wise.* (Ephesians 5:6-15)

Contentment – when enough is enough. (6:6-10)

⁶ But godliness *actually* is a means of great gain *when* accompanied by contentment. ⁷ For we have brought nothing into the world, so we cannot take anything out of it, either. ⁸ If we have food and covering, with these we shall be content. ⁹ But those who want to get rich fall into temptation and a trap, and many foolish and harmful desires which plunge people into ruin and destruction.

¹⁰ For the love of money is a root of all sorts of evil, and some by longing for it have wandered away from the faith and pierced themselves with many griefs.

INTRODUCTION TO 1 TIMOTHY 6:6-10.

A wealthy man was once asked, "How much is enough?" He answered, "Just a little bit more." The pursuit of wealth has been a curse on the human race throughout time. King Solomon was one of the world's wealthiest men. He had it all. When he reached the end of his life he concluded:

> *⁹ Then I became great and increased more than all who preceded me in Jerusalem. My wisdom also stood by me. ¹⁰ All that my eyes desired, I did not refuse them. I did not restrain my heart from any pleasure, for my heart was pleased because of all my labor; and this was my reward for all my labor. ¹¹ So I considered all my activities which my hands had done and the labor which I had exerted, and behold, all was futility and striving after wind, and there was no benefit under the sun.* (Ecclesiastes 2:9-11)

Solomon learned the hard way that our ultimate treasure is the Lord and all other pursuits are like trying to eat the wind. We end up empty. Listen to the last words Solomon wrote:

> *¹³ The conclusion, when everything has been heard, is: fear God and keep His commandments, because this applies to every person. ¹⁴ For God will bring every act to judgment, everything which is hidden, whether it is good or evil.* (Ecclesiastes 12:13, 14)

His last words were to focus on God, not on earthy things which pass away. The Apostle Paul understood that lesson and that is the theme of the verses we will now examine. The entire focus of these instructions is to avoid one of the great temptations, the desire of what Jesus called "all that is in the world." The opposite of "desire" is "contentment." When we are not content in God, we are telling Him that He is not enough. We need more.

CONTENTMENT. [6:6]

> *6 But godliness actually is a means of great gain when accompanied by contentment.*

The greatest gain a person can achieve is being right with God. Godliness, according to verse 6 is the path to the greatest gain. There is no financial gain or status or award from a man that can compare to hearing God say, "Well done, good and faithful servant." True contentment means the search is over, we have found our greatest desire. Paul also wrote to the church in Philippi about where to find true contentment:

> *11 Not that I speak from need, for I have learned to be content in whatever circumstances I am. 12 I know how to get along with little, and I also know how to live in prosperity; in any and every circumstance I have learned the secret of being filled and going hungry, both of having abundance and suffering need. (Philippians 4:11–12)*

ETERNAL PERSPECTIVE. [6:7, 8]

> *7 For we have brought nothing into the world, so we cannot take anything out of it, either. 8 If we have food and covering, with these we shall be content."*

It has been said that you will never see a moving van following a hearse. We came into the world with nothing and go out the same way. Anything we obtain in this life is left behind when we die. Ecclesiastes shows the futility of a life lived for the things that perish. Solomon reflected on the emptiness of life when eternal things are not kept in focus. He reminds his readers that God has set eternity in the heart of man (Ecclesiastes 3:11). Eternity must be kept in perspective, not the temporary things of life that will pass away.

Jesus spent His time on earth telling the world about what matters. The things of earth are what make people worry but when we trust in God, we are securely in His hands. What is there to worry about?

> *²⁵ For this reason I say to you, do not be worried about your life, as to what you will eat or what you will drink; nor for your body, as to what you will put on. Is not life more than food, and the body more than clothing?* (Matthew 6:25)

Then He describes what happens when we trust God. He provides for our daily needs. We need to be content with that. It happens when we keep our eyes on the Lord, an eternal perspective. Our eternal destination is what is real. The world, as we know it, is passing away:

> *" . . . we look not at the things which are seen, but at the things which are not seen; for the things which are seen are temporal, but the things which are not seen are eternal."*
> (2 Corinthians 4:18)

Much of the world strives for the things of this world and clutches on to them until the day they die. Then they have to let go of it all. As believers, we work for that which will never pass away. We have the joy of an eternal perspective on life. We, like Abraham, are looking forward to the better place God has promised:

> *⁸ By faith Abraham, when he was called, obeyed by going out to a place which he was to receive for an inheritance; and he went out, not knowing where he was going. ⁹ By faith he lived as an alien in the land of promise, as in a foreign land, dwelling in tents with Isaac and Jacob, fellow heirs of the same promise; ¹⁰ for he was looking for the city which has foundations, whose architect and builder is God.*
> (Hebrews 11:8-10)

Jesus spoke of that same city, *"¹'Do not let your heart be troubled; believe in God, believe also in Me. [2] In My Father's house are many dwelling places; if it were not so, I would have told you; for I go to prepare a place for you. [3] If I go and prepare a place for you, I will come again and receive you to Myself, that where I am, there you may be also'"* (John 14:1-3).

SEEKING WEALTH LEADS DOWN A PATH OF RUIN. (6:9,)

[9] But those who want to get rich fall into temptation and a trap, and many foolish and harmful desires which plunge people into ruin and destruction."

Notice how the warning is about those who desire or want to be rich. Even if a person never becomes rich in this world, the very desire for wealth is just as destructive as the wealth itself. We are to set our hearts on the things above, not the things below (2 Corinthians 4:18). It is a matter of the heart. It is possible to have wealth and not have that wealth consume us, but that is rare. There were godly, wealthy people in the Bible, like Abraham, who kept his eye on God, not his material blessings. The Psalmist warned *"If riches increase, do not set your heart upon them"* (Psalm 62:10). Even the secular world understands the mirage of wealth:

> *"There are two great tragedies in life. One is not to get your heart's desire. The other is to get it."* (George Bernard Shaw, English writer.)

Riches are described as a trap or snare one would set for a wild animal. In our case, the wealth of this world is the bait on the trap. *"But those who want to get rich fall into temptation and a trap"* (6:9). An animal caught in a trap is headed for destruction. The same language is used for a person who seeks wealth. Hearts that choose that path are embracing *"harmful desires which plunge people into ruin and destruction."* (6:9). If

119

you were hiking on a trail and noticed the path had collapsed and to continue would cause you to fall onto the jagged rocks below, what would you do?

VERSE 10 IS ONE OF THE MOST MISQUOTED VERSES IN THE BIBLE.

> [10] *For the love of money is a root of all sorts of evil, and some by longing for it have wandered away from the faith and pierced themselves with many griefs.*

The usual misquotation is "Money is the root of all evil." Money is not the root of evil, the love of money is the root of all evil. Remember, this is a matter of the heart. Jesus told us that to lust for a woman is to commit adultery in our hearts. To hate our brother is to be guilty of murder (Matthew 5:21-30). If we wish someone dead we are guilty before God. The same principle applies to the one who lusts for wealth. The penalty is the same. The penalty, in this case, is ruin and destruction.

Ancient Greek traditions talked of sirens. They were usually portrayed as beautiful winged-women who sang a song that enchanted the sailors on ships causing the crew to steer their ships onto the rocks. The only way for sailors to pass through the treacherous waters and not be led astray by the song of the sirens was to put wax in their ears so they could not hear the seductive music. The allure of wealth is like the siren's song which can lead a believer off the path and into a life of grief and regret. "some by longing for it have wandered away from the faith and pierced themselves with many griefs" (6:10).

There is, however, a true wealth we are to pursue. It is described in the next verses.

Pursuing the greater things of God, not earthly values. (6:11-16)

11 But flee from these things, you man of God, and pursue righteousness, godliness, faith, love, perseverance, *and* gentleness. 12 Fight the good fight of faith; take hold of the eternal life to which you were called, and *for which* you made the good confession in the presence of many witnesses. 13 I direct you in the presence of God, who gives life to all things, and of Christ Jesus, who testified the good confession before Pontius Pilate, 14 that you keep the commandment without fault *or* reproach until the appearing of our Lord Jesus Christ, 15 which He will bring about at *the* proper time—He who is the blessed and only Sovereign, the King of kings and Lord of lords, 16 who alone possesses immortality and dwells in unapproachable light, whom no one has seen or can see. To Him *be* honor and eternal dominion! Amen.

After warning Timothy about the deceptions of seeking wealth, Paul instructs his young disciple to flee from the dangerous paths around him. He reminded Timothy that he was a *"man of God"* now, no longer an apprentice, but a seasoned warrior for God. He uses a phrase used for Elijah and the powerful prophets that walked the earth calling men to turn from sin. Timothy had come of age. He was a man of God. His maturity in the faith exceeded his earthly age.

Timothy was exhorted to demonstrate the life of a godly man. The world of Ephesus was consumed with philosophy, empty arguments, moral decadence, religious confusion, and too much leisure time on their hands. Timothy was to show them a different life that comes when Jesus Christ is King of our hearts.

Here is the evidence of a Christian the world needs to see:

- **A life of righteousness** (6:11)— Paul contrasted the pursuit of wealth which produces ruin and destruction (6:10) with a life that pursues a godliness that yields the *"peaceable fruit of righteousness"* (Hebrews 12:11). What a choice. A life of tension, turmoil, and unfulfillment vs. a life of purpose, peace, and joy. The Ephesians needed to see that kind of man. The world today does also.

- **Godliness** (6:11)— Philip once asked Jesus, *"Lord, show us the Father, and it is enough for us."* [9] *Jesus said to him, 'Have I been with you for so long a time, and yet you have not come to know Me, Philip? The one who has seen Me has seen the Father'"* (John 15:8, 9). Jesus reflected the nature and person of His Father. We are called to be reflectors of our Lord. As we demonstrate the godly characteristics we honor God and draw others to our Savior.

- **Faith** (6:11)— We are saved by faith; we walk by faith. Paul was reminding Timothy that his calling was to a pagan world that had faith in statues and false teachings. Timothy had the only faith that leads to eternal life. Even if faith is ridiculed, there is no reason to apologize. We all need to cling to our faith. The fruit of the Spirit (Galatians 5:22-23), evidenced in our lives, will demonstrate our faith to the lost around us.

- **Love** (6:11)— It is not easy to love everyone. Some of the depraved pagan practices at the temples in Ephesus would have been shocking to a young believer like Timothy who had been raised in a small Asia Minor town. The world is no friend of God. Yet, God loved the entire world enough to send His Son, who even forgave His murderers while hanging on the cross. Paul was himself a recipient of that love and grace. The stoning of Stephen was a memory Paul carried with him his entire life:

> *58 When they had driven him out of the city, they began stoning him; and the witnesses laid aside their cloaks at the feet of a young man named Saul. 59 They went on stoning Stephen as he called on the Lord and said, 'Lord Jesus, receive my spirit!' 60 Then he fell on his knees and cried out with a loud voice, 'Lord, do not hold this sin against them!' Having said this, he fell asleep.'* (Acts 7:58-60)

- **Gentleness** (6:11)— One of the best solutions we have when being confronted by an angry, uncontrolled person is the gentle answer. *"A gentle answer turns away wrath, but a harsh word stirs up anger"* (Proverbs 15:1). Interestingly, one of the most common images of the Holy Spirit is the dove. A godly man responds to confrontation with supernatural strength to exhibit a calm gentleness. Gentleness is one of the fruit of the Holy Spirit (Galatians 5:22-23). For Timothy and us it is a reminder that we need to daily rely on the Holy Spirit to help us navigate the treacherous waters of attacks that will come.

- **Perseverance** (6:12)— Never give up the good fight. We can be worn down by a constant barrage of skeptics and haters. Paul wrote a letter to encourage the believers in Corinth, a city of similar depravity and beliefs. He emphasized to them to hang in there, never give up. *"58 Therefore, my beloved brothers and sisters, be firm, immovable, always excelling in the work of the Lord, knowing that your labor is not in vain in the Lord"* (1 Corinthians 15:58).

- **A steadfast confidence in our relationship with Christ** (6:13, 14)— When doubters and intellectuals attack our beliefs it can become discouraging, even causing doubts. John the Baptist and Elijah faced moments of discouragement and doubt. Paul reminded Timothy of his changed life, his salvation, and his relationship with Christ. Jesus is the truth and no wisdom of man can change His Lordship over our lives or our relationship with Him. Paul was telling Timothy to cling tightly to Christ during times of attacks that will come. We all need to remember what God has done for us. We have the truth, which is in Christ alone. If we stand on those truths we never need to falter in our faith. We have the last chapter in the Book, and we win.

- **A constant, faithful witness of our salvation** (6:13)— Paul reminded Timothy how he came to faith and encouraged him to keep a strong grip on that faith. *"Take hold of the eternal life to which you were called, and for which you made the good confession in the presence of many witnesses"* (6:12). A soldier in the army first undergoes basic training. After he completes that phase of his preparation, he is ready for battle. Timothy was ready for the next stage of his journey of faith. He would face great struggles and enemies but he had passed his field training. Paul entreated Timothy to remain faithful until the end. He reminded him that Jesus finished His course and His testimony was strong even in His trial before His accusers. *"[13] I direct you in the presence of God, who gives life to all things, and of Christ Jesus, who testified the good confession before Pontius Pilate, [14] that you keep the commandment without fault or reproach until the appearing of our Lord Jesus Christ"* (6:13, 14).

Paul knew Timothy would face great opposition, just as he had in Ephesus. He described his time there as a great struggle. He wrote, *"I fought with wild beasts at Ephesus"* (1 Corinthians 15:32). Paul was speaking of the vicious, attacking enemies he faced. This was part of the job description of bringing the Gospel to a wicked city. In his letter to the Ephesian church he wrote, *"¹² For our struggle is not against flesh and blood, but against the rulers, against the powers, against the world forces of this darkness, against the spiritual forces of wickedness in the heavenly places. ¹³ Therefore, take up the full armor of God, so that you will be able to resist on the evil day, and having done everything, to stand firm"* (Ephesians 6:12, 13).

He told the church they needed to protect their minds with the helmet of salvation and maintain a strong defense against attack with the shield of faith (Ephesians 6:16, 17). The fact of our salvation and the strength of our faith is what we need today, just like Timothy, to endure the heat of battle for the souls of men. A pastor or church planter is on the front line of the greatest of all wars.

- **A consistently, victorious Christian walk** (6:14)— Paul prayed for Timothy that he would endure to the end. With God strengthening him day by day, Timothy would live his life in spiritual consistency and victory until the day he was stoned to death on the streets of Ephesus in his old age (traditional history). He was truly a good and a faithful servant and an example to all pastors of a godly man.

THE SECOND DOXOLOGY – (1 TIMOTHY 6:15, 16).

He who is the blessed and only Sovereign, the King of kings and Lord of lords, [16] who alone possesses immortality and dwells in unapproachable light, whom no one has seen or can see. To Him be honor and eternal dominion! Amen.

The first doxology was a praise to our eternal God and King. It is found in 1 Timothy 1:17:

[17] Now to the King eternal, immortal, invisible, the only God, be honor and glory forever and ever. Amen
(1 Timothy 1:17)

Notice the similarity in the two doxologies. Compare them line by line.

Two Doxologies Compared

1 Timothy 1:17	1 Timothy 6:15, 16
"To the King of the ages	"The King of king and Lord of lords
immortal	who alone has immortality
invisible	who dwells in unapproachable light whom no one has ever seen or can see.
the only God be honor and glory	to Him be honor
forever and ever	and eternal dominion
Amen"	Amen"

Some theologians and historians believe this doxology was an actual Christian hymn sung by the early church.

"The stately and rhythmical doxology with which the solemn charge to Timothy is closed was not improbably taken from a hymn loved by the Ephesian Christians, and often sung in their churches; the words, then, were, likely enough, familiar to Timothy and his people, though now receiving a new and deeper meaning than before."
(Ellicott's Commentary)

The first doxology in Chapter 1 was a praise song to our God and King. It was specifically to God our heavenly Father. The second doxology found in Chapter 6 uses language more familiar with the Lord Jesus Christ. God the Son is truly God as is the Father and the Holy Spirit. Each member of the Trinity is worthy of titles of Deity, but they have different roles in the story of salvation. Jesus is the One referred to as King of kings and Lord of lords (Revelation 1:5; 17:14; 19:16, Philippians 2:8-11). He is the fulfillment of the Davidic Covenant. He is the promised King that will reign over the earth. The phrase "eternal dominion" is also a specific phrase about the One who will reign over the earth one day.

Even though the focus seems to be the Lord Jesus Christ, some descriptions fit both the Father and the Son. Examples are *"invisible"* and *"unapproachable light."* Also, He *"alone has immortality."* Each member of the Triune God fits each of these descriptions. The nature of God remains a mystery so it is not surprising that this early Christian hymn reflects the deep mysteries of the Godhead. We may not be able to adequately understand it, but use it for worship and wonder.

We learn that God alone has all power, rules the universe, and is seated on His throne in the heavens. He is immortal, dwelling in pure unapproachable light. But one day, in our resurrection bodies, we will see God. We can only worship and honor our God and King. Amen.

Help the wealthy to be generous and rich in good works. (6:17-19)

17 Instruct those who are rich in this present world not to be conceited or to set their hope on the uncertainty of riches, but on God, who richly supplies us with all things to

enjoy. [18] *Instruct them* to do good, to be rich in good works, to be generous and ready to share, [19] storing up for themselves the treasure of a good foundation for the future, so that they may take hold of that which is truly life.

Paul had finished warning about the dangers of seeking wealth and then he focused on the value of spiritual wealth in a godly life. Now, he puts the two thoughts together. He told Timothy that the wealthy have a path of redemption by being good stewards of their time and resources. The wealthy were to be instructed that the true nature of riches is not what you have, but what you give away to help others (6:18). There is a strong reminder that the rich have no reason to be arrogant since everything comes from the hand of God (6:17).

The previous doxology was a praise of the glory and power of God. It is a song all men can sing, even the wealthy. Timothy was told to show the wealthy true riches, which means becoming rich toward God. That is ultimately the only riches that have permanent eternal value (6:19). We can't take it with us, but we can send it ahead. The economy of God is very different than the economy of man. The world tells us to accumulate and accumulate and hold on to wealth to consume it ourselves. God tells us to give it away and in letting go of our wealth we "take hold of that which is truly life" (6:19).

We don't increase wealth by holding on to it. We increase it by giving it away. Jesus said the same thing:

> [19] *"Do not store up for yourselves treasures on earth, where moth and rust destroy, and where thieves break in and steal. [20] But store up for yourselves treasures in heaven, where neither moth nor rust destroys, and where thieves do not break in or steal; [21] for where your treasure is, there your heart will be also."* (Matthew 6:19-21)

The best investment is in what lasts, not in what is passing away. This lesson was not given to Timothy just to help the wealthy develop an eternal perspective, but it was also to help Timothy, a young man in ministry, avoid the temptations of greed and stay focused on eternal riches.

Hang tightly on to that which God has given you avoiding worldly distractions. (6:20-21)

[20] Timothy, protect what has been entrusted to you, avoiding worldly, empty chatter and the opposing arguments of what is falsely called "knowledge"— [21] which some have professed and *thereby* have gone astray from the faith. Grace be with you.

Paul's final exhortation in his first letter to his son in the faith was to stay on course and not get distracted by the world and its lusts. Timothy was to guard the great gifts he had been given, his heritage, his salvation, his calling, his purpose, and his training. All of this produced the man God wanted him to become. That is what Paul was saying when he told Timothy, *"[20] Timothy, protect what has been entrusted to you"* (6:20).

Imagine climbing a mountain and when you get close to the summit, you get careless and slip off the edge. So much can be lost in a careless act. Many pastors have learned that the hard way. Paul did not want that to happen to his dearest partner in ministry.

It takes diligence and resolve to stay on God's path when many voices are calling us away. For Timothy, he was young and placed in charge of building a strong Christian community in Ephesus, one of the greatest ancient churches. A person could become proud in such a position. He could also become engaged in a multitude of philosophical arguments to prove his knowledge. Paul's warning was to avoid being drawn into empty discussions which have no ultimate value. Many in that day had lost their way and strayed from the narrow path (6:21).

Paul ended with the same blessing he used to begin this first letter. "*Grace be with you*" (6:21).

> *2 To Timothy, my true child in the faith, "Grace, mercy and peace from God the Father and Christ Jesus our Lord."* (1:2)

FINAL THOUGHTS ON PAUL AND TIMOTHY AND THIS FIRST LETTER.

It was A.D. 62 when Paul left Timothy in Ephesus to get the believers back on track. Paul would go on to Macedonia after he left Timothy in charge of the church he had poured three years of his life into. The relationship between Paul and Timothy was like father and son. Paul loved Timothy like his own flesh. He probably knew his time on earth was closing down. He had already been imprisoned in Rome once. Nero had become the Emporer and hated the Christians. Paul most likely knew he was a marked man, a target of the Roman Empire, an instigator of the group the Romans proclaimed as enemy of the state.

When Paul left Timothy in Ephesus he knew he might never see him again. He wrote Timothy one more letter when he knew he was on death row and the time of his departure had come. He pled with his beloved son in the faith to come to him in Rome. The year was A.D. 64.

> *21 Make every effort to come before winter. Eubulus greets you, also Pudens and Linus and Claudia and all the brethren. 22 The Lord be with your spirit. Grace be with you.* (2 Timothy 4:21, 22).

Those were the last words Paul wrote. Did Timothy get to Rome to see his friend and mentor before he was beheaded by Nero's decree? We have no idea but most likely he did get there to see his friend one last time. This will be discussed in the commentary on 2 Timothy. It would have been a very dangerous trip for Timothy.

If Timothy did go to Rome and see Paul, we can only imagine the tears and joy the two experienced for their last time together on this earth.

Before Paul died he wrote one final Epistle. It was to Timothy. It is the letter of 2 Timothy. We will examine that one next.

2 TIMOTHY

Paul's final instructions to his beloved son in the faith.

"7 For God has not given us a spirit of timidity, but of power and love and discipline."

2 Timothy 1:7

Introduction

NOTE: Please see the introduction at the beginning of the 1 Timothy commentary for a complete timeline of the journeys of Paul and Timothy. This introduction to 2 Timothy is mostly focused on the time between the two books of 1 and 2 Timothy and the unique qualities of 2 Timothy. The first introduction covers the conversion and early travels of Timothy during Paul's three missionary journeys.

When and where Paul wrote his two letters to Timothy.

1 Timothy – The book of Acts ended with Paul in prison in Rome. It was around A.D. 60. He had been arrested following his third missionary journey. Two years later, Paul was released from Roman confinement which is described in Acts 28. The rest of Paul's life is reconstructed from his later writings and traditional history. Paul traveled to Asia, leaving Titus at Crete, and took Timothy back to Ephesus. Paul gave instructions and left him in charge of pastoring the troubled church in Ephesus. Paul then returned to the churches in Macedonia. During his time in Macedonia, he wrote to Timothy with instructions about how to deal with the many problems the church in Ephesus was facing (1 Timothy). He also gave instructions about how to organize the church and appoint elders and deacons.

> *³ Just as I urged you upon my departure for Macedonia, to remain on at Ephesus so that you would instruct certain people not to teach strange doctrines.* (1 Timothy 1:3)

Paul traveled the Macedonian region reconnecting with churches he had founded. He also preached in some new regions. Some believe he went as far as Spain as he had intended. We have some idea of his travels when, at the end of his third missionary journey, he wrote the Book of Romans during a three-month stay in Corinth. Here is some of what he wrote to the Roman church:

22 For this reason I have often been prevented from coming to you; 23 but now, with no further place for me in these regions, and since I have had for many years a longing to come to you 24 whenever I go to Spain—for I hope to see you in passing, and to be helped on my way there by you, when I have first enjoyed your company for a while— 25 but now, I am going to Jerusalem, serving the saints. 26 For Macedonia and Achaia have been pleased to make a contribution for the poor among the saints in Jerusalem.
(Romans 15:22-26)

If Paul did go to Spain, which is unlikely, he returned to Macedonia. It was in Macedonia where Paul was arrested and taken to Rome for a trial as an enemy of the empire. During this time Timothy was also imprisoned, but released (Hebrews 13:23).

Paul's final imprisonment –

The year was probably between A.D. 62-64 when Paul wrote his first letter to Timothy. Paul traveled the Macedonian region and was eventually rearrested by Rome as an insurrectionist, an enemy of the state. Christianity had been ruled by Rome as an illegal religion of the Roman Empire. Paul had a trial, was found guilty of a capital crime and was held in the Mamertine Prison in Rome to await execution. Some historians say Paul may have been held in a secure military house arrest and not in the Mamertine prison. They base this on the number of people that visited Paul, which may have been impossible in the Mamertine. General tradition, however, is that he was held in the Mamertine until his execution. We can't be sure. The time between his first and second Roman imprisonments was four to six years.

Many historians believe the great fire in Rome set by Nero was an excuse to execute Christians.

"The Roman emperor Nero had been slowly descending into madness since his ascent to the throne in A.D. 54, a process exacerbated by the great fire of Rome in A.D. 64

that burned half the city. With the residents of Rome in an uproar, Christians became a convenient target for Nero, who used believers as scapegoats for his city's lack of preparedness. Paul was one of those caught up in this persecution and was beheaded by Roman officials soon after writing this letter." (Chuck Swindoll)

2 Timothy – When Paul reached the end of his final imprisonment he wrote his last epistle, the book of 2 Timothy, sometime around A.D. 66. Timothy, at that time, was either the pastor of the Ephesian house churches, or he had become an over shepherd for the churches in Asian Minor. The church in Ephesus was the hub of his ministry. Paul was executed sometime between A.D. 66-67. This was just before the death of the evil Emporer, Nero, who had Paul executed. Nero died by suicide in June of A.D. 68.

In 2 Timothy, Paul asked Timothy to come to him and bring John Mark, along with a warm coat, and some parchments he had left with another brother for safekeeping. Paul sent Tychicus to be his replacement so he could travel to Rome. The letter of 2 Timothy contained final instructions and warnings a father would give to his son he might not see again. This was the only letter Paul wrote while in his final confinement.

What was the difference between 1 Timothy and 2 Timothy?

1 Timothy was primarily an administrative directive. Paul gave instructions encouraging sound teaching, dealing with false teachers in the church, appointing elders and deacons, and general conduct for believers living in a pagan society. He also addressed the issue of the role of women in the church.

2 Timothy was not written as an administrative directive, but was more like a personal note to his "son in the faith." It was written from a father's heart. It is personal, more like his last will and testament.

2 Timothy Chapter 1
Commentary

An affectionate greeting. (1:1, 2)

¹ Paul, an apostle of Christ Jesus by the will of God, according to the promise of life in Christ Jesus, ² To Timothy, my beloved son: Grace, mercy, *and* peace from God the Father and Christ Jesus our Lord.

The greeting Paul gives Timothy in his second letter is almost identical to the first letter. Here is the first greeting to compare it to the second:

> *¹ Paul, an apostle of Christ Jesus according to the commandment of God our Savior, and of Christ Jesus, who is our hope, ² To Timothy, my true son in the faith: Grace, mercy, and peace from God the Father and Christ Jesus our Lord.* (1 Timothy 1:1-2)

Most of Paul's letters begin the same way, but that is not because it was a habit or a required greeting style in the first century. When we know Paul's conversion story, his journeys, and struggles, we can only assume the words he uses are a true reflection of his heart. He was certain of his calling by the will of God and did not doubt his assignment from God as an Apostle. He also was keenly aware of the grace of God that rescued him from a life of dead religion.

Paul was eternally grateful that God showed him mercy. He was formerly a man of blind ambition who had Stephen murdered and hunted down the followers of Jesus to destroy them. As a result, Paul experienced something he had never felt before his conversion, pure peace in his soul. That is why he prayed for his workers and partners to have that same sense of gratitude and peace of mind. His statement about "the promise of life" is probably a reminder to Timothy that his life was coming to an end, which is clear in Chapter 4. He did not want Timothy to be concerned. He was ending his life's work in with an eternal promise of hope. Paul would soon be leaving his dark and dismal prison cell, and enter the life God intended for his children, a life with glory and light.

An interesting observation about Paul's greetings is that when he wrote to the churches in general he used "grace and peace," yet when he wrote to pastors he used "grace, mercy, and peace." Charles Spurgeon noted, "Did you ever notice this one thing about Christian ministers, that they need even more mercy than other people? Although everybody needs mercy, ministers need it more than anybody else." Whatever the reason, Paul added "mercy" to his greetings to Timothy and Titus.

If there was any doubt Paul was an apostle, this passage removes all doubt. He was an apostle, an ambassador, a spokesman for God. He was led and used by God to write one-half of the New Testament books.

> *"Paul wrote this letter from his second Roman imprisonment, and soon after he wrote this letter he was condemned and executed in Rome at the command of Nero. Paul sensed this; therefore 2 Timothy is not only the last letter we have from Paul, but there is also a note of urgency and passion we might expect from a man who knew he would soon be executed."* (David Guzik)

Cultivating a Godly heritage. (1:3-7)

³ I thank God, whom I serve with a clear conscience the way my forefathers did, as I constantly remember you in my prayers night and day, ⁴ longing to see you, even as I recall your tears, so that I may be filled with joy. ⁵ For I am mindful of the sincere faith within you, which first dwelled in your grandmother Lois and your mother Eunice, and I am sure that *it is* in you as well. ⁶ For this reason I remind you to kindle afresh the gift of God which is in you through the laying on of my hands. ⁷ For God has not given us a spirit of timidity, but of power and love and discipline.

Not everyone is proud of his heritage. Maybe you were raised with an abusive father or one who abandoned your mother. Fortunately, you now have a heavenly Father who will never leave or forsake you. However, in the case of Timothy, he was raised by a godly family with sincere faith (1:5). Paul's heart was warmed when he remembered Timothy's believing mother and grandmother. Timothy was blessed with a godly heritage, one that Paul continually thanked God for in his prayers (1:3).

Paul told the Corinthian church, *"Be imitators of me, just as I also am of Christ"* (1 Corinthians 11:1). He knew all the time that his life was a model to others. We should be conscious of this as well. Do we live in a way we could say that to others? Paul reminds Timothy in verse three, *"³ I thank God, whom I serve with a clear conscience the way my forefathers did, as I constantly remember you in my prayers night and day."* The prayer life of Paul was worth imitation. He had told the church in Thessalonica the same principle: *"¹⁷ pray without ceasing"* (1 Thessalonians 5:17). Martin Luther was the father of the Protestant Reformation. He saw the need to spend long seasons in prayer:

"I have so much to do that I shall spend the first three hours in prayer." (Martin Luther)

If we are too busy to pray, we are too busy. In Verse 4, Paul was touched by the loving heart of Timothy as he recalled tears shed by his special friend. Paul, while in prison and awaiting execution, remembered moments that brought joy to his heart. The tears of Timothy may have been a memory of the time when his third missionary journey was over and he met with the Ephesian leaders for what he thought would be the last time. It was a very beautiful and emotional send-off. Paul knew that the road ahead was going to be difficult.

> *²² And now, behold, bound by the Spirit, I am on my way to Jerusalem, not knowing what will happen to me there, ²³ except that the Holy Spirit solemnly testifies to me in every city, saying that bonds and afflictions await me … ³⁶ When he had said these things, he knelt down and prayed with them all. ³⁷ And they began to weep aloud and embraced Paul, and repeatedly kissed him, ³⁸ grieving especially over the word which he had spoken, that they would not see his face again. And they were accompanying him to the ship.* (Acts 20:22, 23, 36-38)

Tears of joy flooded Paul's jail cell when these memories surfaced. Paul then encouraged Timothy to use his spiritual gifts and keep them fresh and active (1:6). God had led him to lay hands on his young "son in the faith" for a special enabling, a work of the Spirit, to equip Timothy for the work God had for him. Paul did not want Timothy to lose sight of this special blessing he had been given. Paul exhorted Timothy to keep the fire burning, stir up the gifts God had given him. It was also a good reminder of just how much Timothy was dependent on God for the intense warfare and challenges he faced every day. He was equipped and empowered by God for the task.

Because God had gifted and empowered Timothy there was no need to fear anything. *"⁷ For God has not given us a spirit of timidity, but of power and love and discipline"* (1:7). Another translation reads, *"⁷ For God hath not given us the spirit of fear; but of power, and of love, and of a sound mind"* (KJV). Fear does not come from God. The Lord tells his people numerous times to "Fear not." Instead of fear, God has provided:

- **Power.** God gives us the needed resources to defeat our enemies. He makes us strong so we can stand against the storms of attack and accusations. Paul had been a great example to Timothy of a man who stood strong when the difficulties intensified. Paul wanted Timothy to remember that he had the same God on his side and He would always be there. There was no reason to fear anything.

- **Love.** This is a supernatural love that can overcome the evil that seeks to destroy us (1 Peter 5:8-10). John showed us that the lost world will know real Christians by our love one for another (John 13:35). It is that same supernatural love that helps us forgive our enemies and causes us to pray for those who despitefully use us (Matthew 5:44). It is a love the world does not understand but sees and feels the presence of God in us. We are the aroma of God in a rotting world (2 Corinthians 2:15). Timothy would face the lions, the oppositions of Ephesus, armed with the love of God. Once again, what was there to fear?

- **A sound mind.** People that are lost wander through life in a spiritual fog. What a contrast with the one who knows God. *"² The Spirit of the LORD will rest on him— the Spirit of wisdom and of understanding, the Spirit of counsel and of might, the Spirit of the knowledge and fear of the LORD"* (Isaiah 11:2). The Greek word describes a calmness during a storm. It is the one who is not overwhelmed with a present crisis, but sees the way out. It is the opposite of confusion. We can see clearly when the world is in a panic stage. We have no fear, and we can bring calmness to others as well.

Remember: When we allow ourselves to become fearful, we are telling God that He is not enough.

Our Christian heritage is a great treasure to be unashamedly protected and boldly proclaimed. (1:8-14)

8 Therefore do not be ashamed of the testimony of our Lord or of me His prisoner, but join with *me* in suffering for the gospel according to the power of God, 9 who saved us and called us with a holy calling, not according to our works, but according to His own purpose and grace, which was granted to us in Christ Jesus from all eternity, 10 but has now been revealed by the appearing of our Savior Christ Jesus, who abolished death and brought life and immortality to light through the gospel, 11 for which I was appointed a preacher, an apostle, and a teacher. 12 For this reason I also suffer these things; but I am not ashamed, for I know whom I have believed, and I am convinced that He is able to protect what I have entrusted to Him until that day. 13 Hold on to the example of sound words which you have heard from me, in *the* faith and love which are in Christ Jesus. 14 Protect, through the Holy Spirit who dwells in us, the treasure which has been entrusted to *you.*

These verses are an anchor for the soul. If you have ever faced attacks and trials because of your faith, these verses will be a source of great comfort as they were to Timothy. In the previous verse, we learned God is not the source of fear. He is the source of power, love, and a sound mind.

> *"³¹ What then shall we say to these things? If God is for us, who is against us?" (Romans 8:31)*

A CALL TO EMBRACE SUFFERING FOR CHRIST. (1:8)

Jesus promised, *"¹¹ 'Blessed are you when people insult you and persecute you, and falsely say all kinds of evil against you because of Me. ¹² Rejoice and be glad, for your reward in heaven is great; for in the same way they persecuted the prophets who were before you'"* (Matthew 5:11, 12). Jesus called the ones who suffered for Him happy or blessed. Why? Because He knows something we don't understand. Why should we embrace suffering for Him, for righteousness? Because it builds our faith and conforms us to the image of Christ. Jesus died for our sins and forgave those who caused His death (which included us). When we gladly take our stand for Christ and suffer for our faith, Jesus said our reward in heaven is "great!" When the creation of the world was complete, it was declared as "good." But that same Creator calls it "great" when we suffer for His namesake. How big is "great" when the infinite God uses that word? The blessings God will bestow on all who suffer for His name must be beyond measure. Maybe that is why the Lord told the prophet Ananias what He was going to do to His chosen vessel, Paul:

> *. . . he is a chosen instrument of Mine, to bear My name before the Gentiles and kings and the sons of Israel; ¹⁶ for I will show him how much he must suffer for My name's sake.* (Acts 9:15, 16)

Paul suffered much in his life. He described his suffering to the church at Corinth:

> *... In far more labors, in far more imprisonments, beaten times without number, often in danger of death. ²⁴Five times I received from the Jews thirty-nine lashes. ²⁵Three times I was beaten with rods, once I was stoned, three times I was shipwrecked, a night and a day I have spent adrift at sea. ²⁶I have been on frequent journeys, in dangers from rivers, dangers from robbers, dangers from my countrymen, dangers from the Gentiles, dangers in the city, dangers in the wilderness, dangers at sea, dangers among false brothers; ²⁷I have been in labor and hardship, through many sleepless nights, in hunger and thirst, often without food, in cold and exposure. ²⁸Apart from such external things, there is the daily pressure on me of concern for all the churches.* (2 Corinthians 11:23-28)

Paul invited Timothy to join him in suffering for Christ; *"Join with me in suffering for the gospel according to the power of God" (1:8).* Paul had learned the joyful privilege to be called of God to bear His name, which meant it was not going to be easy, but God was with him all along the way, and the best, or "great," was yet to come.

NEVER FORGET OUR GREAT SALVATION AND CALLING. (1:9)

We can take no credit for our salvation. Jesus paid it all, called us to Himself and He alone gets the glory.

> *(He) who saved us and called us with a holy calling, not according to our works, but according to His own purpose and grace, which was granted to us in Christ Jesus from all eternity.* (1:9)

God told Jeremiah that before he was born, from eternity past, he was on God's heart:

Before I formed you in the womb I knew you,
And before you were born I consecrated you;
I have appointed you a prophet to the nations.
(Jeremiah 1:5)

How special we are to God. He chose us from the beginning and gave us a great purpose. How can we fear anything since we have been in the hand of God from the beginning? What a great salvation. What a Savior!

WE ARE CHOSEN TO BE FEARLESS AMBASSADORS OF THE LIFE-CHANGING GOSPEL. (1:10, 11)

[10] but has now been revealed by the appearing of our Savior Christ Jesus, who abolished death and brought life and immortality to light through the gospel, [11] for which I was appointed a preacher, an apostle, and a teacher. (1:10, 11)

Each of these points relates to verse 7. Paul knew Timothy would face great difficulties with the Ephesian silversmiths and others who opposed the Christians. The previous riot in Ephesus (Acts 19:23-41) revealed how extreme, hostile and dangerous it was for a believer to proclaim the gospel in that city. It would have been very encouraging to young Timothy to be reminded of the great salvation he had and that he was chosen to serve God before he was born (1:9). Nothing was going to come to Timothy that wasn't filtered through the protective hands of God. Even death is no threat to the Christian (1 Corinthians 15:55-57). Timothy was with Paul when those words were written. He saw in Paul a man who did not fear death or any man. His anchor was secure in Christ.

Verse 10 is one more reason to live without fear in life. Jesus has abolished death and has given eternal life to all who follow Him (1:10). Paul taught Timothy that *"to live is Christ and to die is* gain" (Philippians 1:21). The guarantee of immortality permeated Paul's teachings:

> *Where, O death, is your victory?*
> *Where, O death, is your sting?* *(1 Corinthians 15:55)*

Jesus taught His disciples the same thing, *"28 Do not be afraid of those who kill the body but cannot kill the soul. Rather, be afraid of the One who can destroy both soul and body in hell"* (Matthew 10:28). The point is clear if we don't fear death, we don't fear life. What is the worst thing that can happen to a believer? We may be killed and then we graduate to eternal life. If that is the worst thing, what can we possibly fear? It is this message that Paul and we have been called to preach.

> *10 but has now been revealed by the appearing of our Savior Christ Jesus, who abolished death and brought life and immortality to light through the gospel, 11 for which I was appointed a preacher, an apostle, and a teacher* (1:11).

Someone might say, "I am not afraid of death, it is the dying that bothers me. Suffering is not something we joyfully anticipate. That is what the next verse addresses.

IN SUFFERING, WE ARE HELD SECURELY IN THE HANDS OF OUR SAVIOR. (1:12)

> *12 For this reason I also suffer these things; but I am not ashamed, for I know whom I have believed, and I am convinced that He is able to protect what I have entrusted to Him until that day. (1:12)*

The Psalmist sang, *"Weeping may last for the night, But a shout of joy comes in the morning"* (Psalm 30:5). Pain and suffering on earth are but for a short season in light of the glory of eternity. Paul wrote to the persecuted believers in Rome who were being tortured and slaughtered, *"18 For I consider that the sufferings of this present time are not worthy to be compared with the glory that is to be revealed to us"* (Romans 8:18).

What is it that gives confidence to the one suffering for Christ? It will all turn out well. It is the unchanging and dependable Word of God. What God has revealed will happen. That was the rock-solid foundation of Paul's faith that drove him to boldly proclaim, *"I am not ashamed, for I know whom I have believed, and I am convinced that He is able to protect what I have entrusted to Him until that day"* (1:12). The world around us is uncertain. People break promises and let us down. We experience betrayal and personal hurt. It is not that way with God. His word is certain. What He says will happen. Paul is saying he has entrusted his life in the hands of God and he is certain God will protect what is His. Once again, for Timothy, the message was that there is simply nothing to fear. God will preserve us until that day when He takes us to glory.

PRINCIPLES TO LIVE BY.

Whatever we give to God for safekeeping will be protected forever. If we give Him our heart, He will keep it forever. If we give God our finances, they will be invested forever. If we hoard things, thieves will steal them or someone else gets them when we die. If we turn our desires over to God, He will one day give us greater things. Our greatest treasure is the Lord. "He is no fool to give up what he can never keep to gain what he can never lose" (Jim Elliot, missionary).

GOD HAS ENTRUSTED US WITH THE GREATEST TREASURE IN THE UNIVERSE. (1:13, 14)

> [13] *Hold on to the example of sound words which you have heard from me, in the faith and love which are in Christ*

Jesus. **[14] Protect, through the Holy Spirit who dwells in us, the treasure which has been entrusted to you.** (1:13, 14)

Paul reminded Timothy he had a great treasure within him. God provided the Holy Spirit to protect that treasure. He was describing Timothy's faith and love that had grown over the years. The teaching and mentoring of Paul and the heritage of his mother and grandmother all helped mold Timothy into the man of God he had become. Timothy lived in a pagan city where truth was overshadowed by the darkness of sin. However, Timothy was well-anchored in the truth, his words were solid, he had learned his lessons well (1:13). The greatest treasure of all was that Timothy was anchored to the rock and would stand firm in all trials.

> *"In times like these, you need a Savior*
> *In times like these, you need an anchor*
> *Be very sure, be very sure*
> *Your anchor holds and grips the Solid Rock."*
> (Old Christian Hymn)

PRINCIPLES TO LIVE BY.

Preach the Word. The Word of God has been described as a lion. We don't need to protect it or defend it, just let it loose. The Word of God is quick and powerful and sharper than any two-edged sword (Hebrews 4:12). The Word can make one wise (2 Timothy 3:15). It is like a mirror that reveals our true self (James 1:23). The Word of God is true, inspired, authoritative, flawless, eternal, unbreakable, perfect, reliable, sufficient, powerful, and a thousand times more. Philosophies will fail, men's wisdom will leave us empty but the one who preaches the Word opens the treasure chest of God for all who will listen.

> *"The grass withers, the flower fades, but the word of our God will stand forever.* (Isaiah 40:8).

The faithful and unfaithful workers will be revealed with the trials of ministry. (1:15-18)

¹⁵ You are aware of the fact that all who are in Asia turned away from me, among whom are Phygelus and Hermogenes. ¹⁶ The Lord grant mercy to the household of Onesiphorus, for he often refreshed me and was not ashamed of my chains; ¹⁷ but when he was in Rome, he eagerly searched for me and found me— ¹⁸ the Lord grant to him to find mercy from the Lord on that day—and you know very well what services he rendered at Ephesus.

THOSE WHO ABANDONED PAUL AND THE MINISTRY. (1:15)

> *¹⁵ You are aware of the fact that all who are in Asia turned away from me, among whom are Phygelus and Hermogenes.* (1:15)

As Paul reached the end of a very productive ministry, he was nearly alone. Have you ever been let down by someone you trusted? Have you ever felt alone when standing for what you believed? Paul lived for three years in Ephesus and taught the people and evangelized daily. He was a tireless worker. Timothy was with him much of the time. Paul reminded him of how many of the people he trusted were a disappointment to him. He had been deserted by all his early contacts in Ephesus, *"all who are in Asia turned away from me"* (1:15).

Paul was sitting in a dungeon prison in Rome awaiting execution with only Luke by his side (2 Timothy 4:11). It is interesting that when Jesus died on the cross, He was alone as well. A few onlookers were there, but the disciples were scattered and hiding. Peter denied him and even God the Father could not

look at His Son when He became our sins on the cross
(2 Corinthians 5:21). It was His darkest, most abandoned
moment in eternal history, yet it was then that He was doing His
greatest work. Paul experienced his greatest abandonment at
the end of his life as well. He would walk alone to his execution.
No awards were given to the world's greatest church planter.
None of his students were there thanking him for writing half of
the New Testament. They had all abandoned him. He had done
more than any follower of Christ to spread the gospel to the
world and he ended up alone at the end. Fortunately, Paul knew
that the applause of men was not what was most important.

> *⁶ For I am already being poured out as a drink offering, and*
> *the time of my departure has come. ⁷ I have fought the good*
> *fight, I have finished the course, I have kept the faith; ⁸ in*
> *the future there is reserved for me the crown of*
> *righteousness, which the Lord, the righteous Judge, will*
> *award to me on that day; and not only to me, but also to all*
> *who have loved His appearing.* (2 Timothy 4:6-8)

PHYGELUS AND HERMOGENES

Paul knew who these two were and Timothy also knew them.
This is the only reference to them in the Bible. They must have
been the worst of the deserters. They have gone down in
history along with Demas as giving up on God (2 Timothy 4:10).
What a horrible way to end a life.

It wasn't just a few that walked away from the ministry but
"all" of them left at some point. We have no record outside of
this passage about "Phygelus and Hermogenes," but we have to
assume that they were the most promising of all the workers.
Paul would have put more time into them and had great hopes
that they would become leaders. In the military, there is nothing
worse than deserters. They abandon their men when the going

gets tough. All the training and time put into them was wasted. These two men Paul named were deserters from God's army.

When Paul wrote Romans he finished with a long list of those who had gone through the fire and were tested, but in the end they were approved. That list is the hall of fame of warriors for God. What a horrible thing for Phygelus and Hermogenes to have their names only mentioned once and they are part of the hall of shame.

Disappointments in ministry are sadly part of the job description. Paul had them and Jesus had them. You will have them. When precious metals are put into a furnace to be purified, the fire reveals the true quality of the metal. The impurities float to the surface and are strained off leaving only pure precious metal. The challenges of ministry and the intensity of spiritual warfare are the furnace and will separate the pure from the impure.

> *But He knows the way I take;*
> *When He has tried me, I shall come forth as gold.*
> (Job 23:10)

PRINCIPLES TO LIVE BY.

Everyone goes through dark tunnels at times. But Jesus is with us in the dark, when we are rejected, abandoned, and alone. He will bring us into the light again. Ministry at times is a lonely journey. Paul kept his eye on the prize. He walked the last road alone, but was victorious. We have the same resources and can also be victorious to the end.

ONESIPHORUS, ONE WHO REMAINED FAITHFUL TO PAUL AND THE MINISTRY. (1:16-18)

> *[16] The Lord grant mercy to the household of Onesiphorus,*
> *for he often refreshed me and was not ashamed of my*

chains; ¹⁷ but when he was in Rome, he eagerly searched for me and found me— ¹⁸ the Lord grant to him to find mercy from the Lord on that day—and you know very well what services he rendered at Ephesus. (1:16-18)

Fortunately, Paul also had some who stood the test of fire. Paul wrote two letters specifically to Timothy, more than any other individual. Timothy was pure gold, a rare find; most didn't stand the test. Another good worker Paul mentioned was a man named Onesiphorus, a worker well known by Timothy (1:18). When others were abandoning Paul, this worker showed hospitality to Paul. He unashamedly embraced the gospel. Paul prayed a special prayer that God would show mercy to his family.

After warning Timothy about the deserters and enemies of the gospel, Paul praised Onesiphorus, one of the most faithful friends he knew. Timothy and Onesiphorus were likely neighbors in Ephesus since Paul reminded Timothy to greet his family at the end of this letter (1:18). Onesiphorus may have already gone to be with the Lord. Some scholars believe that Onesiphorus had died and that is why Paul greets the household and he speaks only in the past tense when he talks of Onesiphorus.

We do know that this family was loyal to Paul even when most had given up on him when he was in Ephesus during his third missionary journey (1 Timothy 1:15).). When Paul was arrested and went to Rome on his final journey, Onesiphorus made the difficult journey to Rome and "*eagerly*" searched for Paul in the maze of prison dungeons and found him. It was a dangerous journey to make. He managed to locate Paul in the dungeon of the Mamertine Prison where Paul was a condemned criminal awaiting execution. Christians had been declared enemies of the state. Paul never forgot the love and concern Onesiphorus showed toward him. His visit "refreshed" Paul in his dreary, underground cell (1:17). *"He often refreshed me and was not ashamed of my chains"* (1:16).

Onesiphorus was a faithful servant. He was like Barnabas, a man of encouragement. Barnabas' name means "son of encouragement." The name "Onesiphorus" means "one who brings help." They both lived up to their names. We who believe in Jesus are called children of the King. We need to live up to our names as well.

PRINCIPLES TO LIVE BY.

The fact that you are reading this means you can choose how you want to finish your course. Will you be inducted into God's Hall of Fame or be recorded into the Hall of Shame as a deserter? What will the furnace of ministry do to you? It is your choice. The final books are written for Phygelus and Hermogenes, but not yet for you. All of us have an opportunity to finish well.

2 Timothy 2

Multiplying disciples, the pastor's role in the Great Commission. (2:1, 2)

[1] You therefore, my son, be strong in the grace that is in Christ Jesus. [2] The things which you have heard from me in the presence of many witnesses, entrust these to faithful people who will be able to teach others also.

This verse contains a very important pattern of ministry. It is a pattern of muliplication. The previous verses described two different kinds of workers Paul encountered, faithful and unfaithful. Chapter 2 picks up from there. Instructions were given to Timothy concerning what to do with faithful workers. Paul gives a simple formula to expand the kingdom of God. It has three steps:

- We need to have the right message.
- We need to find, cultivate and train faithful workers.
- We need to send them out to duplicate the process of teaching others to become multipliers.

Let's examine each of these steps. This pattern is often missing in modern churches that have a strong pastor who does it all. He preaches, he teaches, while the congregation watches and listens, like an audience. That pattern will not build a church that multiplies the body of Christ. We begin by reminding ourselves what this is all about, the Great Commission.

THE GREAT COMMISSION.

> *[18] And Jesus came up and spoke to them, saying, "All authority in heaven and on earth has been given to Me. [19] Go, therefore, and make disciples of all the nations, baptizing them in the name of the Father and the Son and the Holy Spirit, [20] teaching them to follow all that I commanded you; and behold, I am with you always, to the end of the age.* (Matthew 28:18-20)

GRACE AND STRENGTH FROM GOD. (2:2)

In the Great Commission given by Jesus, the main point, and the only command in the text, in the Greek original text, is to "*make disciples of all the nations.*" We do that by going to witness to people, teaching them to follow Christ and accept Him as their savior, and then baptizing them. Chapter 2 in Second Timothy is a reminder of how to accomplish the teaching portion of the Great Commission. Paul starts by using a word he has used over 20 times to Timothy, namely, to *"be strong"* in God's assignment. It is God who provides grace and empo werment to fulfill His will. Ephesus was a tough crowd, as we have seen. Timothy needed the strength and grace (favor) of God. God once told Paul that His grace was sufficient (2 Corinthians 12:9-10). We also need that grace, and His strength, day by day. God's assignments need God's enabling.

THE PROCESS OF DISCIPLESHIP TRAINING. (2:2)

1. We need to have the right message. (*"The things you have heard"*) It all begins with a strong foundation. We can only teach what we know. We can only model how we live. Timothy was encouraged to find his strength in God. *"You therefore, my son, be strong in the grace that is in Christ Jesus."* That strength comes from drawing close to God and relying on Him.

> *²⁹ He gives strength to the weary,*
> *And to the one who lacks might He increases power.*
> *³⁰ Though youths grow weary and tired,*
> *And vigorous young men stumble badly,*
> *³¹ Yet those who wait for the Lord*
> *Will gain new strength;*
> *They will mount up with wings like eagles,*
> *They will run and not get tired,*
> *They will walk and not become weary.* (Isaiah 40:29-31)

Timothy was discipled by Paul during two of his missionary journeys. Timothy was given a very strong foundation in the Word of God as well as watching and working with the greatest church planter of that time. He was given the responsibility to assist the churches in Macedonia. He helped Paul write several books. Even with that strong foundation, Timothy was challenged to continue growing in grace in Christ. Then, when a believer is taught, nourished, and established by Christ, he is ready to do what Paul told the church in Corinth, *"Be imitators of me, just as I also am of Christ"* (1 Corinthians 11:1). We need to pass it on.

You can't expect a house to stand if you build it on a faulty foundation. Jesus described the value of a strong foundation in our lives:

> *²⁴ Therefore everyone who hears these words of Mine and acts on them, may be compared to a wise man who built his house on the rock. ²⁵ And the rain fell, and the floods came, and the winds blew and slammed against that house; and yet it did not fall, for it had been founded on the rock.*
> *²⁶ Everyone who hears these words of Mine and does not act on them, will be like a foolish man who built his house on the sand. ²⁷ The rain fell, and the floods came, and the winds blew and slammed against that house; and it fell— and great was its fall.* (Matthew 7:24-27)

Paul refers to what is to be taught or passed on to others as *"2 The things which you have heard from me in the presence of many witnesses.* These are the apostolic doctrines, the great faiths of the church. These are those matters which many witnesses have verified are the truths of the church.

The foundation every pastor needs, to begin with, is a firm commitment and good knowledge of the Word of God. Any teaching we receive needs to be confirmed with Scripture like the Bereans did (Acts 17:11). We also should have a trusted team of spiritual advisors, mentors. What we teach others should be well-grounded and accurate to the Scriptures. Today we have the same foundation and "witnesses" that Paul had, but we also have a great company over the ages of faithful teachers and writers who honored the Word of God and have left us a heritage of the faith. We have a great foundation to build upon. We need to pass it on.

2. WE NEED TO FIND, CULTIVATE, AND TRAIN FAITHFUL WORKERS ("FAITHFUL MEN").

This step is vital for success, but it is the hardest part. Paul poured his life into many who later deserted the faith, as we have seen. Solomon noted, *"6 Most men will proclaim every one his own goodness: "but a faithful man who can find?"* (Proverbs 20:6). Faithfulness is evidence of a life filled with the Holy Spirit (Galatians 5:22). It is like an exquisite diamond, beautiful, enduring, and rare. Paul had many who failed the test and walked away, but fortunately, he had some like Timothy, Luke, Silas, and others who were faithful. These were the ones that helped change the world.

The big lesson here is that team effort is required, much like a relay race, where the baton is handed off to the next runner.

The great truths of God were never meant to be held on to, but to be shared with others. Think again of the illustration of the relay race. If you were running in an important relay race you would pick your team of runners carefully. They would have to have exceptional speed and running skills, but it would also be important that they had a reputation for showing up. You would not want a runner that did not take the challenge seriously and came late for races or decided to take the day off. He would have to be dependable and dedicated. He would have to be a faithful runner. So it is with the discipling of the nations. We are wise to teach proven and faithful workers who will carry on the work when we are no longer able to do it.

When Paul found faithful workers, he commended them:

> *Now, so that you also may know about my circumstances as to what I am doing, Tychicus, the beloved brother and faithful servant in the Lord, will make everything known to you.* (Ephesians 6:21)

> *. . . just as you learned it from Epaphras, our beloved fellow bond-servant, who is a faithful servant of Christ on our behalf."* (Colossians 1:7)

Jesus walked with His disciples every day for three years. They were taught the Word of God. They followed His teachings. They watched a dedicated life. They learned. They were prepared. Finally, they launched out on their own. Paul followed the same pattern and told the believers to *"Be imitators of me, just as I also am of Christ."* (1 Corinthians 11:1)

Once we have found, trained, and developed faithful men, then what?

3. SEND THEM OUT TO MULTIPLY AND TRAIN OTHERS TO BECOME MULTIPLIERS. *("TEACH OTHERS")*

"... entrust these to faithful people who will be able to teach others also." (2:2)

The people to whom we entrust the great truths of the faith must be faithful, but they must also be *"able to teach."* They must have the spiritual gift of teaching, a requirement for spiritual leaders (1 Timothy 3). Equip them and send them out. Too many churches today have a paid professional staff that does the work of the ministry while the rest are an audience, observers of ministry. This verse tells a different story. The church members are the ministers, the pastor is the trainer/discipler to equip the people to do the work of the ministry.

The role of the leader is to *"entrust"* or hand off the role of spreading the kingdom of God. The things we have learned are not secrets we keep for ourselves. They must be shared. Distribute them to others who can also entrust them to others. The goal is the multiplication of the church. As the workers go out and duplicate the process, they then see new generations of faithful workers doing the same. Instead of adding to the church, it becomes a multiplication system. So the purpose of this passage is to replace addition with multiplication. It is God's new math.

The soldier, the athlete, and the farmer. (2:3-7)

[3] Suffer hardship with *me*, as a good soldier of Christ Jesus. [4] No soldier in active service entangles himself in the affairs of everyday life, so that he may please the one who enlisted *him*. [5] And if someone likewise competes as an athlete, he

is not crowned *as victor* unless he competes according to the rules. ⁶ The hard-working farmer ought to be the first to receive his share of the crops. ⁷ Consider what I say, for the Lord will give you understanding in everything.

In verse 2 we were given a pattern for the multiplication of the church. Faithfulness was the primary character attribute needed. But there are other qualities as well which define a successful Christian worker. In verses 3-7 we find them illustrated by three occupations: a soldier in the army, an athlete in training, and finally a successful farmer.

Before we examine the soldier in the army, let's think about what it was like to be a Roman soldier in the first century.

THE ARMY IN ROME WAS A COMMON SIGHT TO PAUL AND TIMOTHY.

Think of a soldier in the army. What images come to mind. The people in Ephesus were under the authority and control of Rome. The Roman army was the greatest on the earth in Pauls' time. Soldiers were everywhere. Historical writings help us understand what was required of a man to be in the army of the Roman Empire. All Roman citizens were required to participate in the military. They had to prove their worth to be paid their wages, which consisted of bags of salt.

- They were highly respected and honored because they served their Emporer.

- They carried heavy weights long distances over difficult terrain. They had to be in top condition to follow their orders.
- They supplied their own personal clothing, which cost them around 10 percent of their income.
- They were the best. Centurions were chosen for their size, strength, and dexterity. They had to be vigilant, temperate, actively able to execute all orders. They were highly disciplined, clean, well dressed, and maintained battle readiness. (This list was assembled from various historical writings).

These ancient requirements were understood by the people, and help us understand what it means for a Christian to be a soldier for God, our Commanding General.

BELIEVERS ARE LIKE SOLDIERS IN OUR KING'S ARMY. (2:3, 4)

> *24 Then Jesus said to His disciples, "If anyone wishes to come after Me, he must deny himself, and take up his cross and follow Me.* (Matthew 16:24)

Disciplined – A soldier must stay focused on the task in the heat of battle. Christian service is described as a spiritual war.

> *12 For our struggle is not against flesh and blood, but against the rulers, against the powers, against the world forces of this darkness, against the spiritual forces of wickedness in the heavenly places. 13 Therefore, take up the full armor of God, so that you will be able to resist on the evil day, and having done everything, to stand firm.* (Ephesians 6:12, 13)

A Finisher – A soldier stays on the course until the end and does not get distracted along the way. *"4 No soldier in active service entangles himself in the affairs of everyday life."* Paul was the best example of this quality. At the end of his life, he wrote these words:

> *I have fought the good fight,*
> *I have finished the course,*
> *I have kept the faith.*
> (2 Timothy 4:7)

Sacrificial – A soldier had to supply his clothing and live on very basic needs. He considered the purpose of his service more important than personal comfort.

> *Therefore, I urge you, brothers and sisters, in view of God's mercy, to offer your bodies as a living sacrifice, holy and pleasing to God—this is your true and proper worship.*
> (Romans 12:1)

A God-centered life – *"So that he may please the One who enlisted him."* A true soldier does it all for the glory of king and country. A true believer does it all for the Glory of our King and His kingdom.

> *[31] Whether, then, you eat or drink or*
> *whatever you do, do all to the glory of God.*
> *(1 Corinthians 10:31)*

BELIEVERS ARE ALSO LIKE AN ATHLETE. (2:5)

> *[5] And if someone likewise competes as an athlete, he is not crowned as victor unless he competes according to the rules. (2:5)*

The first Olympics were held in Greece and continued into the Roman Empire. Great stadiums and colosseums were built for sport and entertainment. Everyone that lived then understood what it took to become a great athlete and why they did it.

Imagine an athlete running against the world's best and breaking the world record. Then It is discovered when he goes to the awards stand to receive his crown that he was not officially registered  for the games. He will be disqualified and no crown will be given him. He will be disgraced in front of everyone. Jesus described a scene like that when the great judgment happens:

> [21] *"Not everyone who says to Me, 'Lord, Lord,' will enter the kingdom of heaven, but the one who does the will of My Father who is in heaven will enter.* [22] *Many will say to Me on that day, 'Lord, Lord, did we not prophesy in Your name, and in Your name cast out demons, and in Your name perform many miracles?'* [23] *And then I will declare to them, 'I never knew you; leave Me, you who practice lawlessness.'*
> (Matthew 7:21-23)

He lacked the one basic thing that God required, faith, true faith. Without faith, we cannot please God (Hebrews 11:6).

Paul wanted Timothy to run the course well and finish well. That was how Paul finished. Here is how he described it in his final words before his death:"

> [6] *For I am already being poured out as a drink offering, and the time of my departure has come.* [7] *I have fought the good fight, I have finished the course, I have kept the faith; in the future there is laid up for me the crown of righteousness, which the Lord, the righteous Judge, will award to me on that day; and not only to me, but also to all who have loved His appearing.*
> (2 Timothy 4:6-8)

That is how to finish a race!

BELIEVERS ARE ALSO LIKE A FARMER. (2:6, 7)

> *⁶ The hard-working farmer ought to be the first to receive his share of the crops. ⁷ Consider what I say, for the Lord will give you understanding in everything.* (2:6, 7)

Paul sent a letter to the church in Galatia with a reference to farmers and the joy of a successful harvest season:

> *⁷ Do not be deceived, God is not mocked; for whatever a person sows, this he will also reap. ⁸ For the one who sows to his own flesh will reap destruction from the flesh, but the one who sows to the Spirit will reap eternal life from the Spirit. ⁹ Let's not become discouraged in doing good, for in due time we will reap, if we do not become weary. ¹⁰ So then, while we have opportunity, let's do good to all people, and especially to those who are of the household of the faith.* (Galatians 6:7-10)

In farming it is all about preparing the soil, planting the seed, and harvesting the crops. As Christians, the gospel is the seed and the harvest is the souls of men. Jesus used a very familiar parable to say that very same thing when He explained the parable of the sower:

> *¹⁸ Listen then to the parable of the sower. ¹⁹ When anyone hears the word of the kingdom and does not understand it, the evil one comes and snatches away what has been sown in his heart. This is the one sown with seed beside the road. ²⁰ The one sown with seed on the rocky places, this is the one who hears the word and immediately receives it with joy; ²¹ yet he has no firm root in himself, but is only tempo-rary, and when affliction or persecution occurs because of the word, immediately he falls away. ²² And the one sown with seed among the thorns, this is the one who hears the word, and the anxiety of the world and the deceitfulness of wealth choke the word, and it becomes unfruitful. ²³ But*

the one sown with seed on the good soil, this is the one who hears the word and understands it, who indeed bears fruit and produces, some a hundred, some sixty, and some thirty times as much. (Matthew 13:18-23)

The farmer in this passage to Timothy works dilegently at an unseen task. He is not performing like an athlete, and he does not get a medal like the military commander. He labors hard because he is committed to seeing a great harvest and there is no shortcut for work. Ministry is not for people who are lazy, seeking recognition, or those who are apathetic toward people. True character has been described as what you do when nobody is watching.

Paul wrote to the church in Corinth and described how, like a good farmer, he toiled in the field until the spiritual harvest came in:

⁹ For I am the least of the apostles, and not fit to be called an apostle, because I persecuted the church of God. ¹⁰ But by the grace of God I am what I am, and His grace toward me did not prove vain; but I labored even more than all of them, yet not I, but the grace of God with me. ¹¹ Whether then it was I or they, so we preach and so you believed. (1 Corinthians 15:9-11)

Just as the farmer gets to benefit from the crops when they come in, so God's faithful workers in God's fields will be rewarded in the final harvest

Timothy was to find faithful workers he could teach and pour into their lives. They should be like disciplined soldiers, ready to take the heat of battle. It's like the great athlete who runs to the finish and ends in victory. Like the patient farmer, they need to be willing to work hard when nobody is watching, rising early and toiling until late in the day to see a great harvest. We each need this challenge to reset our personal goals to become the kind of leader that truly makes a difference and will not be ashamed when we stand before Christ at the judgment seat.

The prize awaits all who finish well. (2:8-13)

8 Remember Jesus Christ, risen from the dead, descendant of David, according to my gospel, 9 for which I suffer hardship even to imprisonment as a criminal; but the word of God is not imprisoned. 10 For this reason I endure all things for the sake of those who are chosen, so that they also may obtain the salvation which is in Christ Jesus *and* with *it* eternal glory. 11 The statement is trustworthy:

For if we died with Him, we will also live with Him;
12 If we endure, we will also reign with Him;
If we deny Him, He will also deny us;
13 If we are faithless, He remains faithful, for He cannot deny Himself.

Paul encouraged Timothy to be a good soldier for Christ, stay disciplined, and endure hardships. He needed the stamina of a strong athlete to finish the race and receive the prize. He needed the patience of the farmer who expectantly sowed his crops and waited for the harvest. The fruits of his labors would come, but later. Timothy was exhorted to not give up. It is all worth it. Remember who we serve, "Jesus Christ, risen from the dead, descendant of David."

When Jesus came to earth, He came to suffer and die for sins. He fulfilled the Abrahamic covenant that a Savior would come to rescue His people from sin. The other national covenant was given to King David. The promise was that a son from the line of David, a son of the tribe of Judah would one day rule on the thone over the nations. This One would be the King of kings and Lord of all lords. Both covenants were about Jesus the Messiah. He came the first time to pay for sins, the son of Abraham. He is coming again as the son of David to take His rightful throne. He suffered and then He reigns forever.

AN EARLY HYMN OF THE FIRST-CENTURY CHURCH

Many church historians understand Verses 12 and 13 as the words of a first-century hymn sung in the house churches. As persecuted Christians, they would sing of the great hope that was promised to all who would endure to the end. Because Christ had died and we have identified with Him, our sins are forgiven and all believers would one day live with Him. Not only that, but when we suffer for Him we will reign with Him. That would have been a great encouragement for a suffering church to sing those words. The words also follow the pattern of the three previous illustrations. We should live like disciplined soldiers, hard-working athletes, and patient farmers. The reward in the end is worth it.

That is why Paul quoted the lines of that early Christian hymn:

> *For if we died with Him, we will also live with Him;*
> *¹² If we endure, we will also reign with Him.* (2:11, 12)

The second part of the hymn has at times been a bit confusing and has even caused some controversy today.

> *If we deny Him, He will also deny us;*
> *¹³ If we are faithless, He remains faithful, for He cannot deny Himself.* (2:12, 13)

"If we deny Him, He will also deny us." Some think this means that if we fail to endure to the end, we will lose our salvation.

"He will deny us" eternal life. The poetic style of the hymn is similar to the writings of the Biblical prophets who used what is referred to as Synonymous parallelism (the repetition in the second part is what has already been expressed in the first). It is important to read both lines, not just the first line. In this grammatic style commonly used in the Old Testament, the second line often amplifies the first line. The second line tells us if *"we are faithless, He remains faithful, for He cannot deny Himself."* Remember, it is important to read all of the lines together. When we trusted Christ, we were joined together with Him. We died with Him and because of that, we will one day live with Him. This is a forever act. We are in Christ and we know from Paul's letter to Rome that, *"There is, therefore, no condemnation for those who are in Christ and nothing will separate us from the love of Christ"* (Romans 8:1, 39). That is our position as a believer.

The next statement in the first stanza of the hymn is about the blessings of the believer who endures suffering for Christ. That believer will have a great reward; he will reign with Christ. But not everyone will complete the race victoriously, or endure the attacks. Some will fall short, and that is the second part of the hymn.

> *If we deny Him, He will also deny us;*
> *13 If we are faithless, He remains faithful, for He cannot deny Himself.*

Just as Peter denied Christ three times and John the Baptist questioned his faith in prison, so there will be believers who fail in their faith at times. But even if we, as God's born again children, fail in our walk, He will always remain faithful to us. *"13 If we are faithless, He remains faithful, for He cannot deny Himself."* We remain in Christ where there is no eternal condemnation. He denies us the reward of reigning with Him, but our position is never lost. Nothing will separate us from His love (Romans 8). This hymn is saying the same thing Paul wrote to the church at Corinth.

> *10 According to the grace of God which was given to me, like a wise master builder I laid a foundation, and another is building on it. But each person must be careful how he builds on it. 11 For no one can lay a foundation other than the one which is laid, which is Jesus Christ. 12 Now if anyone builds on the foundation with gold, silver, precious stones, wood, hay, or straw, 13 each one's work will become evident; for the day will show it because it is to be revealed with fire, and the fire itself will test the quality of each one's work. 14 If anyone's work which he has built on it remains, he will receive a reward. 15 If anyone's work is burned up, he will suffer loss; but he himself will be saved, yet only so as through fire.* (1 Corinthians 3:10-15)

> *9 Therefore we also have as our ambition, whether at home or absent, to be pleasing to Him. 10 For we must all appear before the judgment seat of Christ, so that each one may receive compensation for his deeds.* (2 Corinthians 5:9, 10)

There is a great reward for those who suffer for Christ and a loss of reward for those who fail to diligently follow Him. But never is loss of salvation mentioned.

We need to be faithful soldiers, disciplined athletes, and hard-working farmers. Paul was telling Timothy that it was worth it all. That is why he said, *"10 For this reason I endure all things for the sake of those who are chosen, so that they also may obtain the salvation which is in Christ Jesus and with it eternal glory"* (2:10). Paul lived and died with an eternal perspective, not focussing on the difficulties of the day. A greater day is coming when all the suffering will be worth it all. Our salvation is based on the work of Christ, not our efforts. He is faithful to us even when we struggle in our faith. But the overall lesson is it will be worth it all when we see Jesus.

Paul reminded his younger disciple that even though he was suffering in a Roman prison, the word of God was not imprisoned, but had an eternal impact (2:9). Paul, we know, was chained to one of the palace guards, but because of that, the gospel reached the very household of Caesar himself.

> *12 Now I want you to know, brothers and sisters, that my circumstances have turned out for the greater progress of the gospel, 13 so that my imprisonment in the cause of Christ has become well known throughout the praetorian guard and to everyone else, 14 and that most of the brothers and sisters, trusting in the Lord because of my imprisonment, have far more courage to speak the word of God without fear."* (Philippians 1:12-14)

> *21 Greet every saint in Christ Jesus. The brothers who are with me greet you. 22 All the saints greet you, especially those of Caesar's household.*
> (Philippians 4:21, 22)

Paul learned to embrace suffering for Christ and knew the eternal benefits far outweighed the temporary pain. That lesson is what he is passing on to Timothy, his closest friend, and co-worker in the world. For us, the message is the same.

Summary. The main takeaway from this portion of Scripture can be summed up with what Paul told the suffering church in Rome.

> *16 The Spirit Himself testifies with our spirit that we are children of God, 17 and if children, heirs also, heirs of God and fellow heirs with Christ, if indeed we suffer with Him so that we may also be glorified with Him. 18 For I consider that the sufferings of this present time are not worthy to be compared with the glory that is to be revealed to us.*
> (Romans 8:16-18)

Now, that is something to sing about.

The Word of God was not given for academic arguments, but for life change. (2:14-19)

14 Remind *them* of these things, and solemnly exhort *them* in the presence of God not to dispute about words, which is useless *and leads* to the ruin of the listeners. 15 Be diligent to present yourself approved to God as a worker who does not need to be ashamed, accurately handling the word of truth. 16 But avoid worldly *and* empty chatter, for it will lead to further ungodliness, 17 and their talk will spread like gangrene. Among them are Hymenaeus and Philetus, 18 *men* who have gone astray from the truth, claiming that the resurrection has already taken place; and they are jeopardizing the faith of some. 19 Nevertheless, the firm foundation of God stands, having this seal: "The Lord knows those who are His;" and, "Everyone who names the name of the Lord is to keep away from wickedness."

The challenge is clear. Choose which side you will be on and stay the course. The previous verses ended with a Christian hymn that had a great promise to all who faithfully followed God and warnings to those who did not. Verse 14 begins with Paul reminding Timothy that he needed to remind the believers how important it was for them to understand this. He was also exhorted by Paul to take care of a serious problem in the church. A group had become argumentative over the truths of the Word of God and had caused damage to the body of Christ. Paul feared it would drive the entire church to ruin (2:14). Discussions are fine, but argumentative people were causing great unrest. Maybe you know people like this, always looking for problems.

> *"Paul is here combating those who like to get into intellectual banter over obscure points of doctrine, but who*

are not seeking to grow in obedience to God. These scholars like to prove their superior intelligence by winning theological debates. But the point of Scriptural knowledge is not to fill our heads, but to change our lives. To use the Bible for knowledge without application is to misuse it." (OBible.org)

HANDLE THE WORD OF GOD CORRECTLY. (2:15)

Paul wanted Timothy to be a strong, diligent master of the Scriptures so he could answer and refute false teaching with authority. The people causing the damage were not careful in handling the Word of God so Paul's word to Timothy was to *"15 Be diligent to present yourself approved to God as a worker who does not need to be ashamed, accurately handling the word of truth"* (2:15). We find in this verse a few important guidelines on how we as pastors and teachers should approach the Word of God:

- **Study the Word with diligence** – Bible study is a sacred trust and privilege. Just as the soldier, athlete, and farmer were discussed earlier, we need those positive traits in our lives applied to the study of the Word of God. Diligence means the Scriptures are a high priority. It requires time and work. It is not something we add to a busy day, it is first on the list every day. *"Be diligent."*
- **Our approval comes from God, not man.** We don't study to impress our crowd, but to honor our God. We only need to be *"approved to God."*
- **Don't be ashamed of the message.** The Word of God will be mocked and ridiculed as foolishness. It will be reviled by philosophers as uneducated. It will be hated by idolaters. It will be considered subversive by the government. It will be accused as confrontational and rigid. In all this, recognize it is the truth and worth dying for. The truth is nothing to be ashamed of and all who

mock will be the ones ashamed as they stand before God in judgment. We need to be *"as a worker who does not need to be ashamed."*

- **Be respectful and careful when handling the Scriptures.** We need to be in the Word each day for devotions, growth in our Christian life, and to prepare what we will share. All of it takes time. Our goal is to get into the Word until the Word gets into us. Be familiar with the great voices of the past that have proven records of diligent study. If we are to be accused of anything, may it be for *"accurately handling the word of truth."*

15 Be diligent to present yourself approved to God as a worker who does not need to be ashamed, accurately handling the word of truth" (2:15).

AVOID EMPTY AND USELESS CONVERSATIONS. (2:16-18)

16 But avoid worldly and empty chatter, for it will lead to further ungodliness, 17 and their talk will spread like gangrene. Among them are Hymenaeus and Philetus, 18 men who have gone astray from the truth, claiming that the resurrection has already taken place; and they are jeopardizing the faith of some."

After Paul told Timothy what he was to do, he then told him what not to do. The *"empty and worldly chatter"* is more than a warning about talking about the weather or other everyday events. The conversations described here result in leading people to "further ungodliness" which means the discussions were ungodly themselves. Paul further tells Timothy they lead people astray and gives the name of two from the church who have become guilty of this form of destructive speech. The danger, Paul warns, is that this form of talk spreads *"like gangrene,"* which requires amputation to save the body. In all, Paul was very concerned that the church in Ephesus may be in trouble. There was a pattern of destructive speech that needed to be stopped right away. Dangerous speech is a challenge to the truth of the Word of God. The two people listed, Hymenaeus and Philetus, had been caught up in the errors and were now starting to pull others away from the faith. They *"have gone astray from the truth, claiming that the resurrection has already taken place; and they are jeopardizing the faith of some"* (2:18).

What were these dangerous conversations? Another Bible version translates it as "profane and idle babblings" which produce ungodliness. We don't have any other information about the content, but it has to do with denial of God's Word. They are described as "ungodly" and also empty or useless, having no value in the long run. The visual image which comes to mind is a great sailing vessel in the harbor which was anchored to the rocks, but a storm has broken the chains and it has drifted out to sea with no one at the helm. Unless someone gets back on that ship and sails it back to port the great vessel will be lost at sea. Paul's language indicates that this situation was serious. We see that in his descriptive language, "gangrene," "ungodliness," "gone astray," and "jeopardizing the faith."

The first letter Paul wrote to Timothy contained warnings of false prophets in Ephesus and now it seems that problems may have worsened. Here is what Paul wrote in his first letter alerting Timothy to potential danger:

> **3 Just as I urged you upon my departure for Macedonia, to remain on at Ephesus so that you would instruct certain people not to teach strange doctrines, 4 nor to pay attention to myths and endless genealogies, which give rise to useless speculation rather than advance the plan of God, which is by faith, so I urge you now. 5 But the goal of our instruction is love from a pure heart, from a good**

conscience, and from a sincere faith. ⁶ Some people have strayed from these things and have turned aside to fruitless discussion, ⁷ wanting to be teachers of the Law, even though they do not understand either what they are saying or the matters about which they make confident assertions. (1 Timothy 1:3-7)

In both instances, the warning is about the danger of empty or world conversations becoming the center of activity in the church. These useless discussions lead to unhealthy speculations which give birth to false leaders who control the message and pull people away from the truth of the gospel. In the second letter, they had been led astray in the fundamentals of the gospel, even denying a future resurrection of the body (2:18). There were no doubt other primary doctrines being attacked.

One of the men listed, Hymenaeus, was already known by Paul earlier as one who blasphemed God. Paul said, *"Hymenaeus and Alexander, whom I delivered to Satan that they may learn not to blaspheme"* (1:20). He never learned his lesson.

Both of these passages together help us to understand the environment of the church in Ephesus. The pagan people that had become converted were very prone to be lured into philosophical arguments which were common in the culture. They were highly influenced by the pagan world of Ephesus. Many fell away. Paul, earlier, mentioned that all of them from Asia had deserted him (1:15). It must have been very frustrating for Paul and Timothy to work so hard and have so many serious struggles with the people losing their faith

Timothy was a very faithful, mature, and hard worker for the gospel. However, he was like a firefighter in the middle of a large forest fire putting out the fires he could reach, but new hot spots kept bursting forth.

174

A small problem in the church may seem like something that can be handled later. That would be like a small skin cancer showing up. It is so small it can be handled later. Much of the danger of skin cancer is that most of it is under the layers of the skin and not visible. Skin cancers are like icebergs that have most of their bulk underwater. If cancer is not dealt with immediately, it will be a much larger problem very soon. One author of a book on cults gave this definition of a cult, "they are the unpaid bills of the church." Like cancer, error in the church, will spread and *"jeopardize the faith"* of the body like in Paul's writings to Timothy. Radical surgery is the only answer. All false teachings need to be handled quickly and removed.

GOD'S FOUNDATION STILL STANDS. (2:19)

> *19 Nevertheless, the firm foundation of God stands, having this seal: "The Lord knows those who are His;" and, "Everyone who names the name of the Lord is to keep away from wickedness.*

After all the warnings of the dangers of false teachers, Paul closes these thoughts with a promise of hope. No matter what attacks come against the people of God, one thing is certain. God will stand and His true believers will prevail. He is the Rock of Ages and His children are anchored to the Rock. "The firm foundation of God stands." His kingdom cannot be moved or shaken. It will weather any storm.

After reading about the false prophets in Ephesus and the number of people led astray by them, it can sound hopeless and depressing. Not only is God unshakable with the attacks against His kingdom, but we are also told, *"The Lord knows those who are His."* The false teachers may confuse some people, but not God. He knows who are His children and who are not no matter what they claim. Not only is God secure, but so are His children. This statement is described as a "seal."

> *"In ancient buildings, the builder placed an inscription on a foundation stone—much as modern builders do today. That inscription indicated the purpose of the builder and identified the worthiness of the building. The same is true for the Lord's great house. Paul describes it as 'having this seal. The Lord knows those who are His,'"*
> (Bethany Bible Church commentary)

The book of Ephesians contains a similar promise to the believers in Ephesus:

> *¹³ In Him, you also, after listening to the message of truth, the gospel of your salvation—having also believed, you were sealed in Him with the Holy Spirit of the promise.*
> (Ephesians 1:13)

The Old Testament prophet predicted the coming destruction of Nineveh, but gave assurance to the true believers that He knew who they were:

> *Who can stand before His indignation?*
> *Who can endure the burning of His anger?*
> *His wrath gushes forth like fire,*
> *And the rocks are broken up by Him.*
> *⁷ The Lord is good,*
> *A stronghold in the day of trouble,*
> *And He knows those who take refuge in Him.*
> (Nahum 1:6, 7)

The second part of this seal is *"Everyone who names the name of the Lord is to keep away from wickedness."* This sounds very similar to what God told the Israelites in the camp during the rebellion of Korah. Before God destroyed the rebels, He warned the people:

> *26 and he spoke to the congregation, saying, "Get away*

now from the tents of these wicked men, and do not touch anything that belongs to them, or you will be swept away in all their sin! (Numbers 16:26)

This verse is an interesting combination of the full knowledge of God and the responsibility of man. God knows His own and they are to turn from sin.

> *"Some might say, "I belong to the Lord, I know I'm His. I am going to heaven. It doesn't matter so much how I live." Yet, such a son has forgotten that there are two inscriptions on the foundation of God. There are two – and those who are His will have the desires and the actions to depart from iniquity. If someone does not have the desire or the actions to depart from iniquity, it is fair to ask if he really belongs to Jesus or if he has just deceived himself."*
> (Blue Letter Bible Commentary)

The final verses in this chapter will describe in more detail what it means to keep away from wickedness

Qualities of a godly leader. (2:20-26)

20 Now in a large house there are not only gold and silver implements, but also *implements* of wood and of earthenware, and some *are* for honor while others *are* for dishonor. 21 Therefore, if anyone cleanses himself from these *things*, he will be an implement for honor, sanctified, useful to the Master, prepared for every good work. 22 Now flee from youthful lusts and pursue righteousness, faith, love, *and* peace with those who call on the Lord from a pure heart. 23 But refuse foolish and ignorant speculations, knowing that they produce quarrels. 24 The Lord's bond-servant must not be quarrelsome, but be kind to all, skillful in teaching, patient when wronged, 25 with

gentleness correcting those who are in opposition, if perhaps God may grant them repentance leading to the knowledge of the truth, [26] and they may come to their senses *and escape* from the snare of the devil, having been held captive by him to do his will.

Timothy was a young man working in a world of great temptations. These verses are like a father-son chat about the dangers lurking around every corner of the city and even within the church. Paul counseled his *"son in the faith"* with a loving concern for his spiritual growth. He speaks with the wisdom of a man who has lived through the battles and has emerged victoriously. He wants to pass these five lessons on before he died.

LESSON ONE – WHY IT IS IMPORTANT TO LIVE A LIFE SEPARATED FROM THE EVIL WORLD. (2:20, 21)

[20] Now in a large house there are not only gold and silver implements, but also implements of wood and of earthenware, and some are for honor while others are for dishonor. [21] Therefore, if anyone cleanses himself from these things, he will be an implement for honor, sanctified, useful to the Master, prepared for every good work.
(2:20, 21)

Just as there are different kinds of containers found in a large house, so we expect to find different kinds of people in a church. A container or vessel is meant to hold something. Some hold the finest of wines and others hold refuse or waste oil. Fine china is used for special guests and everyday plates are used so much they are chipped and weathered. You would not use old beaten-up plates and clay service vessels to host the King, but you would use your finest dinner ware and gold pitchers. What if you were hosting God? In Paul's llustration we are the vessels, the great house is the church and God is the guest of honor. We should be the most honorable vessels fit for filling with the Holy Spirit. This makes the church fit to serve the King who is the One honored.

The Holy Spirit can only fill a clean and empty vessel, not a polluted one. *"18 And do not get drunk with wine, in which there is debauchery, but be filled with the Spirit,"* (Ephesians 5:18). The way we do that is to keep short accounts with God. When we sin, we need to repent and be cleansed. *"9 If we confess our sins, He is faithful and righteous, so that He will forgive us our sins and cleanse us from all unrighteousness"* (1 John 1:9). Walk close to God and we will never find ourselves far from Him. *"21 Therefore, if anyone cleanses himself from these things, he will be an implement for honor, sanctified, useful to the Master, prepared for every good work."*

Why should we want to avoid the paths of sin? To be honorable vessels God can use for every good work. For Timothy, this was a call to fully commit to being that kind of person. It is up to each of us what kind of vessel we will be, one for dishonor or honor.

LESSON TWO – DEALING WITH THE TEMPTATIONS OF LUST. (2:22)

22 Now flee from youthful lusts and pursue righteousness, faith, love, and peace with those who call on the Lord from a pure heart. (2:22)

The command seems simple, *"Now flee from youthful lusts and pursue righteousness, faith, love, and peace."* But it is probably the most common struggle and source of downfall any of us face. It is a choice between two paths, one downward, and the other upward. God created us as passionate beings. In Paul's list of cleansing ourselves so we will be *"an implement for honor, sanctified, useful to the Master, prepared for every good work"* (2:21), the first item that needed to be addressed was the matter of *"youthful lusts" (2:22).* Timothy was in his early 30's and single at the time.

Paul had given the same instruction to the church at Corinth, which was known for its carnality:

> **¹⁸ Flee immorality. Every other sin that a man commits is outside the body, but the immoral man sins against his own body."** (1 Corinthians 6:18)

Paul also gave the same warnings to the believers in Rome,

> **"¹⁴ But put on the Lord Jesus Christ, and make no provision for the flesh in regard to its lusts."** (Romans 13:14*)*

"Lusts—we all have them and we're all susceptible to them. We can never be safe from them while we're in these earthly bodies. This is because, in the fall of the entire human race, the perfect physical body God created for us became the sinful flesh, full of lusts.

> **"We believers are not exempt from this fact. Certainly, when we believed in Jesus Christ, we were forgiven of our sins and saved eternally. We became God's children, born again with His divine life. But though our spirit was regenerated, our body was not. The sinful lusts in our flesh remain."** (Bibles for America commentary*)*

We know clearly that we live in a dangerous place, a world filled with lusts of every kind. We lust for the flesh, we lust for things we don't have and we lust for personal greatness.

> **¹⁶ For all that is in the world, the lust of the flesh and the lust of the eyes and the boastful pride of life, is not from the Father, but is from the world"**
> (1 John 2:16).

The command has two parts, what not to do, and what to do. The first is an unguarded fall and second is an intentional pursuit. One is dishonoring to our body and God, and the other is honoring God with a heart that is pure in its pursuit.

From what we know there are several instructions about how we are to handle lusts. We should never make plans or provisions which would place us in the position of lust. We also are told to flee lusts. We are not told to fight them or struggle with them but to flee, get away, leave immediately. The Old Testament story of Joseph is one of the best to illustrate this:

> *Now Joseph was well-built and handsome, ⁷ and after a while, his master's wife took notice of Joseph and said, "Come to bed with me!"*
> *⁸ But he refused. "With me in charge," he told her, "my master does not concern himself with anything in the house; everything he owns he has entrusted to my care.*
> *⁹ No one is greater in this house than I am. My master has withheld nothing from me except you, because you are his wife. How then could I do such a wicked thing and sin against God?" ¹⁰ And though she spoke to Joseph day after day, he refused to go to bed with her or even be with her.*
> *¹¹ One day he went into the house to attend to his duties, and none of the household servants was inside. ¹² She caught him by his cloak and said, "Come to bed with me!" But he left his cloak in her hand and ran out of the house.*
> (Genesis 39:6-12)

We are also told to build up our immune system against lust, which is weak, by staying strong in the Word of God:

> *9 How can a young man keep his way pure?*
> *By keeping it according to Your word. (Psalm 119:9)*

The Bible will keep us from sin or sin will keep us from the Bible. We all wish there was a vaccine or pill or treatment to stop this pandemic of the flesh which has infected the entire world, but there is not a one-time fix. It will remain a battle for our duration in this journey of life. We know what we should not be doing or planning and we know where we need to invest our precious time. It is up to us what pursuit we will choose.

> *22 Now flee from youthful lusts and pursue righteousness, faith, love, and peace with those who call on the Lord from a pure heart."*

LESSON THREE – KEEPING FOCUSED ON THE IMPORTANT THINGS, AVOIDING DISTRACTIONS. (2:23)

> *23 But refuse foolish and ignorant speculations, knowing that they produce quarrels.* (2:23)

There are times when we need to defend our faith:

> *15 but sanctify Christ as Lord in your hearts, always being ready to make a defense to everyone who asks you to give an account for the hope that is in you, yet with gentleness and reverence.* (1 Peter 3:15)

> *2 preach the word; be ready in season and out of season; reprove, rebuke, exhort, with great patience and instruction.* (2 Timothy 4:2)

What Paul is talking about in verse 23 is not one of those times. "Foolish and ignorant speculations" are not defending our faith, it is wasting time that could be used for valuable conversations. Paul's point to young Timothy was to be careful to pick our battles. You don't have to be a Christian very long before you know some issues and even some doctrinal disputes either have no answers or are not worth fighting over. Strong convictions are things we would die for, they are the essentials of our faith.

Personal preferences are not worth an argument. They have no eternal value.

If you had been on the Titanic when it was sinking in 1912, do you think you would have been out on the deck arranging deck chairs while people were screaming and trying to get into lifeboats? No, there was only one priority at the moment, saving the lives of as many passengers as possible.

An illustration from the world of time management seminars is helpful here. A presenter had completed his course on time management when he set a large glass jar on the table in front of him. He then took out a bag of large rocks and filled the jar to the brim. He asked the attendees of his conference if the jar was full. They all agreed that it was. Then he took out another bag which contained small pebbles and he poured that into the jar filling all the voids between the large rocks. Then, he asked the same question, "Is the jar full now?" Most became quiet, only a few agreed that the jar was full. Then he took a sack of sand and poured it in filling the smallest spaces. This time no one said anything when he asked his question. Finally, he took out a jug of water and poured it in until it reached the brim of the jar. Then he said, "What lesson do we learn from this?"

Someone said, "No matter how busy we are, we can always fit something else in."

He responded, "No, the main lesson here is if you don't put the large rocks in first, you will never get them in later."

In our lives, there are main things and lesser things. The main things have to always go in first in our life or they never will. God, prayer, Bible study, and family are large rocks. If you don't put them in first, the day will fill up with insignificant pebbles and sand and there will be no time for what matters later. The main thing is to keep the main thing the main thing.

LESSON FOUR – HOW TO BE AN EFFECTIVE TEACHER OF THE WORD. (2:24, 25)

> *24 The Lord's bond-servant must not be quarrelsome, but be kind to all, skillful in teaching, patient when wronged, 25 with gentleness correcting those who are in opposition.*
> (2:23, 25)

Both 1 and 2 Timothy contained warnings about false teachers in the church in Ephesus. This issue needed to be confronted. False teachers needed to be corrected or removed if they could not accept their errors or their domineering attitudes. It was a challenging problem for a young pastor. This was very different from the previous warning about getting involved in a useless argument and trivial matters. The matter of false teaching is not trivial. It is like poisonous snakes that have been unleashed into the congregation. The snakes need to be removed.

In these verses, the emphasis is training and correction and how to do these things. We are told in another passage, *"18 If possible, so far as it depends on you, be at peace with all men."* (Romans 12:18). That is the tone here. Wrong teaching must be corrected while maintaining peace if possible. If that does not work, then we confront it and even remove it. But, for now, the first approach is to be skillful in the use of the Word of God to expose the errors. The Word will do that:

16 All Scripture is inspired by God and beneficial for teaching, for rebuke, for correction, for training in righteousness; 17 so that the man or woman of God may be fully capable, equipped for every good work.
(2 Timothy 3:16, 17)

The key concept in this passage is to handle opposition with gentleness. Gentleness is a fruit of the Spirit; God is available at all times to help us. Gentleness calms the rough waters:

> *A gentle answer turns away wrath,*
> *But a harsh word stirs up anger. (Proverbs 15:1)*

We must be *"able to teach,"* which is a requirement for a pastor (1Timothy 3:2). We need to be able to handle opposition without becoming quarrelsome (2:24). These qualities are found in great servants of God. Timothy was such a man. There are times during these potentially hostile sessions when God brings supernatural calmness and clarity to the shepherd. Many of us can attest to that.

Jesus told the crowds, *"43 You have heard that it was said, 'You shall love your neighbor and hate your enemy.' 44 But I say to you, love your enemies and pray for those who persecute you,'"* (Matthew 5:43, 44). It takes humility to be *"patient when wronged, 25 with gentleness correcting those who are in opposition."* Without God's help, we will never be able to handle adversity and accusations with a gentle spirit. Thankfully, we have that help.

LESSON FIVE – IT IS WORTH IT TO LIVE A DISCIPLINED AND DEDICATED LIFE. (2:25, 26)

> *. . . if perhaps God may grant them repentance leading to the knowledge of the truth, 26 and they may come to their*

senses and escape from the snare of the devil, having been held captive by him to do his will. (2:25, 26)

Finally, If we do all that Paul instructed Timothy, we will be like a farmer who patiently planted and waited and then rejoiced greatly at the harvest that came. Living a disciplined life takes continual effort. Allowing God to mold and shape us into the image of His Son is a painful process. Holding our tongue when falsely accused is very hard, but wise. Staying focused on the most important things and not wandering off onto an easier path is worth the investment. Fleeing lustful temptations, when everyone around us is giving in, is very frustrating. The struggle can make one want to give up, but we know it would only be worse is we did. Living a life separate from the evil world makes for a lonely journey. Paul certainly knew he was asking a lot from his young disciple.

Paul also knew something more important than any of that. He knew that when Timothy lived a life as a dedicated overcomer and solid disciple of Christ, the fragrance of that life would attract others who are weary of the stench of sin and guilt. That is the reward. When we live lives based on truth, the world will notice and some will become convicted of their shallow lives. They will want the abundant life as they see in us:

> *"Perhaps God may grant them repentance leading to the knowledge of the truth, [26] and they may come to their senses and escape from the snare of the devil, having been held captive by him to do his will."* (2:25, 26)

2 Timothy 3

Evil, difficult days are coming. (3:1-9)

¹ But realize this, that in the last days difficult times will come. ² For people will be lovers of self, lovers of money, boastful, arrogant, slanderers, disobedient to parents, ungrateful, unholy, ³ unloving, irreconcilable, malicious gossips, without self-control, brutal, haters of good, ⁴ treacherous, reckless, conceited, lovers of pleasure rather than lovers of God, ⁵ holding to a form of godliness although they have denied its power; avoid *such people as these.* ⁶ For among them are those who slip into households and captivate weak women weighed down with sins, led on by various impulses, ⁷ always learning and never able to come to the knowledge of the truth. ⁸ Just as Jannes and Jambres opposed Moses, so these men also oppose the truth, men of depraved mind, worthless in regard to the faith. ⁹ But they will not make further progress; for their foolishness will be obvious to all, just as was that also of Jannes and Jambres.

When we see a beautiful valley with a river winding its way through majestic trees, we forget that we are only looking at the ruins of a world that once was. God created the universe and our earth in perfection. He said it was all good. But sin came and everything went down from there. God, who is holy, was offended by the evil that sin brought into His perfect creation. The curses on the serpent, the woman, the man, and the entirety of creation remain with us today. We live in a world of disease, pollution, sins of every kind, broken marriages, nations at war, rampant crime, and the list goes on and on. Everything is broken. When Paul wrote to the church in the depraved city of Rome he reminded them that they lived in a place of curse and pain:

> **20 For the creation was subjected to futility, not willingly, but because of Him who subjected it, in hope 21 that the creation itself also will be set free from its slavery to corruption into the freedom of the glory of the children of God. 22 For we know that the whole creation groans and suffers the pains of childbirth together until now. 23 And not only that, but also we ourselves, having the first fruits of the Spirit, even we ourselves groan within ourselves, waiting eagerly for our adoption as sons and daughters, the redemption of our body.** (Romans 8:20-23)

We are all looking forward to that glorious day when *"3 There will no longer be any curse"* (Revelation 22:3). Until that day the world will continue its spiral downwards. Paul told Timothy in the first century these very things. These verses are a journey into the dark heart of a fallen man. There is nothing new under the sun, evil continues its reign and its influence is increasing.

> *"1 But realize this, that in the last days difficult times will come." (3:1)*

Before we examine the list of sins, let's first understand what the "last days" means.

THE LAST DAYS. (3:1)

Peter addressed the crowds on Pentecost (Acts 2). He quoted a prophecy from Joel about the *"last days"* and indicated that part of it was fulfilled at that time and part of it was reserved for the latter times.

> *"In the last days: This is a broad term in the New*

Testament, broad enough to where one could say that **the last days** *began with the birth of the Church on the Day of Pentecost* (Acts 2:17*). The days of the Messiah mark* **the last days; yet the term is especially appropriate to the season immediately before the return of Jesus and the consummation of all things.*** (Enduring Word Commentary)

Since Paul was writing 2 Timothy at the end of his life and uses the future tense, we must assume that he is looking to a future day when the days will be characterized by a very depraved human condition. It is also likely, understanding the fallen nature of man, that the world conditions will not all of a sudden become very wicked but will continually move in a downward trajectory through time. If anyone has a theology, or hope, that the world will become better and better and then one day Jesus will come, they simply have no basis for that belief. Jesus will not return to a beautiful, loving world. When Jesus the King returns He appears in glory at the end of the Great Tribulation when the entire world will be at war against Israel and is following the Antichrist. It is the reign of evil and will be destroyed by Christ:

> *"11 And I saw heaven opened, and behold, a white horse, and He who sat on it is called Faithful and True, and in righteousness He judges and wages war. 12 His eyes are a flame of fire, and on His head are many diadems; and He has a name written on Him which no one knows except Himself. 13 He is clothed with a robe dipped in blood, and His name is called The Word of God. 14 And the armies which are in heaven, clothed in fine linen, white and clean, were following Him on white horses. 15 From His mouth comes a sharp sword, so that with it He may strike down the nations, and He will rule them with a rod of iron; and He treads the wine press of the fierce wrath of God, the Almighty. 16 And on His robe and on His thigh He has a name written, "KING OF KINGS, AND LORD OF LORDS." 17 Then I saw an angel standing in the sun, and he cried out with a loud voice, saying to all the birds which fly in*

midheaven, "Come, assemble for the great supper of God,
18 so that you may eat the flesh of kings and the flesh of
commanders and the flesh of mighty men and the flesh
of horses and of those who sit on them and the flesh of all
men, both free men and slaves, and small and great."
(Revelation 19:11-18)

As we look at the list of sins Paul described to Timothy we have
a glimpse of the heart of fallen man. It was bad in Timothy's city
of Ephesus and it would continue through the centuries to our
time today. It will continue until Jesus returns to end the
madness of sin and He will reign forever one day on a new earth
and heaven where sin and curse will be no more.

THE CONDITION OF HUMANITY IN THE LAST DAYS. (3:2-9)

For people will be lovers of self – Many self-centered,
self-absorbed people will arise. Scripture warns us about
thinking too highly about ourselves (Romans 12:3). This is the
first on the list because it is the beginning of a departure from
loving God and others. It is a violation of the total Law of God,
to love God and our neighbor as ourselves. The opposite of
self-centeredness is love; it is Jesus who went to the cross to die
for our sins and the ones who crucified Him.

For people will be lovers of money – The only love they
express is greed for more money. Money is to be used and
people to be loved. These people love money and use people.
When we are full of ourselves, there is no room for anyone else.
A very selfish world will be a sign of the last days. Paul
discussed this danger in his first letter to Timothy. See the
commentary on 1 Timothy 6 for more.

> *⁹ But those who want to get rich fall into temptation and a*
> *snare and many foolish and harmful desires which plunge*
> *men into ruin and destruction. ¹⁰ For the love of money is*

a root of all sorts of evil, and some by longing for it have wandered away from the faith and pierced themselves with many griefs. ¹¹ *But flee from these things, you man of God, and pursue righteousness, godliness, faith, love, perseverance and gentleness.* (1 Timothy 6:9-11)

Boastful - It is bad enough when we sin, but to be proud of it and boast about it is worse. When there is no sorrow for sin, it is indicative of a seared conscience, without sensitivity towards those we hurt. They are like the ones described in Romans One.

> *"³² although they know the ordinance of God, that those who practice such things ae worthy of death, they not only do the same, but also give hearty approval to those who practice them."* (Romans 1:32)

Arrogant - God resists the proud (arrogant) but gives grace to the humble (James 4:6). Pride is the root of sin. It was what brought about the fall of Lucifer (Isaiah 14:13, 14). King Nebuchadnezzar became very arrogant in his life and God humbled him publically. When he repented and was restored to his position of King, he said: *"³⁷ Now I, Nebuchadnezzar, praise, exalt and honor the King of heaven, for all His works are true and His ways just, and He is able to humble those who walk in pride"* (Daniel 4:37).

Slanderers – An arsonist burns a building down, a slanderer burns a life or reputation down. Slander is the act of harming a person's reputation by telling one or more other people something untrue and damaging about that person. It is a violation of one of the Ten Commandments, *"¹⁶ You shall not bear false witness against your neighbor"* (Exodus 20:16). These are lies that can destroy others. God is clear about what he thinks of slander, *"Whoever secretly slanders his neighbor, him I will destroy"* (Psalm 101:5).

Disobedient to parents – This is another violation of the basic moral Law of God. *"12 Honor your father and your mother, that your days may be prolonged in the land which the Lord your God gives you"* (Exodus 20:12). *"My son, observe the commandment of your father, and do not forsake the teaching of your mother"* (Proverbs 6:20). Children who are raised without respect for God will not respect His creation or anyone, including their parents.

Ungrateful - These are the words listed as synonyms: thankless, unthankful, careless, demanding, dissatisfied, faultfinding, forgetful, grasping, grumbling, heedless, ingrate, insensible, oblivious, self-centered, unmindful, unnatural, and unappreciative. Would you want to work with a person like that? Someone always finds fault, paying no attention to those around him, unhappy with everything, complaining, criticizing, and demanding. What about a world with people like that? Those days are coming and some are showing these signs now.

Unholy - Filled with everything that God hates. In a recent political election, one candidate referred to the supporters of their opponent as being a "basket of deplorables." That is an accurate description of the unholy crowd in the last days. *"15 To the pure, all things are pure; but to those who are defiled and unbelieving, nothing is pure, but both their mind and their conscience are defiled"* (Titus 1:15). Since Holiness is the fundamental description of the nature of God, the opposite of God must be the word "unholy."

Unloving - mankind was created in love by God. We are made in His image and love is a necessary part of our experience. It is built into our being, our soul. We are made to love God and love our neighbors. When we fulfill this basic purpose we are most alive. Sin is a darkness that dims the soul, shrivels up the heart, and makes us cold like a corpse. Without love, we are walking dead, unconscious of the needs around us. Today we see more and more people that have lost a sense of conscience, they have no remorse for their actions nor do they care who they hurt. These are the beginnings of the coming difficult times in the last days.

Irreconcilable - We tend to think that no one is outside of the saving grace of God. But what if a person chooses to no longer want anything to with God. A well-known agnostic wrote a book called "Farewell to God," which stated that he could never have anything to do with the God of the Bible. He got his wish when he died. If a person mocks the blood of Christ and willfully rejects God's salvation, God will ultimately grant his desire. There is only one way to be reconciled to God and if that is rejected completely, then he is irreconcilable. The one who chooses to live as an enemy of God will die an enemy of God. Militant atheism is growing in the world. Sociologists estimate that number at 500 million, 7% of the world's population. In the last days, it will be the true believers who are in the minority (Luke 18:8).

Malicious gossips - People that spread scandalous information about the private lives of others. This problem is not just found in political contests or tabloid newspapers, but it applies to anyone who smears another's reputation to make themselves look good, or just to injure the other. *"A perverse man spreads strife,and a slanderer separates intimate friends"* (Proverbs 16:28). We are not to listen to these people; *"An evildoer listens to wicked lips, a liar pays attention to a destructive tongue"* (Proverbs 17:4). This will also increase greatly in the last days.

Without self-control – This describes the person who can't say "No." The opposite is a disciplined life. There have always been destructive behaviors in society and crowds who have been attracted to them. Many become addicted or controlled by these behaviors or substances. Paul, in the first century, recognized the dangers around him and wrote: *"27 but I discipline my body and make it my slave, so that, after I have preached to others, I myself will not be disqualified"* (1 Corinthians 9:27). Paul did not want anyone or anything in control of his body or soul. Self-control is the ability to recognize how important it is to say "no" to anything that stands in the way of being able to serve God with a clean heart and clear conscience. Satan wants to side-track as many people as he can from God's path. The last days will be marked by a great increase of people who will be like mindless sheep following false shepherds and destructive habits, unable to simply say "No!"

Brutal - (Savage physical violence; great cruelty) The first two children born on the earth gave us a hint of what society would become in the centuries to follow. Cain brutally killed his younger brother Abel. And since then there has not been peace on earth. The history of mankind is a story of greed, conquest, and brutality. Up to the end, we will have wars and rumors of war (Matthew 24:8). The last days will come to an end with one great battle where blood will flow like a river. When Jesus reigns it will be the first time mankind can honestly say, "goodbye cruel world." The dictionary tells us the opposite of "brutality" is "kindness" or "gentleness" which are fruit of the Spirit (Galatians 5:22, 23). Brutality is a fruit of the unholy spirit who will be ruling when the last days come.

Haters of good - It is hard for us to imagine how anyone can hate a good thing. It gets even worse. There will be those who will call good "evil," and call evil "good," a complete reversal of what is real and true. *"Woe to those who call evil good, and good evil; who substitute darkness for light and light for darkness; Who substitute bitter for sweet and sweet for bitter"* (Isaiah 5:20). Only minds darkened by sin would see something

194

good and despise it but that will be a sign of the last days. It will be a day when right is wrong and wrong is right. This is why there will be great persecution of Christians in that day, *"9 Then they will deliver you to tribulation, and will kill you, and you will be hated by all nations because of My name. 10 At that time many will fall away and will betray one another and hate one another"* (Matthew 24:9, 10).

Treacherous - (Guilty of, or involving betrayal, or deception). When you hear the word "Judas," what image comes to mind? The ultimate betrayal. He was trusted among the followers of Christ but turned against Him. Jesus referred to him as a devil. The last days will be a time when those you thought were your friend will turn against you. During the communist regimes of Russia and Romania, the churches lived in fear and suspicion. They never knew who they could trust. A church member might be a spy for the state and have a pastor arrested. The last days will be times like that when betrayal and suspicion will be common.

Reckless – (Without thinking or caring about the consequences of an action). When a person does not believe in God, they do not believe in consequences for their actions. They fit the old philosophy, "Eat, drink and be merry for tomorrow we die." They are their own god. A society with this philosophy would be lawless since each person makes his own rules. In the Old Testament, there was a time when *"25 In those days there was no king in Israel; everyone did what was right in his own eyes"* (Judges 21:25). The last days will be a society under the law of man, not the Law of God.

Conceited - Mankind will not only live lawlessly, hate good, and treat others brutally, but he will be proud of doing it. God tells us, *"Whoever secretly slanders his neighbor, him I will destroy; No one who has a haughty look and an arrogant heart will I endure"*

(Psalm 101:5). In Romans, the Gentiles had become conceited knowing that God had cut off unbelieving Israel and opened the doors to the Gentiles. God had strong words to the Gentiles for their attitude: *"Do not be conceited, but fear; [21] for if God did not spare the natural branches, He will not spare you, either"* (Romans 11:20, 21).

Lovers of pleasure rather than lovers of God - Jesus warned that just before the world is judged there would be days like those of Noah when the whole world was judged because of the sins of the people. *"[37] For the coming of the Son of Man will be just like the days of Noah. [38] For as in those days before the flood they were eating and drinking, marrying and giving in marriage, until the day that Noah entered the ark, [39] and they did not understand until the flood came and took them all away; so will the coming of the Son of Man be"* (Matthew 24:37-39). The known world was swept away by a flood because man pursued pleasure and ignored God. It will happen again only the next, and final time, the world will be destroyed in a fiery battle at the second coming of Christ.

Holding to a form of godliness although they have denied its power; avoid such people as these – The reason Jesus was so angry with the Pharisees was that they were custodians of the Law of God. They were the religious leaders of the nation. When they failed in their calling they led the people of God astray. Christians, in a similar way, are held to a high standard. We represent the King of kings. God hates hypocrisy. *"Let not many of you become teachers, my brethren, knowing that as such we will incur a stricter judgment"* (James 3:1). There are many leaders today that have the appearance of godliness but are not genuine. Jude described these false leaders and their destiny in powerful words: *"[12] These are the men who are hidden reefs in your love feasts when they feast with you without fear, caring for*

*themselves; clouds without water, carried along by winds;
autumn trees without fruit, doubly dead, uprooted; ¹³ wild waves
of the sea, casting up their own shame like foam; wandering stars,
for whom the black darkness has been reserved forever"* (Jude
12, 13). When asked about the end of days, Jesus mentioned
several signs of the last days and his coming but the first one
He warned about was deception. *"Tell us, when will these things
happen, and what will be the sign of Your coming, and of the end
of the age?" ⁴ And Jesus answered and said to them, "See to it that
no one misleads you. ⁵ For many will come in My name, saying, 'I
am the Christ,' and will mislead many"* (Matthew 24:3-5).

**For among them are those who slip into households and
captivate weak women weighed down with sins, led on by
various impulses** - This sin was about those who claim to be
religious or followers of God but are false. They are empty of
true faith inside. The fake believers do not have the power of
God and therefore have no restraint for their desires. They fool
women who are weak and control them. They prey on the weak
to fulfill their lusts. We know cults tend to convert weak
religious people who have no defenses. These people are
predators going after gullible women. That is why it is so
important to be familiar with the Word of God. That is our
first defense.

**Always learning and never able to come to the knowledge
of the truth** – One additional characteristic of false leaders is
that their deception runs deep. They can study and study, but
their minds only see what they are looking for. They are not
interested in truth, but only to fulfill their lusts and maintain
power over people. Any information they can find to reinforce
their false teaching is what they absorb. They are constantly
learning but learning the wrong things. They are not capable of
learning truth because God is Truth and they have denied His

power. This will be the spirit of the last days. They may sound intellectual and persuasive when they speak, yet their words are hollow, lacking truth.

Just as Jannes and Jambres opposed Moses, so these men also oppose the truth, men of depraved mind, worthless in regard to the faith. ⁹ But they will not make further progress; for their foolishness will be obvious to all, just as was that also of Jannes and Jambres – Paul used an illustration of this type of dangerous leaders from an Old Testament story. Just because a person has power or impresses does not mean they are of God. This story is about the magicians in Pharaoh's court that did magic to oppose Moses. When Moses threw his staff down it became a serpent. The magicians of Pharoah did the same thing using the power of Satan. They duplicated the miracles of Moses up to a point but could not do everything Moses did. Satan may be powerful but he is not God. They were counterfeits. Here is what God told Moses:

> ⁹ *"When Pharaoh speaks to you, saying, 'Work a miracle,' then you shall say to Aaron, 'Take your staff and throw it down before Pharaoh, so that it may turn into a serpent.'* ¹⁰ *So Moses and Aaron came to Pharaoh, and so they did, just as the Lord had commanded; and Aaron threw his staff down before Pharaoh and his servants, and it turned into a serpent.* ¹¹ *Then Pharaoh also called for the wise men and the sorcerers, and they too, the soothsayer priests of Egypt, did the same with their secret arts.* ¹² *For each one threw down his staff, and they turned into serpents. But Aaron's staff swallowed their staffs.* ¹³ *Yet Pharaoh's heart was hardened, and he did not listen to them, just as the Lord had said."* (Exodus 7:9-13)

NOTE: The names of Jannes and Jambres are only found in Paul's second letter to Timothy, nowhere else in the Bible. Exodus tells the story but does not give the names of the magicians. We know the names because of ancient historical and apocryphal writings which identify their names. Their names were known to the early church fathers and found in non-Biblical Hebrew historical manuscripts. Paul verifies this fact when he names of the magicians.

There is no protection for a Christian leader except to walk close to God and stay in His Word. The path of evil is alluring and wide, many choose to go that way. Many temptations attack us each day but we know that God will provide a way of escape. *"13 No temptation has overtaken you but such as is common to man; and God is faithful, who will not allow you to be tempted beyond what you are able, but with the temptation will provide the way of escape also, so that you will be able to endure it"* (1 Corinthians 10:13).

> *"This is the message of great hope in the midst of this great darkness – the spirit of the last days has an answer to it in Jesus Christ. The spirit of the last days is not stronger than the power of Jesus. The glorious truth is that we don't have to be bound by the spirit of our times; we don't have to be slaves to self and have our universe revolve around something as puny as ourselves. There is hope, triumphant hope, in Jesus."* (David Guzik)

Exhortation to Timothy to remain faithful to God's matchless Word. It will provide our strength through all trials. (3:10-17)

10 Now you followed my teaching, conduct, purpose, faith, patience, love, perseverance, 11 persecutions, *and* sufferings, such as happened to me at Antioch, at Iconium,

and at Lystra; what persecutions I endured, and out of them all the Lord rescued me! ¹² Indeed, all who want to live in a godly way in Christ Jesus will be persecuted. ¹³ But evil people and impostors will proceed *from bad* to worse, deceiving and being deceived. ¹⁴ You, however, continue in the things you have learned and become convinced of, knowing from whom you have learned *them*, ¹⁵ and that from childhood you have known the sacred writings which are able to give you the wisdom that leads to salvation through faith which is in Christ Jesus. ¹⁶ All Scripture is inspired by God and beneficial for teaching, for rebuke, for correction, for training in righteousness; ¹⁷ so that the man *or woman* of God may be fully capable, equipped for every good work.

EXAMPLE OF TRUE DISCIPLESHIP. (3:10, 11)

> ¹⁰ *Now you followed my teaching, conduct, purpose, faith, patience, love, perseverance,* ¹¹ *persecutions, and sufferings, such as happened to me at Antioch, at Iconium, and at Lystra; what persecutions I endured, and out of them all the Lord rescued me!* (3:10, 11)

If you want to know what discipleship means, read verses 10 and 11. Paul taught and lived as a model for Timothy to follow. He could honestly say *"Be imitators of me, just as I also am of Christ"* (1 Corinthians 11:1). Timothy did not learn these life skills and character traits by sitting in a classroom. He followed Paul day by day. Timothy observed, imitated his mentor, and learned to walk as a disciple of Christ.

Paul was an example in each of these ways he listed, in *his* *"teaching, conduct, purpose, faith, patience, love, perseverance,* ¹¹ *persecutions, and sufferings."* Let's briefly look at each of them.

- **Paul's teaching** - Paul spent many years teaching

Timothy the great truths of the faith. He took Timothy along with him from city to city as he taught. Like Christ with his disciples, Paul was with Timothy along the way between church plants, and as a father with his son, he passed on what he had to his disciple. He then sent Timothy to different church plants to disciple the believers.

- **Paul's conduct** – Timothy was either with Paul or knew about all the struggles and trials Paul experienced. He saw how Paul responded to poor treatment by the churches, the Jews, and the Romans. Paul's life was a living lesson for Timothy about how to handle the challenges of life and ministry. Here is the list Paul wrote about what he went through:

> *[24] Five times I received from the Jews thirty-nine lashes. [25] Three times I was beaten with rods, once I was stoned, three times I was shipwrecked, a night and a day I have spent in the deep. [26] I have been on frequent journeys, in dangers from rivers, dangers from robbers, dangers from my countrymen, dangers from the Gentiles, dangers in the city, dangers in the wilderness, dangers on the sea, dangers among false brethren; [27] I have been in labor and hardship, through many sleepless nights, in hunger and thirst, often without food, in cold and exposure. [28] Apart from such external things, there is the daily pressure on me of concern for all the churches.* (2 Corinthians 11:24-28)

Paul's conduct was daily training for Timothy to handle any trial that might come his way. Paul reminded his disciple how he had carefully followed him (3:10). Timothy had learned from the best.

- **Paul's purpose** - Timothy followed Paul's life, example, and purpose of his mentor through his entire life and even died a martyr's death as did Paul. What was his purpose? He wrote, *"²¹ For to me, to live is Christ and to die is gain"* (Philippians 1:21). A more expanded statement of Paul's life purpose can be found in Colossians:

  > **²⁵ Of this church I was made a minister according to the stewardship from God bestowed on me for your benefit, so that I might fully carry out the preaching of the word of God, ²⁶ that is, the mystery which has been hidden from the past ages and generations, but has now been manifested to His saints, ²⁷ to whom God willed to make known what is the riches of the glory of this mystery among the Gentiles, which is Christ in you, the hope of glory. ²⁸ We proclaim Him, admonishing every man and teaching every man with all wisdom, so that we may present every man complete in Christ. ²⁹ For this purpose also I labor, striving according to His power, which mightily works within me.** (Colossians 1:25-29)

- **Paul's faith** - Paul demonstrated and passed on how to trust God in everything. He was an example of one who could rejoice in all situations. He wrote, *"²⁷ Only conduct yourselves in a manner worthy of the gospel of Christ, so that whether I come and see you or remain absent, I will hear of you that you are standing firm in one spirit, with one mind striving together for the faith of the gospel"* (Philippians 1:27). According to verse 10, Timothy followed Paul's faith.

- **Paul's patience** – We can learn about faith and teaching from school or others but patience comes from facing trials. It comes from life and believing that God will forge us into a man or woman of faith.

² Consider it all joy, my brethren, when you encounter various trials, ³ knowing that the testing of your faith produces endurance. ⁴ And let endurance have its perfect result, so that you may be perfect and complete, lacking in nothing." (James 1:2-4)

- **Paul's love** – Paul was a man of high standards and was demanding but that does not mean he was not a loving man. Remember it was Paul who penned what has become one of the world's most memorable statements about love:

  ¹ If I speak with the tongues of men and of angels, but do not have love, I have become a noisy gong or a clanging cymbal. ² If I have the gift of prophecy, and know all mysteries and all knowledge; and if I have all faith, so as to remove mountains, but do not have love, I am nothing. ³ And if I give all my possessions to feed the poor, and if I surrender my body to be burned, but do not have love, it profits me nothing. ⁴ Love is patient, love is kind and is not jealous; love does not brag and is not arrogant, ⁵ does not act unbecomingly; it does not seek its own, is not provoked, does not take into account a wrong suffered, ⁶ does not rejoice in unrighteousness, but rejoices with the truth; ⁷ bears all things, believes all things, hopes all things, endures all things. ⁸ Love never fails; . . . ¹³ But now faith, hope, love, abide these three; but the greatest of these is love.
  (All of 1 Corinthians 13, sample verses selected)

Paul loved God, he loved the church, and he loved Timothy like a son. Every aspect of Timothy's life was molded by love from his mother and grandmother, from Paul and ultimately from God.

² To Timothy, my beloved son: Grace, mercy and peace from God the Father and Christ Jesus our Lord. ³ I thank God, whom I serve with a clear conscience the way my

forefathers did, as I constantly remember you in my prayers night and day, 4 longing to see you, even as I recall your tears, so that I may be filled with joy."
(1 Timothy 1:2-4)

- **Paul's perseverance** – No matter what the challenges Paul faced, he never gave up. Many of Paul's workers quit and abandoned him (1:15), but Paul was a finisher, not just a starter. He knew it was worth the struggle:

  58 Therefore, my beloved brothers and sisters, be firm, immovable, always excelling in the work of the Lord, knowing that your labor is not in vain in the Lord.
  (1 Corinthians 15:58)

Paul will complete his journey how he began and ran, strong and with a view to the prize. This is what he wrote Timothy at the end of this letter. It is not surprising Timothy was strong and courageous to the end of his life. He died at an old age in Ephesus confronting a pagan festival. They stoned him to death. He finished the course like his mentor and hero, Paul. These are Paul's final words:

  6 For I am already being poured out as a drink offering, and the time of my departure has come. 7 I have fought the good fight, I have finished the course, I have kept the faith; 8 in the future there is reserved for me the crown of righteousness, which the Lord, the righteous Judge, will award to me on that day; and not only to me, but also to all who have loved His appearing. (2 Timothy 4:6-8)

- **Paul's persecutions, and suffering –**

  "such as happened to me at Antioch, at Iconium, and at Lystra; what persecutions I endured, and out of them all the Lord rescued me" (3:11).

Despite the difficult journey, Paul continued teaching, maintained good conduct, never was distracted from his purpose, kept the faith, and showed the virtues of patience, love, and perseverance throughout it all. He reminded Timothy of how it all started at Lystra when they first met and how the angry mobs from Antioch and Iconium tried to kill him. God, in the end, delivered Paul from the evil men who plotted against him. Just as Paul suffered, so would Timothy and all who follow Jesus will as well. He summarizes these thoughts in the next two verses.

PERSECUTIONS WILL COME. (3:12, 13)

12 Indeed, all who want to live in a godly way in Christ Jesus will be persecuted. 13 But evil people and impostors will proceed from bad to worse, deceiving and being deceived. (3:12, 13)

When Jesus prayed the night before He was to die on the cross for the sins of the world, He sweat blood in Gethsemane. The Holy One was the next day going to be crushed with the wickedness of the fallen world. *"21 He made Him who knew no sin to be sin on our behalf so that we might become the righteousness of God in Him"* (2 Corinthians 5:21). He prayed to the father, saying, *"42Father, if You are willing, remove this cup from Me; yet not My will, but Yours be done"* (Luke 22:42). His death and resurrection are the doorway to eternal life to all who would believe. It was purchased at an infinite cost. Paul, Timothy, and all who would come after them who want to live for God's glory will walk a path of persecution. Some will find life through the gospel message, but many will reject and persecute the messengers.

The lives of Paul and Timothy are great encouragements to us. We can all finish the course and help others across the finish line.

PRINCIPLES TO LIVE BY.

Pastors, every aspect of your life is on display and impacts your church and those you disciple. They listen to what you believe, watch how you walk, and face persecution. Determine to be the best you can be for God. Make sure you are a man of the Word. That is what the final verses of this chapter are about.

TIMOTHY WAS REMINDED OF HIS GODLY HERITAGE AND TRAINING. (3:14-15)

> *14 You, however, continue in the things you have learned and become convinced of, knowing from whom you have learned them, 15 and that from childhood you have known the sacred writings which are able to give you the wisdom that leads to salvation through faith which is in Christ Jesus.* (3:14, 15)

In contrast to the false teachers and persecutors, Paul told Timothy, *"14 You, however, continue in the things you have learned and become convinced of, knowing from whom you have learned them"* (3:14). Timothy was reminded that he had a wonderful heritage. He was raised by a godly mother and grandmother. He learned at an early age that the Scriptures were the inspired Word of God. Timothy had faith as a young boy and he never departed from that faith. When he heard the message of salvation from Paul when he came through Lystra, Timothy was a prepared vessel to follow Christ (3:15). Paul reminded Timothy that he had a role in his journey to salvation. Timothy was loved and discipled.

With that trip down memory lane, the main message to Timothy from Paul was, "Don't waste your privileged preparation. The time has come for you to *continue in the things you have learned."* Timothy was going to be on his own from that point on. He had his foundations strongly established. The one final foundation that needed to be emphasized was the importance of the Word of God in all ministry that was coming.

THE INCOMPARABLE WORD OF GOD. (3:16, 17)

> *16 All Scripture is inspired by God and beneficial for teaching, for rebuke, for correction, for training in righteousness; 17 so that the man or woman of God may be fully capable, equipped for every good work. (3:16,17)*

This is possibly the most comprehensive description of the Bible found within Scripture. We learn how the Word of God was accurately communicated to mankind. We also learn four different functions of the Bible. It establishes the doctrinal foundations of what we believe. It also convicts and confronts our sins. It leads us back on the path of righteousness and it provides instruction so we can remain on the right path. We also learn what the results are for the one who abides by the Scriptures. We will look at each of these revelations about the greatest Book in the world, God's Holy Word.

All Scripture *is given by inspiration of God, (3:16)*

If you read the average doctrinal statement of an evangelical church you will find a statement of belief about the Bible. They normally begin with "We believe in the verbal, plenary inspiration of the Bible . . ." What do those three descriptive words mean?

- **Verbal -** means the very words themselves in the original languages.
- **Plenary -** means all, or every word, not just parts of it.
- **Inspiration – "means this:**

  > "God the Holy Spirit superintended the human writers of the 66 books of the Bible such that what they wrote were God's inerrant words to humanity in the original writings. In doing so, God did not violate the respective personalities, abilities, and contexts of the human authors from which they wrote." (Crosswalk.com commentary)

Let's look at what we can learn about the Bible from 2 Timothy 3:16, 17.

"ALL SCRIPTURE"

Every description found in these verses applies to every part of the Bible, not just certain parts. The Bible is complete in itself. It is the Word of God that He intended us to have, every part, every word in the original languages, every teaching, everything. The Greek word translated means the writings which make up the whole of the Word of God given to man. The very words are what make up the whole. This is where we get the word, "verbal" in the doctrinal statements. This means every single word that makes up the entire work or the 66 books.

God used the apostle Paul to write one half of the New Testament. Before that time only the 39 books of the Old Testament existed. Paul was aware of the special assignment he had been given by God. When he wrote to the church which he planted in Thessalonica, he called his letters God's Word. The final section of the story was in the process of being written.

13 For this reason we also constantly thank God that when you received the word of God which you heard from us, you accepted it not as the word of men, but for what it really is, the word of God, which also performs its work in you who believe.(1 Thessalonians 2:13)

Not only had the chosen prophets given us the Old Testament, but Paul wrote to the church in Ephesus that the Apostles were also chosen to be a part of God's amazing program by adding the Gentiles to the story and the final 27 books of Holy Scripture. In the second chapter of the letter to the Ephesians, Paul described the Gentile connection, the church, and its foundation included both the prophets of old and the apostles:

17 And He came and preached peace to you who were far away, and peace to those who were near; 18 for through Him we both have our access in one Spirit to the Father. 19 So then you are no longer strangers and aliens, but you are fellow citizens with the saints, and are of God's household, 20 having been built on the foundation of the apostles and prophets, Christ Jesus Himself being the corner stone, 21 in whom the whole building, being fitted together, is growing into a holy temple in the Lord, 22 in whom you also are being built together into a dwelling of God in the Spirit. (Ephesians 2:17-22)

The apostle Peter, in his writings, testified that the letters of Paul were part of "all Scripture." In Peter's second letter, he reminded the believers that the whole of Scripture was special and came through God's anointed servants, the holy men of God:

20 But know this first of all, that no prophecy of Scripture is a matter of one's own interpretation, 21 for no prophecy was ever made by an act of human will, but men moved by the Holy Spirit spoke from God. (2 Peter 1:20, 21)

Peter in this same letter then named Paul as one of those specially chosen people God called to record Scripture. Here is his authentication of Paul as an inspired author of Scripture:

> *[15] and regard the patience of our Lord as salvation; just as also our beloved brother Paul, according to the wisdom given him, wrote to you, [16] as also in all his letters, speaking in them of these things, in which are some things hard to understand, which the untaught and unstable distort, as they do also the rest of the Scriptures, to their own destruction. (2 Peter 3:15, 16).*

All, not just parts, but all of Scripture is the very Word of God. But what makes it all the Word of God? Didn't man write it just as men had written the 12,000 manuscripts which the Library of Celsus displayed in Ephesus? The unique difference is that as inspirational as some of these works may be, they are not "INSPIRED" directly from God.

"IS GIVEN BY INSPIRATION BY GOD"

Inspiration means that the full contents of the Scripture were "God-breathed." The source of the words was from God and He breathed them into His chosen authors. The same Greek word is also used to describe a wind filling the sails of a sailing ship. The wind drives the vessel where the wind blows it. Inspiration by the living God sets the Bible apart from all other writings in the world. The people of Ephesus understood the value of history. They assembled some of the world's greatest collections of historians, philosophers, poets, architects, political leaders, and others into a great library.

The Library of Celsus in Ephesus was one of the most famous libraries in the world. It contained 12,000 scrolls. It was completed shortly after the death of Timothy but we can understand the culture by what they valued and read.

The Library of Celsus today in the ruins of Ephesus

Wisdom and knowledge were highly esteemed in the Greek world. There were four statues in the Celsus Library: Sophia (wisdom), Episteme (knowledge), Ennoia (intelligence), and Arete (excellence).

Ephesus, Rome, and Athens were all great cities influenced by the Greek empire. Paul had a fascinating experience with that culture when he traveled to Athens and had discussions with the scholars and leaders:

> *18 And also some of the Epicurean and Stoic philosophers were conversing with him. Some were saying, "What would this idle babbler wish to say?" Others, "He seems to be a proclaimer of strange deities,"—because he was preaching Jesus and the resurrection. 19 And they took him and brought him to the Areopagus, saying, "May we know what this new teaching is which you are proclaiming? 20 For you are bringing some strange things to our ears; so we want to know what these things mean." 21 (Now all the Athenians and the strangers visiting there used to spend their time in nothing other than telling or hearing something new.)* (Acts 17:18-21)

Because of this emphasis on learning and knowing all knowledge, much of the conversations of the people were consumed with the pursuit of new knowledge. Paul described them as "*⁷ always learning and never able to come to the knowledge of the truth*" (3:7). This also explains why there are so many warnings about false teachers.

Why bring up the Library of Celsus when discussing the inspiration of the Bible? Paul made sure Timothy did not get discouraged with the constant barrage of philosophies and new teachings. The Ephesians may have had thousands of scrolls but truth does not come from much speaking and the various philosophies of men, it comes from God. Timothy had the truth. He had the Word of God. Nothing compares to the Bible. Only the Word of God is inspired.

Not only is the Bible the only source of written truth, but it also provides very important guidance for the Body of Christ.

"BENEFICIAL FOR TEACHING, FOR REBUKE, FOR CORRECTION, FOR TRAINING IN RIGHTEOUSNESS; ¹⁷ SO THAT THE MAN OR WOMAN OF GOD MAY BE FULLY CAPABLE, EQUIPPED FOR EVERY GOOD WORK"

The Bible is unique, it stands alone and far above any other writing in the history of mankind.

Unique in development.

Forty different authors over 1,500 years wrote a single storyline, each contributing to the unfolding drama. It was one connected story assembled like a complex puzzle with no missing pieces. No other book is like that. Many of the authors never knew the other authors. God was the Inspiration and the General Editor of the work, not man.

Unique in diversity of writers.

They came from Mesopotamia, the Roman Empire, the Hebrew nation, Greece, and Persia. They were Jew and Gentile but all wrote the one connected story of God and mankind, of a fallen race and a Savior. There was unity in the message from a diversity of people. The authors were kings, soldiers, shepherds, fishermen, priests, prophets, a fig farmer and a doctor. They were like different colored paints God used to craft His masterpiece.

Unique in writing style.

It is history, law, poetry, songs, parables, letters, biography, memoirs, allegory, and more. It contains the greatest stories ever told and none of these things are found in any other place.

Unique in languages and cultures.

The Bible is written in three different languages — Hebrew, Aramaic, and Greek. Each adds its distinct traits to the overall work. Each culture from Mesopotamia to Rome to Asia Minor to Macedonia to Jerusalem adds unique insights and accurate history to the combined work.

Unique in range of teachings.

We would not know the true God except for the Bible. *"160 The sum of Your word is truth, and every one of Your righteous ordinances is everlasting"* (Psalm 118:160). We learn about the attributes of God, the nature of man, the spiritual world, the physical world, the way man fell, and how we can be reconciled to God, the church, prophecies about the end of the age, and what happens into eternity. What other book covers such a range of the human experience?

Unique in survival and influence.

The Bible has been and still is under constant attack and criticism. It has been described as the anvil that has worn out all the critics' hammers. It is a lighthouse that has endured every storm. Many peoples have attempted to silence it but they are gone and it is still here. It is the sole source of the person of Jesus Christ who alone has had more influence on the course of the world than any other person. It is the most rejected yet best-selling book of all time. The Bible societies report that the Bible, in whole or part, has been translated into **more than 3,000 languages and still growing.** It has had a profound influence on art and literature, history, governments, law, the justice system, and much more.

Unique in purpose.

Let's examine these four purposes from 2 Timothy that also make the Bible unique, teaching, rebuking, correcting and training in righteousness.

- **TEACHING**

  Teaching is also translated as "doctrine" in some Bible versions. The word means "that which is taught." It is referring to the truths of the Christian faith or doctrines. The first unique purpose of Scripture is to lay a foundation of Biblical truth to it's readers. This of course builds faith since *"17 faith comes from hearing, and hearing by the word of Christ"* (Romans 10:17). Timothy lived in a world dedicated to learning and knowledge. All the knowledge of the Ephesian pagan world was dedicated to demons and false teachers. Paul was clear to Timothy that the only things worth teaching are from the Scriptures. They alone are valuable, profitable.

- **REBUKING**

  When any believer gets off track, the Word of God is fully equipped to confront the sin and convict the heart.

Timothy was to preach the Word and it would accomplish what God intended. The Holy Spirit is the convincer of sin through the Scriptures:

> *"¹¹ So will My word be which goes forth from My mouth;*
> *It will not return to Me empty,*
> *Without accomplishing what I desire,*
> *And without succeeding in the matter for which I sent it."* (Isaiah 55:11)

The word is like a searchlight that illuminates the hidden deeds of the heart. It exposes us. It rebukes us.

- **CORRECTING**
  The Word of God not only exposes what we have done wrong but also shows us what is right, what we need to do to return to a right relationship again with God. The Greek word means restoration to an upright or right state. It describes something that had fallen over and is put upright again. God never wants us to stay in a sinful condition. God's Word puts us back on our feet.

- **TRAINING IN RIGH-TEOUSNESS**
  The word means "The whole training and education of children (which relates to the cultivation of mind and orals." (Thayer's Greek Lexicon). God's word becomes our schoolmaster or parent whose role is to

restore us to proper behavior. God is holy and righteous. He wants us to be restored in righteous standing before Him. The Word of God is a great gift of grace to us from a God who never gives up on us.

- **SO THAT THE MAN OR WOMAN OF GOD MAY BE FULLY CAPABLE, EQUIPPED FOR EVERY GOOD WORK.**
  This is the goal of God's teaching, rebuking, correction, and training in righteousness. If we submit to God's correcting and training we will be complete, lacking in nothing. This reconnection and guidance is a supernatural work of the Holy Spirit. He convicts of sin, He teaches and corrects, restores, and trains us to walk following the will of God.

Here is a diagram of the purpose of God's Word as described in 2 Timothy 3:16, 17.

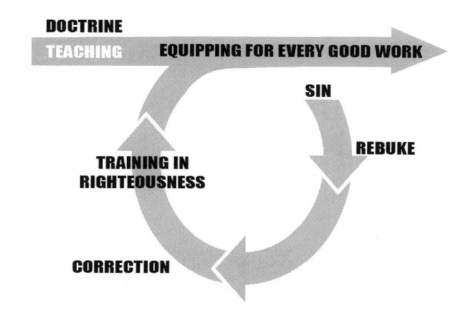

DOCTRINE
TEACHING   EQUIPPING FOR EVERY GOOD WORK

SIN

REBUKE

TRAINING IN
RIGHTEOUSNESS

CORRECTION

IMPORTANT: Before you read Chapter 4, here are a few things to think about. Suppose you knew you only had a very short time to live, maybe days or weeks but you were certain you would die shortly. What would you do? Who would you write or call? What would you want to say? Take time to think about this before you continue. You have learned many lessons in your life but now only the most important ones can be communicated. What are they? What you are about to read are the last things Paul wrote before he died. He wrote them to Timothy. He could have written to one of the churches, or Luke or Silas, or any number of people. We know from what Paul says in this chapter that he knew his death was very close. Let's examine his last words.

2 TIMOTHY 4

Preach the Word faithfully even when people reject the message. (4:1-5)

¹ I solemnly exhort *you* in the presence of God and of Christ Jesus, who is to judge the living and the dead, and by His appearing and His kingdom: ² preach the word; be ready in season *and* out of season; correct, rebuke, *and* exhort, with great patience and instruction. ³ For *the* time will come when they will not tolerate sound doctrine; but *wanting* to have their ears tickled, they will accumulate for themselves

teachers in accordance with their own desires, [4] and they will turn their ears away from the truth and will turn aside to myths. [5] But *as for* you, use self-restraint in all things, endure hardship, do the work of an evangelist, fulfill your ministry.

As you will see, Paul's final words to his son in the faith are the words of a loving parent to a child. They are not given lightly, *"[1] I solemnly exhort you in the presence of God and of Christ Jesus."* They are the most important final instructions he could give to the one person he chose to write to before he was beheaded in Rome. These final words are filled with loving advice, concerning warnings, and triumphant praise. This is how Paul finished. He finished well. May each of us complete the work God has assigned to each of us. Now let's look at the final words of Paul.

PAUL BEGINS WITH THE GREATNESS OF GOD. (4:1)

[1] I solemnly exhort you in the presence of God and of Christ Jesus, who is to judge the living and the dead, and by His appearing and His kingdom. (4:1)

Paul had a challenging word to give Timothy but he first gave a comparison. When one considers the greatness of Christ, there is nothing that is a problem. Timothy need not fear any man, only God should be feared. It is the living God who called Paul and Timothy to do His assigned work. We only have to account to Him, not to any man. Our Savior is also the one who will judge all men when He appears to rule in His eternal Kingdom. It is this eternal perspective Timothy needed because the road ahead for him would be difficult. We need to remember these things as well. It is the same perspective Paul gave to the persecuted church in Rome:

31 What then shall we say to these things? If God is for us, who is against us? 32 He who did not spare His own Son, but delivered Him over for us all, how will He not also with Him freely give us all things? 33 Who will bring charges against God's elect? God is the one who justifies; 34 who is the one who condemns? Christ Jesus is He who died, but rather, was raised, who is at the right hand of God, who also intercedes for us. 35 Who will separate us from the love of Christ?
(Romans 8:31-35)

It was like Paul saying, "Timothy, do you understand how great God is and He loves you and how He holds you securely in His hands? His will for you may be hard but it is perfect. You will never regret following Him. Now, here are my final instructions for you."

PAUL EXHORTS TIMOTHY TO PREACH GOD'S WORD AND NOT FEAR THE MANY ENEMIES HE WOULD FACE. (4:2-5)

2 preach the word; be ready in season and out of season; correct, rebuke, and exhort, with great patience and instruction. 3 For the time will come when they will not tolerate sound doctrine; but wanting to have their ears tickled, they will accumulate for themselves teachers in accordance with their own desires, 4 and they will turn their ears away from the truth and will turn aside to myths. 5 But as for you, use self-restraint in all things, endure hardship, do the work of an evangelist, fulfill your ministry.

This first of Paul's final instructions reveals that the stresses and duties of a pastor are non-stop. Timothy had to "*be ready in season and out of season*" (4:2). Judging by previous comments in both 1 and 2 Timothy, Paul had been abandoned by most of those he had trained and worked with. The false teachers were abundant and the people spent much of their days in useless and even destructive speech. Timothy was the one that could be trusted. He had a huge task at hand to get the church back on track and to evangelize the masses who mostly did not want the gospel message. He was almost on his own. That is why Paul told him he would have to work overtime, even when inconvenient. It will take great patience and tireless instruction (4:2) if he expects to reap a harvest of souls and disciplined soldiers for God's army.

The people of Ephesus were not looking for a difficult path but an easy one. The message of the gospel is a call to follow Christ which means rejection. That was not going to go over well. They wanted to find teachers that appeased them, not challenged them to live sacrificially. They wanted to feel good, to have "their ears tickled," so they found teachers who would fulfill *"their own desires"* even if it meant rejecting the truth and turning to myths (4:4). We still have that same problem today. If you look at the list of the largest mega-churches in the world, you frequently will find a compromised gospel, which is no gospel at all. People want to go to a church where they will not feel guilty.

The message to Timothy was to preach Christ and do it in two seasons, *"in season and out of season"* (4:2). Timothy was to do it with *"great patience"* expecting resistance and persecution. Young pastors often have great plans and visions for their church but often they are disappointed. One pastor was asked if his church had any problems. He said, "Yes, the people." The Ephesians, Paul warned, *"will accumulate for themselves teachers in accordance with their own desires, ⁴ and they will turn their ears away from the truth and will turn aside to myths"* (4:3, 4). If anyone knew the Ephesians, it was Paul, having worked tirelessly with them for three years. He was ultimately abandoned by most of them (1:15).

The warnings of Paul were a dose of reality, however, he did not want Timothy to quit, but to be aware of the real battle that comes with ministry. The next words were a challenge to stand strong and fulfill the calling of God:

⁵ But as for you, use self-restraint in all things, endure hardship, do the work of an evangelist, fulfill your ministry. (4:5)

PRINCIPLES TO LIVE BY.

Preach the Word. Regardless of the audience, preach the Word of God. You will be rejected but stay faithful to the Word. Some will fall away but never stop preaching the Word. Some will use fancy words to impress. Others will claim that philosophy answers life's questions. Keep on preaching the Word. God's Word is empowered by the God of the universe and it will accomplish all that God intends. Preach the Word.

Paul tells of his soon coming death and his eternal hope. (4:6-8)

⁶ For I am already being poured out as a drink offering, and the time of my departure has come. ⁷ I have fought the good fight, I have finished the course, I have kept the faith; ⁸ in the future there is reserved for me the crown of righteousness, which the Lord, the righteous Judge, will award to me on that day; and not only to me, but also to all who have loved His appearing.

It is the last lap in the race that Paul has been running. He knows his death is at the door. There is not a hint of concern or fear as he faces his beheading under Nero. He had been imprisoned in a dungeon on death row awaiting the final moment. He had written his last letters, shared the gospel for the last time to the guards, and now it was time to face the end of his mortality. How did he feel? Triumphant! He is transferring from a dark and dingy Roman dungeon to the light of glory in the presence of his Savior.

THE END HAS COME. (4:6)

> **⁶ For I am already being poured out as a drink offering, and the time of my departure has come.**

What is "a drink offering?" The first time we see it in the Old Testament was when God changed Jacob's name to Israel and reaffirmed the covenant He had made with Abraham. Jacob's response is recorded in Genesis 35:

> **¹⁴ Jacob set up a pillar in the place where He had spoken with him, a pillar of stone, and he poured out a drink offering on it; he also poured oil on it. ¹⁵ So Jacob named the place where God had spoken with him, Bethel."**
> (Genesis 35:14, 15)

Jacob was acknowledging that he was going to follow God's will. He was giving himself over to God.

When God gave Moses the blueprints and instructions to build the Tabernacle in the wilderness, He also established the Levitical priesthood. The priests were consecrated (set apart) for their special calling. The drink offering was a symbol of complete surrender to the will of God and the commitment to faithfully honor God with their service. Here is how the consecration service was described:

> **⁴⁰ and there shall be one-tenth of an ephah of fine flour mixed with one-fourth of a hin of beaten oil, and one-fourth of a hin of wine for a drink offering with one lamb. ⁴¹ The other lamb you shall offer at twilight, and shall offer with it the same grain offering and the same drink offering as in the morning, for a soothing aroma, an offering by fire to the Lord.** (Exodus 29:40, 41)

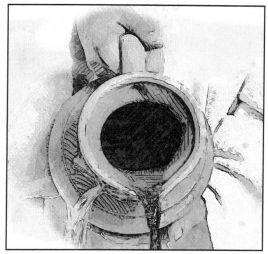

The drink offering was later included in the Jewish sacrificial system as a part of the grain, or meal offering. This particular offering was a consecration offering. The worshipper brought the first fruits of his harvest and offered it to God and symbolically he was offering his life as a worship offering. The wine was poured out on the ground indicating that the consecration was complete. Leviticus 23 describes how the grain offering was part of the feast of First Fruits which had the same meaning but on a national level. The sheaf of the first harvest was brought to the priests and waved before God, a burnt offering (a worship offering) was offered and then the drink offering was poured out (a consecration offering).

> *12 Now on the day when you wave the sheaf, you shall offer a male lamb one year old without defect for a burnt offering to the Lord. 13 Its grain offering shall then be two-tenths of an ephah of fine flour mixed with oil, an offering by fire to the Lord for a soothing aroma, with its drink offering, a fourth of a hin of wine.*
> (Leviticus 23:12, 13)

Paul was a Pharisee before his salvation. He was very familiar with his heritage of Jacob, Moses, and the feasts of Israel. He knew very well what it meant to do a drink offering. It meant full consecration to God. All of it was poured out into the sand. He now uses that beautiful image to say his life was the drink offering and his blood would be poured into the sand as an offering of a life that honored God to the very end.

⁶ For I am already being poured out as a drink offering, and the time of my departure has come. (4:6)

One more thing before we move on. Paul said the time of his departure had come. We may not know the date and time of our departure but we all have one assigned:

²⁷ And inasmuch as it is appointed for men to die once and after this comes judgment, ²⁸ so Christ also, having been offered once to bear the sins of many, will appear a second time for salvation without reference to sin, to those who eagerly await Him. (Hebrews 9:27, 28)

Have you ever boarded a train, subway, or plane? Your ticket tells you the time and place to board and the destination. You had to be at the boarding gate or platform on time to get to your destination. Life is like that. You have a boarding time assigned and the gate you will use to board. One difference is that there are two destinations, heaven, and hell. The choice is yours what the destination will be.

FINISHING WELL. (4:7)

⁷ I have fought the good fight, I have finished the course, I have kept the faith. (4:7)

This should be the goal of every Christian, to finish well. Paul mentions many who did not finish the course on faith. His greatest enemies were often the ones who had religion without a relationship with God or those who could not stand the heat so they climbed out of the furnace. Some wanted the comforts of the world rather than take the persecution that comes to believers. Paul wanted Timothy to know that he had kept the faith and accomplished all he was assigned to do. Paul finished the course.

In a baseball or softball game, there are three bases and then the runner goes home. Paul touched every base, he fought the good fight, finished the course, and kept the faith. Then he went home. It was a strong fight but he won. He had a difficult course to follow but he finished it all. He was challenged in his faith on many occasions but never gave up. So, what was it like when Paul went home? He had an idea of what was coming for him. That is the next point.

PAUL'S CONFIDENCE IN HIS FUTURE HOPE. (4:8)

> *8 in the future there is reserved for me the crown of righteousness, which the Lord, the righteous Judge, will award to me on that day.* (4:8)

Home to Paul was where Jesus lived and that is where he knew he was going. He said he had a reservation there (4:8). He had an appointed departure and he had a reserved reward awaiting his arrival. The reward was guaranteed by the Lord Jesus Himself (4:8).

His reward is described as a crown. In the Bible, crowns normally designate royalty. Kings have crowns. There is another crown in the Bible that is used as a reward like a trophy for achievement. That is the word Paul used when he said a crown of righteousness awaited him. Paul excelled in living a godly life against all odds and would be honored for that. Interestingly, the Greek word for crown is *"Stephanos."* It is identical to the name of the first martyr of the church, Stephen, who Paul was responsible for having killed for his faith. Here is one commentary on that similarity:

> *"Before Paul was a Christian he supervised the execution of the first martyr and then began to kill as many other Christians as he could. But now at the end of his life, he was*

*ready to receive a crown – a stephanos. **He likely
remembered the name of the first martyr, who died at
Paul's own hands:** Stephanos **(Stephen)."***
(Enduring Word Commentary)

The name Stephen means "crowned." Strong's concordance compares the crown Paul mentioned and Stephen the martyr:

> **"Stéphanos (crown) , stef'-an-os; the same as** G4735;
> **Stephanus, a Christian:—Stephen.**

Paul began his illustrious career with the murder of Stephanos (Stephen) and in the end, he knows he will receive the crown (Stephanos) of life. These were like two bookends of his life. Both Stephen and Paul were martyrs who died in faith.

There are other references to crowns in Scripture. Here are two of them:

> **[25] Everyone who competes in the games goes into strict
> training. They do it to get a crown that will not last, but we
> do it to get a crown that will last forever.**
> (1 Corinthians 9:25)

> **[4] And when the Chief Shepherd appears, you will receive the
> crown of glory that will never fade away.** (1 Peter 5:4)

There are five crowns mentioned in the Bible. They all signify a reward for faithfulness. They are not physical crowns like a king would have on his head but spiritual blessings. We can only trust God as to what they mean. Since the crowns come from God they must be worth the sacrifice of a faithful life.

- Crown of righteousness – 2 Timothy 4:8
- Incorruptible crown - 1 Corinthians 9:24–25
- Crown of life - Revelation 2:10
- Crown of glory -1 Peter 5:4
- Crown of rejoicing – 1 Thessalonians 2:19

The amazing thing is the crown of righteousness, as well as the others, are available to us as well. That is the next point.

HOPE FOR ALL WHO FOLLOW CHRIST. (4:8)

. . . and not only to me, but also to all who have loved His appearing. (4:8)

"All who live in expectation of the coming of Christ, who anticipate it with joyfulness, having buried the world and laid up all their hopes above. Here is a reward, but it is a reward not of debt but grace; for it is by the grace of God that even an apostle is fitted for glory. And this reward is common to the faithful; it is given, not only to apostles but to all them that love his appearing. This crown is laid up-it is in view, but not in possession. We must die first."
(Adam Clarke commentary)

Enemies of the gospel are all around us and even our friends sometimes desert us. (4:9-18)

9 Make every effort to come to me soon; 10 for Demas, having loved this present world, has deserted me and gone to Thessalonica; Crescens *has gone* to Galatia, Titus to Dalmatia. 11 Only Luke is with me. Take along Mark and bring him with you, for he is useful to me for service. 12 But I have sent Tychicus to Ephesus. 13 When you come, bring the overcoat which I left at Troas with Carpus, and the books, especially the parchments. 14 Alexander the coppersmith did me great harm; the Lord will repay him according to his deeds. 15 Be on guard against him yourself too, for he vigorously opposed our teaching. 16 At my first defense no one supported me, but all deserted me; may it not be counted against them. 17 But the Lord stood with me

and strengthened me, so that through me the proclamation might be fully accomplished, and that all the Gentiles might hear; and I was rescued out of the lion's mouth. [18] The Lord will rescue me from every evil deed, and will bring me safely to His heavenly kingdom; to Him *be* the glory forever and ever. Amen.

THE ROMAN PRISON WAS A LONELY PLACE FOR PAUL. (4:9)

[9] *Make every effort to come to me soon.* (4:9)

This chapter will list many of Paul's fellow workers and associates who have been sent out to various places. It will also list some who didn't finish the course and were a disappointment to Paul. Except for Luke, Paul is alone, locked up in the Mamertine prison in Rome. Those awaiting execution were kept in the cold, damp, lowest level of the stone structure.

Mamertine Prison

Paul's most beloved traveling companion was Timothy. Paul's execution was a certainty. He was lonely and wanted to see his "son in the faith" one more time before he died. He wrote, *"⁹ Make every effort to come to me soon."* From what we know of Timothy, he would have made every effort to get to Rome and see Paul. Since Christians had been declared enemies of the state, it would have been a dangerous venture. Paul knew that but missed his beloved Timothy. There are no known historical records or statements within the Scripture that tell us if Timothy was able to see Paul or even travel to Rome. It will remain a mystery. Having said that, there is one small hint and it will be found in verses 12 and 13. We will get to that shortly.

MOST OF PAUL'S WORKERS WERE SCATTERED OR SENT OUT. (4:10-12)

> *¹⁰ for Demas, having loved this present world, has deserted me and gone to Thessalonica; Crescens has gone to Galatia, Titus to Dalmatia. ¹¹ Only Luke is with me. Take along Mark and bring him with you, for he is useful to me for service.* (4:10-12)

Demas - His was a sad story. He traveled with Paul, had seen miracles, and conversions among the Gentiles. Demas was part of Paul's ministry team during Paul's house arrest in Rome.

> *¹⁴ Luke, the beloved physician, sends you his greetings, and also Demas.* (Colossians 4:14)

> *²³ Epaphras, my fellow prisoner in Christ Jesus, greets you, ²⁴ as do Mark, Aristarchus, Demas, Luke, my fellow workers.* (Philemon 1:23, 24)

He traveled with Paul and was well known among the brethren. He was numbered with the greatest. But along the way, he left the work and returned home to Thessalonica. Maybe he had tasted persecution and sacrifice and had enough. We aren't told but we are told that he deserted Paul because he loved this world. He didn't return home to evangelize. He was a deserter. How sad to have this written about you. Paul said he finished the course and kept the faith. Then the next thing he mentions is one who did not finish the course well. He chose to go back to the world rather than follow the Lord.

This is the last we hear of Demas. The one hope in this story is that he went to Thessalonica which was one of the greatest and most impactful churches in the first century. Maybe the church in Thessalonica helped Demas find his way home. There is no doubt, the demands of discipleship are high; not everyone survives the test.

> *"We must not suppose that he altogether denied Christ or gave himself up either to ungodliness or to the allurements of the world; but he merely preferred his private convenience, or his safety, to the life of Paul."* (John Calvin)

Crescens – We can only assume he was sent to Galatia to assist the church there. This is the only mention of him in the Scriptures.

Titus – Titus was a trusted partner of Paul in church planting. His sending Titus to Dalmatia would have been for a new evangelistic outreach. When you look at the map you will see the general zone of church planting Paul and his team focussed on. Dalmatia was not in that region. Paul, however, when he wrote to the Romans, indicated that he went into that region at one time:

> *19 in the power of signs and wonders, in the power of the Spirit; so that from Jerusalem and round about as far as Illyricum I have fully preached the gospel of Christ.*
> (Romans 15:19)

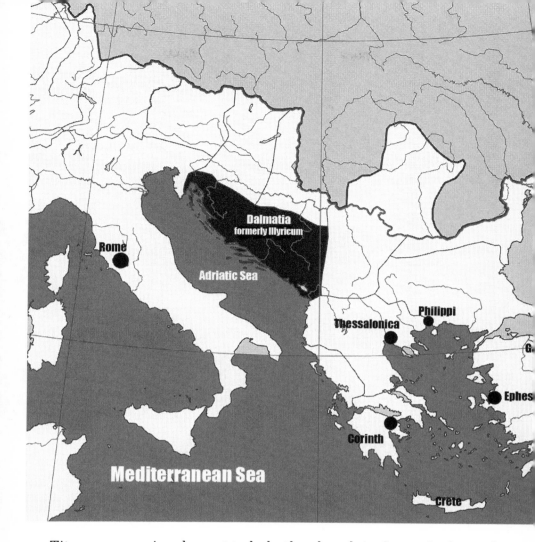

Titus was previously sent to help the church in Crete. At the end of Paul's life, it seems that he sent him to complete the work of evangelizing and church planting in Dalmatia. Today, that would include Albania and Serbia.

Luke – The only Gentile to write a gospel. Luke was a physician by trade but became one of Paul's most faithful companions. Luke was a careful researcher and detailed person in his writings. Even more than that, he was the historian helping Paul in recording the book of Acts along with the gospel bearing his name. He was the only one who remained with Paul when he wrote 2 Timothy, his final work.

Mark – Paul requested Timothy to bring Mark with him to Rome. He was the immature one who accompanied Barnabas and Paul on their first missionary journey. He deserted Paul and Barnabas and became the source of the split-up of the team (Acts 15:36-40). Mark has at this time become a man of God. This was a work of grace in both Mark's and Paul's life. It was a wonderful resolution to an earlier problem. Demas started well and ended badly, but Mark started poorly and ended well. Mark is the greater story.

THE ONE HINT THAT TIMOTHY MAY HAVE GONE TO ROME. (4:12, 13)

[12] But I have sent Tychicus to Ephesus. [13] When you come, bring the overcoat which I left at Troas with Carpus, and the books, especially the parchments. (4:12)

Paul had been very clear that he missed his friend and coworker, Timothy. He urged him to come to Rome, *"[9] Make every effort to come to me soon"* (4:9). There are no historical records that mention if Timothy saw Paul one more time before his death. Timothy was in Ephesus when he got Paul's second letter with the request. So, did he make it to Rome or not? We don't know. There is, however, one small hint that he might have made it.

Titus had been sent to Crete to organize the church, set things in order. Paul wrote the following to Titus while he was in Crete doing ministry: *"When I send Artemas or Tychicus to you, do your best to come to me at Nicopolis, for I have decided to spend the winter there"* (Titus 3:12). Paul sent a replacement to Crete to free up Titus to travel to Nicopolis to assist him there. He most likely chose Artemas because as we will see, he would decide to send Tychicus to Ephesus.

"Paul requested Titus to meet him in Nicopolis, a city on the Macedonian coast (mentioned only in Titus

*3:12) to help him minister during the winter. Some
writers think it was in Nicopolis that Paul was again
arrested and sent back to Rome. Titus is mentioned in
Paul's last letter, as having gone to Dalmatia
(2 Timothy 4:10), a Roman province just northwest of
Macedonia, presumably to evangelize and organize
churches in that unreached area."*
(Institute for Creation Research commentary)

It appears that Paul did the same thing with Timothy. He wrote
to Timothy, *"¹² But I have sent Tychicus to Ephesus."* It was most
likely to replace him so he could come to Rome. Timothy was to
bring along with him some important items:

> *¹³ When you come, bring the overcoat which I left at Troas
> with Carpus, and the books, especially the parchments.*

It was winter and Paul was in the lowest level of the dark, damp
Mamertine Prison in Rome with Luke. That is why he wanted
his coat. The books and parchments would have been of
importance to both Paul and the historian Luke. Some items
were in Troas, left in the possession of a trusted believer named
Carpus. We have seen an example in Paul's life of a man who
learned that God was most important. He warned Timothy
about the dangers of money and wealth and Paul lived those
principles out. He was at the end of his life and he only had one
cloak. He also requested manuscripts, the Word of God which
he had entrusted with a brother for safekeeping. He wanted to
travel through life as lightly as he could.

> *"In addition to a cloak, Paul had left two other items in the
> possession of Carpus: scrolls and parchments. The scrolls
> may have been Old Testament scrolls or the Torah or other
> books, though this is uncertain. The parchments were flat,
> book-like materials, used for writing. These were either
> parchments already written upon or perhaps referred to
> blank parchment Paul wanted for writing new materials.*

Even during imprisonment, and facing the end of his own life, Paul is still emphasizing the importance of reading and studying the Word of God." (Bibleref.com)

Conclusion. Tychicus probably arrived in Ephesus because he was the one carrying the book of 2 Timothy with him to give to Timothy. Tychicus then took Timothy's place as pastor while Timothy went to Rome as Paul urged him to come to him. The books and parchments were handed to Luke for his records after Paul died. Yes, there is this hint that Timothy did go to Rome before he returned to Ephesus where he lived out his life as the main pastor of the believers there.

PRINCIPLES TO LIVE BY.

Ministry teams are critical. Paul multiplied himself many times by first discipling a faithful, qualified group of believers. As his ministry grew, so did his team. He could confidently send different team members to assist or replace others to free them up for new assignments. And Paul was able to coordinate much of it while in prison. Pastor or church planter, don't try to do it all alone.

Paul's final warning to Timothy. (4:14-18)

[14] Alexander the coppersmith did me great harm; the Lord will repay him according to his deeds. [15] Be on guard against him yourself too, for he vigorously opposed our teaching. [16] At my first defense no one supported me, but all deserted me; may it not be counted against them. [17] But the Lord stood with me and strengthened me, so that through me the proclamation might be fully accomplished, and that all the Gentiles might hear; and I was rescued out of the lion's mouth. [18] The Lord will rescue me from every evil

deed, and will bring me safely to His heavenly kingdom; to Him *be* the glory forever and ever. Amen.

ALEXANDER THE COPPERSMITH OPPOSED PAUL AND THE GOSPEL. (4:14, 15)

> *¹⁴ Alexander the coppersmith did me great harm; the Lord will repay him according to his deeds. ¹⁵ Be on guard against him yourself too, for he vigorously opposed our teaching.* (4:14, 15)

Have you ever made someone angry and after that, they did everything they could to make you miserable or hurt you? Paul had that happen a lot, but we know that Jesus said the unbelievers would hate us because they hated Him first (John 15:18). Even Paul, before his conversion, hated those who followed Christ and even used murder to silence them. The man named Alexander was mentioned in Timothy's first letter. He had professed Christ but had turned away from God:

> *... which some have rejected and suffered shipwreck in regard to their faith. ²⁰ Among these are Hymenaeus and Alexander, whom I have handed over to Satan, so that they will be taught not to blaspheme.* (1 Timothy 1:19, 20)

Alexander was a metal worker, a coppersmith, who had professed faith in Christ but fell back into sin, even blaspheming Christ. When disciplined by Paul, he proceeded to cause harm to Paul. He may have become a government informer or just told lies about Paul. We know he caused Paul a lot of problems. Paul first left Ephesus because of another metalworker named Demetrius who was angry that Paul's message was causing his idol-making business to suffer. He incited a riot which resulted in Paul being sent out of Ephesus (Acts 19). Everywhere Paul went he caused riot or revival, sometimes both.

Even in these difficult attacks, Paul was more interested in warning Timothy to be cautious of Alexander because he was a persistent hindrance to the gospel, *"he vigorously opposed our teaching"* (4:15). Paul did not seek revenge but left that to God, *"the Lord will repay him according to his deeds"* (4:14). He warned Timothy and then he moved on. A good lesson for each of us.

PAUL WAS ABANDONED AT HIS TRIAL, BUT THE LORD STOOD WITH HIM. (4:16, 17)

> *16 At my first defense no one supported me, but all deserted me; may it not be counted against them. 17 But the Lord stood with me and strengthened me, so that through me the proclamation might be fully accomplished, and that all the Gentiles might hear; and I was rescued out of the lion's mouth.* (4:16, 17)

The *"defense"* Paul references was most likely describing his recent trial in Rome. He was given a death sentence and was awaiting execution when he wrote 2 Timothy. His second trial, or hearing, came after his arrest in Macedonia and ended up with him on death row in the Mamertine prison in Rome.

Even though many of his co-workers abandoned Paul, the grace of God was evident within him. He said, *"may it not be counted against them. (4:16).* Paul had been deserted by his friends and was going to die and he forgave the weakness of his disciples. This story sounds familiar. Remember what Stephen said as he was being stoned to death:

> *58 When they had driven him out of the city, they began stoning him; and the witnesses laid aside their cloaks at the feet of a young man named Saul. 59 They went on stoning Stephen as he called on the Lord and said, "Lord Jesus, receive my spirit!" 60 Then he fell on his knees and*

cried out with a loud voice, "Lord, do not hold this sin against them!" Having said this, he fell asleep. (Acts 7:58-60).

Of course, Stephen was echoing the words of Christ on the cross, *"Father, forgive them; for they do not know what they are doing"* (Luke 23:34). As Christians, we are being conformed into the image of Christ (Romans 8:29). There is nothing more Christlike than to forgive those who persecute us. This grace was demonstrated at the cross, seen in Stephen as he was being stoned to death, and proclaimed by Paul as he faced his beheading.

Paul knew it was the presence of God that took him safely through every trial. He was in the hands of the Lord so he could finish his course which was to proclaim the gospel to the Gentiles (4:17). His deliverances were like being in a lions' den and rescued. *"That all the Gentiles might hear; and I was rescued out of the lion's mouth."* (4:17). Paul knew he was immortal until his time was done. Now, his time was done.

It was time to praise God

EVEN IN TRIALS, PAUL KEPT HIS EYES ON THE PRIZE OF HIS HEAVENLY CALLING. (4:18)

> **[18] The Lord will rescue me from every evil deed, and will bring me safely to His heavenly kingdom; to Him be the glory forever and ever. Amen.**

>> **"To Him be glory forever and ever: This reflects an unreasonable optimism and joy. Paul faced his last moments of this life and he was, by many accounts, penniless, mostly friendless, without valuable possessions, cold, without adequate clothing, and destined for a soon death. Yet, especially knowing the**

heavenly reward waiting for him, he would not trade his place with anyone." (David Guzik)

MY PERSONAL TESTIMONY ABOUT FACING DEATH.

As the author of this commentary, I can attest that over the years I have been with quite a few people during their last days on earth, some at their last minutes. A dying nominal Christian told me that he was so ashamed that he had neglected the most important things. He could not remember where his Bible was. Another man, a next-door neighbor, was not a believer. I shared with him but he refused to consider Christ at the end and died the next day a bitter, lost man. I have stood by victims badly burned in a fire who in fear were crying out for help. They died within an hour. I have been in the home for the destitute dying in Calcutta, India with over 100 Hindus on their death beds, many would die that day. As we walked among them, they reached out their hands with absolute fear in their eyes. Hinduism was of no help to them. There are others, but with committed Christians it is different. Paul said with confidence that God *"will bring me safely to His heavenly kingdom" (*4:18).

In my own life, many years ago, I was given two months to live. I had an acute form of leukemia that had very low survivability. After I was given the diagnosis and the bad news that I was most likely not going to survive, I sent an email out to our support and prayer team (We are missionaries). I have kept that email that I sent two hours after getting the "bad news." I want you to read what emotions were going through my head having just found out I had a terminal disease.

"I still can't believe how I am doing. I should be a basket case but I am absolutely triumphant. I am actually happy and enjoying the witnessing opportunities. I think I have shocked the doctors with the peace that God has given me. His hands are embracing me so strong and with such love that this is one of the most thrilling things I have ever gone

through. The world calls this denial but they are wrong. When the doctor first told me I had acute Leukemia I joked that I was glad it wasn't an ugly one." (Ed Landry, 2001)

It has been over 20 years since that moment and I look forward to glory even more today. That is how I felt and what I wrote just after I got the "news." Seven months in the hospital was a thrilling part of my life's journey. My wife and I have lived and worked in third-world countries over the past 20 years and to us, this was just another chapter in the incredible journey with God we have experienced. Even if it was the last chapter I was determined to make sure it was the best. I grew up during the turmoil of the infamous 1960s and one day I saw a poster in a home that said, "Death is the greatest trip of all; that is why God saved it until last!"

I think Paul would have liked that poster.

Paul's last greetings and final words. (4:19-22)

[19] Greet Prisca and Aquila, and the household of Onesiphorus. [20] Erastus remained at Corinth, but I left Trophimus sick at Miletus. [21] Make every effort to come before winter. Eubulus greets you, also Pudens, Linus, Claudia, and all the brothers *and sisters.*

Paul customarily sent greetings from co-workers to the person or church he was writing to. It is the same thing we do when we visit someone and a friend tells us to be sure and say "Hi" to them. Paul had seen various people during his final arrest. Even though he was alone at the end, he still sent greetings to his

friends who had worked with him. The fellowship was close and sweet between the faithful co-workers of Paul. They had gone through much
persecution together. The family bond was intense.

PRISCA AND AQUILA. (4:19)

Paul began with two of his closest friends, co-workers on every level. They taught together, planted churches together, loved the lost together, and made tents together to support the ministry. The husband and wife team of Priscila and Aquilla were so much a part of Paul's life that they were like-minded and glued together as one family. Paul made sure when Timothy got the final letter he would write to be sure and tell his friends, Priscila and Aquilla that he would have to see them again in Heaven. As Paul faced the certain gallows, his heart was blessed with the memory of special people God had graciously put into his life. Timothy was no doubt in contact with the couple who lived in Corinth but traveled to Ephesus and other places building the body of Christ.

ONESIPHORUS. (4:19)

Next was the household of Onesiphorus. We know very little about this man and his family but we do get a glimpse of how special Paul was treated by them by what Paul wrote in the first verses of this second letter to Timothy:

> *"16 The Lord grant mercy to the household of Onesiphorus, for he often refreshed me and was not ashamed of my chains; 17 but when he was in Rome, he eagerly searched for me and found me — 18 the Lord grant to him to find mercy from the Lord on that day — and you know very well what services he rendered at Ephesus."*
> (2 Timothy 1:16-18)

Some scholars believe that Onesiphorus had died and that is why Paul greets the household and he speaks only in the past tense when he talks of Onesiphorus. What we can be sure of is that this family was loyal to Paul when most had given up on him when he was in Ephesus during his third missionary journey (1 Timothy 1:15). Onesiphorus also made the long and dangerous journey from Ephesus to Rome and managed to locate Paul in prison. Paul was a condemned criminal in Rome awaiting execution. Christians had been declared enemies of the state. Paul never forgot the love and concern Onesiphorus showed toward him. His visit "refreshed" Paul in his dreary underground cell. Jesus gave a special appreciation for those who do this:

> [34] *"Then the King will say to those on His right, 'Come, you who are blessed of My Father, inherit the kingdom prepared for you from the foundation of the world.* [35] *For I was hungry, and you gave Me something to eat; I was thirsty, and you gave Me something to drink; I was a stranger, and you invited Me in;* [36] *naked, and you clothed Me; I was sick, and you visited Me; I was in prison, and you came to Me.'* [37] *Then the righteous will answer Him, 'Lord, when did we see You hungry, and feed You, or thirsty, and give You something to drink?* [38] *And when did we see You a stranger, and invite You in, or naked, and clothe You?* [39] *When did we see You sick, or in prison, and come to You?'* [40] *The King will answer and say to them, 'Truly I say to you, to the extent that you did it to one of these brothers of Mine, even the least of them, you did it to Me.'* (Matthew 25:34-40)

This was Onesiphorus. It is obvious that Timothy knew him well, "18 the Lord grant to him to find mercy from the Lord on that day—and you know very well what services he rendered at Ephesus." With all the deserters that Paul mentions in his letter, it is a shaft of light to meet the ones that were faithful to Paul and the Gospel.

ERASTUS OF CORINTH (4:20)

Paul met many different people in his journeys, both Jew and Gentile. He even preached the gospel to the special palace guards in Caesar's household (Philippians 1:13). One government official he met was in Corinth when he lived in that city for 18 months on his second missionary journey. We know a few things about him from the greetings Paul sent from the believers in Corinth to the believers in Rome at the end of his letter to the Romans:

> *"23 Gaius, whose hospitality I and the whole church here enjoy, sends you his greetings. Erastus, who is the city's director of public works, and our brother Quartus send you their greetings." (Romans 16:23)*

It was very risky and unusual for a high-level Roman government official to not only align himself with Christians but we know he ministered with Timothy. Paul sent Timothy and Erastus from Ephesus into Macedonia to help the churches there. Luke wrote this:

> *"22 And having sent into Macedonia two of those who ministered to him, Timothy and Erastus, he himself stayed in Asia for a while." (Acts 19:22)*

In 1929, an inscription mentioning an Erastus was found near a paved area northeast of the theater of Corinth. It has been dated to the mid-first century and reads "Erastus in return for his **"aedileship"** paved it at his own expense."

> Note: *An "Aedile" was an elected office of the Roman Republic. Based in* Rome, *the aediles were responsible for the maintenance of public buildings (aedēs) and the regulation of public festivals. They also had powers to enforce public order to ensure the city of Rome was well supplied and its civil infrastructure well maintained, akin to modern local government."* (Wiki History)

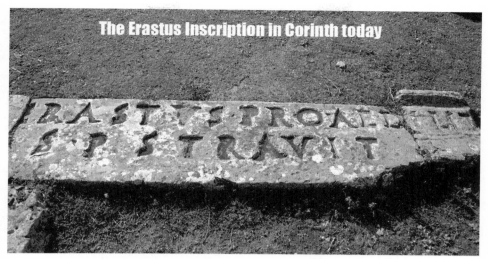

(Latin: ERASTVS. PRO. AED. S. P. STRAVIT[2] abbreviated for
ERASTUS PRO AEDILITATE SUA PECUNIA STRAVIT.)

TROPHIMUS. (4:20)

God did great miracles through the Apostles and some of the
early prophets. In the later days of Paul, the miracles were
fewer and fewer as faith became the way of life for the
first-century church. Theologians have noted that there were
very few seasons of miracles in Scripture. They usually
authenticated some great event or new beginning like the
Exodus, the coming of the Messiah, the birth of the church, etc.
They were never meant to be everyday occurrences. Paul told
the Corinthians, *"7 for we walk by faith, not by sight"*
(2 Corinthians 5:7). Jesus even warned about this:

> *The Pharisees and Sadducees came up, and testing Jesus,
> they asked Him to show them a sign from heaven. 2 But He
> replied to them, "When it is evening, you say, 'It will be fair
> weather, for the sky is red.' 3 And in the morning, 'There will
> be a storm today, for the sky is red and threatening.' Do you
> know how to discern the appearance of the sky, but cannot
> discern the signs of the times? 4 An evil and adulterous*

243

generation seeks after a sign; and a sign will not be given it, except the sign of Jonah." And He left them and went away. (Matthew 16:1-4)

Paul, who had seen people raised from the dead and sickness, told Timothy, who suffered from a stomach ailment, *"23 No longer drink water exclusively, but use a little wine for the sake of your stomach and your frequent ailments"* (1 Timothy 5:23). Paul did not pray for his healing nor could he help his co-worker Trophimus. *"I left Trophimus sick at Miletus"* (4:20). Both of these occurred at the latter time of Paul's life. Even Paul who had personal miracles in his life was afflicted with a *"thorn in the flesh"* which God used to teach him that the grace of God was enough.

> *7 Because of the surpassing greatness of the revelations, for this reason, to keep me from exalting myself, there was given me a thorn in the flesh, a messenger of Satan to orment me—to keep me from exalting myself! 8 Concerning this I implored the Lord three times that it might leave me. 9 And He has said to me, "My grace is sufficient for you, for power is perfected in weakness."* (2 Corinthians 12:7-9)

"I left Trophimus sick at Miletus" (4:20). Sometimes it is the will of God to heal and do miraculous things but we don't live at that level every day. Sometimes God removes a person when it seems like it was too soon. Sometimes He allows His children to experience great losses, like health and family. Sometimes good men like Trophimus will remain sick. In all of life's hardships, we must trust God, His grace is sufficient.

EUBULUS GREETS YOU, ALSO PUDENS, LINUS, CLAUDIA, AND ALL THE BROTHERS AND SISTERS. (4:21)

Paul was writing from a Roman prison. He had contact with the Christian brothers and sisters in the church in Rome. He names four in this verse who are not mentioned anywhere else in the New Testament. When Paul wrote to the church in Rome many years earlier he listed around 30 people he knew and sent greetings from Corinth to them. None of these listed in letters he wrote to Timothy included the four. One assumption is that these had become new believers since Paul was last connected to Rome. Paul wanted to have Timothy hear about how new believers were do

Paul also passed along greetings to *"all the brothers."* There appear to have been many more Christians in Rome than when Paul had written his letter to the Romans approximately a decade earlier. The first four must have been special to Paul. The ministries of Paul, Peter (1 Peter 5:13), and other Christians had led to rapid growth among believers in the Empire's capital. Little is known about these four individuals except for Linus. In the writings of the church father, Irenaeus, Linus is mentioned as the first bishop of Rome after the deaths of Peter and Paul. Timothy already knew these four people. There were also a good number of women who served Paul. He mentions the "sisters" who send greetings to Timothy.

Yes, Timothy knew them. And one more person knew them, God. For most of us, we will never have our names in lights. We may never do the showy things or be popular but it only matters if God knows us. And He knows those that are not, but call themselves Christians

> *19 Every tree that does not bear good fruit is cut down and thrown into the fire. 20 So then, you will know them by their fruits. 21 "Not everyone who says to Me, 'Lord, Lord,' will enter the kingdom of heaven, but he who does the will of My Father who is in heaven will enter. 22 Many will say to Me on that day, 'Lord, Lord, did we not prophesy in Your name, and in Your name cast out demons, and in Your name perform many miracles?' 23 And then I will declare to them, 'I never knew you; depart from Me, you who practice lawlessness.'* (Matthew 7:19-23)

MAKE EVERY EFFORT TO COME BEFORE WINTER. (4:21)

As we previously mentioned, It is highly likely that Timothy, once relieved by Tychicus, was free to travel to Rome to see his friend and mentor before his execution. Paul was cold. It was winter, so he asked for his coat. His death was at hand so Timothy may have been with him to the end. If he didn't get there, Paul would have known that he tried.

THE LAST WORD.

> [22] *The Lord be with your spirit. Grace be with you.*

A simple farewell from the greatest church planter in history and it was over. He put his pen down for the final time. It had all been said. He finished the course and kept the faith. A final prayer closes the life of Paul. It was not just for Timothy, but for us as well. May we carry the torch with the Lord's presence in our spirit. May grace strengthen us for every task until the day when we all meet on the other side and rejoice over what God has done.

Amen and Amen!

Mattia Preti - The Martyrdom of Saint Paul - 17th Century

TITUS

The Making of a Pioneer Cross-Cultural Missionary.

Ancient Manoan Palace on Crete

⁵ For this reason I left you in Crete, that you would set in order what remains and appoint elders in every city as I directed you.

Titus 1:5

Introduction

The Pastoral Epistles.

It is unfortunately common for us to link both Timothy and Titus as pastors. They are together traditionally listed as part of what has become called the Pastoral Epistles (the books of 1 and 2 Timothy and Titus).

Timothy was a young Jewish teenager when he was introduced to Christ and discipled by Paul. He was later assigned the task of correcting and shepherding churches. He became a faithful church leader who tirelessly exercised his pastoral gifts in the face of constant attack and challenging environments in both Macedonia and Asia Minor. This was Timothy the faithful pastor.

Titus was a Gentile who Paul discipled to become a missionary church planter. ew be As apostle Paul's ministry partner, Titus followed up with church plants and even expanded them. He primarily worked in Macedonia and the surrounding region. Paul assigned him to take charge of the struggling churches on the island of Crete. Titus did that until the day when Paul transferred him to Dalmatia to complete the pioneer church plant he had begun in Illyricum. After Paul was arrested, to the best of our knowledge, Titus continued the work of evangelizing and establishing new church plants in that region.

Timothy was a faithful pastor who at times did the work of an evangelist. Titus was an evangelist/church planter who at times did the work of a pastor. When Paul needed a man to rebuke false teachers and develop the long-term church growth of an established church, like Ephesus, he sent Timothy. When Paul needed to expand the growth of a primitive church, reprove entrenched false teachers, plant and evangelize the region, he sent Titus, the trusted missionary pioneer.

Even though Timothy and Titus are commonly linked together, they were quite different people with different personalities (or character qualities), gifts, and roles, yet they were workers together for the Kingdom of God.

The limited New Testament information about Titus.

The ministry of Titus in the New Testament has only four recorded major events. We know he was involved in many more, however, these are all that have been recorded. One of the reasons is that Luke makes no mention of him in Acts, even though he was a major player in the church planting ministry of Paul. The reason for this is quite interesting and will be explained later. Here are the four ministries described in the New Testament:

1. The Jerusalem Council. When Paul went to Jerusalem to deal with the problem of the Judaizers, he took Titus with him. There were Jews who were insisting that new Gentile believers be circumcised to be Christians. Titus was taken to the Council in Jerusalem as an example of an uncircumcised follower of Christ. His presence helped the early church to realize that salvation was by faith alone and not by the works of the Law. The church became unified in the understanding that God was doing great work among the uncircumcised Gentiles. Titus was an outstanding living example. (Galatians 2:1-3)

2. Titus ministry assignment at Corinth. He was sent to strengthen and encourage the carnal and discouraged Corinthian church. He was a fellow worker with Paul in growing and building the believers in Corinth. (2 Corinthians 2:13; 7:6; 7:13; 7:14; 8:6; 8:16; 8:23; 12:18) **Note:** Paul sent

Timothy to Corinth with his first letter (as some believe), but Timothy didn't get anywhere with them. False teachers were turning the church against Paul. Then he sent Titus into that dark spiritual stronghold and God used him to turn the hearts back to Paul and the Lord.

3. Titus' work on the Island of Crete. Paul gave Titus several assignments on the Island of Crete. He was to put things that were broken and in disarray back in order and visit the various cities establishing church leadership. He was sent to organize and strengthen the scattered believers on Crete and confront false teachings. (Titus 1:4, 5)

4. Titus' church planting assignment in Illyricum and Dalmatia. He was sent to complete the outreach of the gospel in the Illyricum/Dalmatia region in western Macedonia where Paul had visited but was unable to adequately penetrate the region. (2 Timothy 4:10)

Titus, the pioneer missionary.

Titus was an early Gentile church leader who had been led to faith and discipled to maturity by Paul, Barnabas, and the Antioch church. He became a trusted traveling companion of Paul and a devoted servant of the Lord. He was a pioneer missionary church planter and regional overseer of new growing churches. He was a defender of the faith.

> *"He was drawn into the ministry in Antioch. He became part of Paul's ministry team through the discipling and mentoring he received from Paul and the healthy church community that Paul helped establish with Barnabas in Antioch. It takes a healthy church to nurture new believers into strong and courageous gospel workers. Paul groomed Titus to become an effective missionary!"*
> (Nelson Reed, mission director)

The character of Titus is observed in his four known ministries.

THE JERUSALEM COUNCIL.

Titus, a strong believer and an example of a Gentile follower of Christ, was taken by Paul to Jerusalem to attend the Jerusalem Council (Acts 15; Galatians 2:1-3). As a Gentile, he was living proof to the council that God was calling Gentiles to be fellow heirs of His kingdom. Titus refused to be circumcised. The council was debating whether a new believer needed to be circumcised and Titus was a living example of a godly, uncircumcised Gentile believer who was strong in his faith, even a co-worker with Paul. His life was a convincing testimony of the saving grace of God to all peoples, Jew and Gentile.

> *Then after an interval of fourteen years, I went up again to Jerusalem with Barnabas, taking Titus along also. ² It was because of a revelation that I went up; and I submitted to them the gospel which I preach among the Gentiles, but I did so in private to those who were of reputation, for fear that somehow I might be running, or had run, in vain. ³ But not even Titus, who was with me, though he was a Greek, was compelled to be circumcised. ⁴ Yet it was a concern because of the false brothers secretly brought in, who had sneaked in to spy on our freedom which we have in Christ Jesus, in order to enslave us. ⁵ But we did not yield in subjection to them, even for an hour, so that the truth of the gospel would remain with you.* (Galatians 2:1-5)

Titus showed his strength and trust in the Lord early in his Christian walk. He stood strong against the cultural traditions of the influential Jews and was unshakeable from attacks that came from the pagan Roman pressures and false teachers who surfaced early in the first century. Titus was an important coworker Paul could depend upon to resist the evil of the times. He stood fearlessly against the false teachers that arose in Jerusalem. Each furnace of trial Titus went through only served to purify his character until he came forth as pure gold. He was the kind of man Paul could send anywhere, whether it was pastoral duties or igniting a church planting movement on Crete, or a pioneer church planting assignment in Dalmatia. He may have been more like the Apostle Paul than any of his other co-workers.

The encounters Titus faced at the Jerusalem Council with the Apostle Paul etched into his soul an incredibly important Christian truth – the Word of God is absolutely reliable! By faith, Paul and Titus proclaimed and stood on the truth of the gospel when faced with great opposition from the apostles, and leaders of the Jerusalem church. They believed in the Word and God prevailed in those pivotal meetings. This helped establish Titus' boldness for the gospel throughout his ministry.

Titus had the complete spiritual toolbox. He could refute the false religions, build the body of Christ, shepherd the weak churches, defend the faith, and do pioneer church planting. He had been discipled by the best — Paul.

We know Paul had a very special relationship with Timothy whom he viewed as a son. Paul also had no other dependable co-worker like Titus who he could confidently send as a pioneer missionary church planter in his place. Timothy and Titus were both Paul's true sons in the faith. Paul always had great affection for both of these men. They were different people with different assignments.

THE CHALLENGES OF CORINTH.

The deeply pagan city of Corinth was not as brutal as Crete, but it posed immense challenges. The church had become infected

with the immorality practiced by the false temple worship carried
on throughout the city. Romans 1 provides a revealing picture of
the Roman Empire's multitude of sins. It was a moral sewer. Read
1 Corinthians for details about the church which had become a
catastrophe. It was not a church where you would send a new
believer. This task required a tested servant of Christ. It needed
a man of trusted moral character who would be respected for his
wisdom, strength, and compassion. This church needed Titus.

Ruins today of the Temple of Apollo in Corinth

Paul sent Titus and Luke (2 Corinthians 8:18) to handle some
pressing matters in Corinth. Paul, in the letter of 2 Corinthians,
described Titus with these words, *"As for Titus, he is my partner
and fellow worker"* (2 Corinthians 8:23). Titus was successful
in reconciling the church and winning them as partners in the
ministry. The effectiveness of Titus with the Corinthians was a
blessing to Paul and the entire church.

> *⁶ But God, who comforts the discouraged, comforted us by
> the arrival of Titus; ⁷ and not only by his arrival, but also by
> the comfort with which he was comforted among you, as he*

reported to us your longing, your mourning, your zeal for me; so that I rejoiced even more. (2 Corinthians 7:6-7)

Titus' ministry of reconciliation and encouragement adds to our profile of this amazing man. We see in his time in Corinth a motivational speaker, peace-maker, influencer, fundraiser, establishing a team for financial accountability and integrity, founding a partnership that involved intercultural ministry development, etc. He had grown into a well-rounded, multi-gifted influencer. Titus became a disciple-maker. He had been discipled by Paul. It would only be natural for him to carry on the Apostle's example. Titus became a powerful leader in developing sustainable church multiplication movements. That is who Titus was.

THE CHALLENGES OF CRETE.

Ancient Gortina church in Southern Crete

Titus was the person who came to Paul's mind when someone was needed to go to the island of Crete, set things in order, unravel the issues facing the church, and motivate the body of Christ to live as Christians in an ungodly world. In a world that was known for doing every imaginable bad thing, it was time to show the Cretans what it meant for Christians to do good deeds (or good things). Titus was the one equipped for the task. Titus went as a missionary to Crete.

Titus was the model missionary. Where there were no churches throughout the island, he started a church-multiplying movement. He went to fix churches that were broken. He addressed problems with leaders and false teachers. The book of Titus lays out an outline of a cross-cultural missionary focusing his attention on establishing a Biblically strong, solid-faith church in a new region. Paul sent Titus to Crete to engage in vigorous teaching, modeling, rebuking, reproving, correcting, strengthening, and accountability training! Titus did all this in under a year on the island. That meant he traveled very much on the rugged island 75 miles long and 30 miles wide. It was a torturous task.

Theseus, a prince from Athens, whose father was an ancient Greek king named **Ageaus** -whom the Greek sea is named after- sailed to **Crete**, where he was forced to fight a terrible creature called **Minotaur**.

Crete was a rugged land but there was one thing even more rugged, the people of Crete. There is a fascinating connection between the Cretans and one of the greatest enemies of Israel, the Philistines. The Cretans were also called "Minoans" and the "Sea People." Some of them settled in the southern coastal region of Israel; (The Gaza strip today). The Philistines were a people very different from other tribal groups in Canaan. They were known as warring people, very brutal. Current archeology has concluded a strong connection between the people that inhabited Crete and the Philistines:

> *"According to the Bible, the Philistines originated in "Caphtor" (Jeremiah 47:4; Amos 9:7), identified as the island of Crete"* (Hess 1992)
> .

Here is a recent study about the relationship between Cretans and Philistines:

> *"The first-ever study of DNA recovered from an ancient Philistine site is providing a unique genetic insight into the origins of some of the most notorious troublemakers of the Old Testament.*
> *"The authors of the Hebrew Bible made it clear that the Philistines were not like them: This "uncircumcised" group is described in several passages as coming from the "Land of Caphtor" (modern-day Crete) before taking control of the coastal region of what is now southern Israel and the Gaza Strip. They warred with their Israelite neighbors, even seizing the* Ark of the Covenant *for a time. Their representatives in the Bible include the giant Goliath, who was felled by the future king David, and Delilah, who robbed the Israelite Samson of his strength by cutting his hair."* (Article cited by author Kristin Romey about recent discoveries in Askelon, the capital city of ancient Philistia, in southern Israel).

The point is, Paul sent Titus to be a missionary to a brutal people. These same people, the Philistines, were one of the greatest enemies of God. They were known as warring people and very deceptive. We know from the content of the book of Titus that in the first century the Cretans were unsteady, insincere, quarrelsome, greedy, immoral, liars, and prone to drunkenness. Their ungodly lifestyle had influenced the believers living on the island. When you add to that the pagan temples and beliefs in Greek mythology, the challenges were extreme.

Knossos Palace, Crete
The hub of Minoan civilization

Civic, religious, and economic center of Knossos.

Paul could not send just anyone to Crete. He needed a warrior church planter. He needed a man who could stand the heat of battle. He chose Titus. As one great Bible school founder once noted, *"The toughest test, calls for the best"* (L.E. Maxwell, founder of Prairie Bible Institute).

THE CHALLENGES OF DALMATIA.

Dalmatia was a thorn in the side of Rome. It was Paul's final known assignment for Titus. Rome was never able to subdue it except along the coastlands. The natives conducted guerrilla-type warfare against Rome's fortresses for centuries. Interestingly, Paul sent Titus to this rebellious, barbaric land! That alone gives a hint about the personal qualities of Titus. This was Titus the pioneer missionary church planter who had the courage of a military general. After his boot camp of dealing with the Cretans, or Philistines, he was ready for spiritual warfare with the people that even the Roman Empire could not handle.

Temple of Jupiter in ancient Dalmatia

One final thing - Titus had a very important brother.

One additional word about Titus is that he had a very important brother (or uncle). This brother, mentioned by Paul, has been most commonly identified as Luke (the author of Acts and the Gospel of Luke). It was traditional for writers to not mention the names of their family members in their writings. The Apostle John did not even mention his name but called himself the one Jesus loved. Luke did not discuss himself when he recorded the history of the early church in Acts. He mentioned many of Paul's co-workers by name, but he left out one of the most important. He never mentioned the name of Titus, even once, in the book of Acts. Why would he omit Titus who was such a significant person in the early church movement?

When Paul wrote his second letter to the Corinthian church he commended Titus to them and made a veiled reference to the famous brother of Titus. Titus' brother had been a faithful helper to Paul but Paul chose not to give his name, just called him the brother of Titus. When we read what Paul wrote about the brother of Titus, the only name that seems to fit the description is Luke. If it was not Luke, it seems strange that when Luke recorded these events in Acts, he failed to mention one of the most well-known people that traveled with Paul.

> *¹⁶ But thanks be to God who puts the same earnestness in your behalf in the heart of Titus. ¹⁷ For he not only accepted our appeal, but being himself very earnest, he has gone to you of his own accord. ¹⁸ We have sent along with him the brother whose fame in the things of the gospel has spread through all the churches; ¹⁹ and not only that, but he has also been appointed by the churches to travel with us in this gracious work, which is being administered by us for the glory of the Lord Himself, and to show our readiness, ²⁰ taking precaution so that no one will discredit us in our administration of this generous gift; ²¹ for we have regard for what is honorable, not only in the sight of the Lord, but also in the sight of other people. ²² We have sent with them our brother, whom we have often tested and found diligent in many things, but now even more diligent because of his great confidence in you. ²³ As for Titus, he is my partner and fellow worker among you; as for our brothers, they are messengers of the churches, a glory to Christ. ²⁴ Therefore, openly before the churches, show them the proof of your love and of our reason for boasting about you.*
> (2 Corinthians 8:16-24)

Here is how the International Standard Bible Encyclopedia describes Luke and Titus:

LUKE THE PHYSICIAN

"Paul (Col 4:14) expressly calls him "the beloved physician." He was Paul's medical adviser, and doubtless prolonged his life and rescued him from many a serious illness. He was a medical missionary, and probably kept up his general practice of medicine in connection with his work in Rome (compare Zahn, Intro, III, 1). He probably practiced medicine in Malta (Ac 28:9 f). He naturally shows his fondness for medical terms in his books."

LUKE AND TITUS

"It is possible, even probable (see Souter's article in DCG), that in 2Corinthians 8:18 "the brother" is equivalent to "the brother" of Titus just mentioned, that is, "his brother." If so, we should know that Paul came into contact with Luke at Philippi on his way to Corinth during his 2nd tour (compare also 2Co 12:18). It would thus be explained why in Acts the name of Titus does not occur since he is the brother of Luke the author of the book."

(source, International Standard Bible Encyclopedia)

Although we cannot be certain that Luke and Titus were in the same family, it appears they were. The Gentile family lived in the Antioch region, part of Syria. It was there that the church at Antioch was born. It was there that believers were first called Christians. It was there that Paul found a home church that would send him on his missionary journeys. It was there that he met the family that would help him change the world, the family of Luke and Titus. An unbreakable bond began. Luke traveled with Paul as a close companion and accurate historian and was the only one with him at the end of his life (2 Timothy 4:11). When Paul was going to his death, Titus was in Dalmatia completing and expanding the work Paul had begun there. Titus was Paul's number one partner in church planting expansion. The three together were an inseparable partnership taking the gospel to new regions. Of course, there were other incredible relationships Paul would develop as well, including Timothy, Barnabas, Silas, Priscilla and Aquila, Lydia, Erastus, and others.

When Paul was released from his first Roman imprisonment, he took Titus to Crete and left him there. He later wrote to Titus with special instructions about the work in Crete. This was the book of Titus. Later he sent a replacement for the pastoral duties on Crete to release Titus to travel to Dalmatia and complete the church planting saturation of the region (2 Timothy 4:10). They were all one great family of God. They encouraged each other, toiled together in the gospel fields, suffered together, loved God together, defended each other, and enriched every church they worked with. To borrow the words of the writer of Hebrews when describing the Old Testament prophets, The family of God in the New Testament were *"38 people of whom the world was not worthy"* (Hebrews 11:38).

> *11 And He gave some as apostles, some as prophets, some as evangelists, some as pastors and teachers, 12 for the equipping of the saints for the work of ministry, for the building up of the body of Christ; 13 until we all attain to the unity of the faith, and of the knowledge of the Son of God, to a mature man, to the measure of the stature which belongs to the fullness of Christ. (Ephesians 4:11-13)*

Now, let's begin our study of the only letter we know Paul wrote to Titus. Titus was on Crete assigned there by Paul. The believers on the island needed order and strengthening. Titus had an enormous task on his hands. Paganism and brutality were all around. Paul's timely letter would have been a great encouragement and a breath of fresh air to both Titus and the church.

Sphinx from ancient Crete depicted on a storage jar

Titus Chapter 1
Commentary

Paul's' greeting and our eternal hope. (1:1-4)

¹ Paul, a bond-servant of God and an apostle of Jesus Christ, for the faith of those chosen of God and the knowledge of the truth which is according to godliness, ² in the hope of eternal life, which God, who cannot lie, promised long ages ago, ³ but at the proper time manifested, *even* His word, in the proclamation with which I was entrusted according to the commandment of God our Savior, ⁴ To Titus, my true child in a common faith: Grace and peace from God the Father and Christ Jesus our Savior.

PAUL, BOND SERVANT AND APOSTLE OF CHRIST. (1:1)

> *¹ Paul, a bond-servant of God and an apostle of Jesus Christ, for the faith of those chosen of God and the knowledge of the truth which is according to godliness,* (1:1)

A BONDSERVANT. (1:1)

A servant is someone who serves another. He or she can be a

hired helper or a volunteer, helping just to help. That is a servant. Imagine that you worked for a person and your paid job was to serve the guests of your employer. You were paid to do this. Also, imagine, your boss is a good person and treats you well. When the contract runs out and you have fulfilled the commitments you have been paid to do, you are free to find other employment. Your boss tells you that you can now leave; you are free from the contract. Even though you are no longer under his employment, what if you decide to stay and work for free because you like your boss? You decide that you would rather give up your freedom to do the will of your boss.

You are in essence becoming a slave to him by choice. You would no longer be a hired helper, you would be a *"doulos."* The Greek word "doulos" describes a person who gives all his time and energy to benefit another. It is a person who voluntarily gives up his own time, energy, and interests to serve another. When Paul used the word to describe himself, he is saying he no longer is pursuing his own will but has made a decision to follow and serve Christ, giving up his personal goals. He has committed to a life of service to Christ alone. Paul chose to be the life-long slave, or servant, of the Lord. He chose to be a "doulos," a bond servant by choice for his King.

Paul's assignment was to serve Christ by serving the church and building the *"faith of those chosen of God"* (1:1). He taught, wrote, visited, and encouraged the churches to live godly lives by diligently teaching them the Word of God (1:1).

AN APOSTLE. (1:1)

Paul made it clear he was picked by God to be part of the very foundation of the first-century church. He was more than a teacher, he was a special messenger of the Lord. He was placed by God to be part of the select company of apostles. He also had a particular ministry as the messenger to the Gentiles. In addition, he was assigned to become an author of the very Word of God itself. Peter recognized that the writings of Paul were part of the Scriptures.

> *15 and regard the patience of our Lord as salvation; just as also our beloved brother Paul, according to the wisdom given him, wrote to you, 16 as also in all his letters, speaking in them of these things, in which there are some things that are hard to understand, which the untaught and unstable distort, as they do also the rest of the Scriptures, to their own destruction.* (2 Peter 3:15, 16)

OUR ETERNAL HOPE. (1:2, 3)

> *2 in the hope of eternal life, which God, who cannot lie, promised long ages ago,*

We might think, "What a simple verse. God cannot lie and He has promised the hope of eternal life." But put yourself in the place of Titus for a moment if you can. You are on the island of Crete. The Cretans had pagan mythology that dated back centuries. The early Minoan culture was an abomination, filled with pagan temples and practices. Their false gods offered false hope.

> *"Minoan religion closely linked humans and nature, which the Minoan's believed to be infused with the divine. Frescos frequently show sacrifices and worship taking place beneath or next to images of the sacred tree, a symbol of nature that was also part of the sacred precincts of Minoan palaces.*
>
> *Animals were also of divine significance, symbolizing manifestations of divine presence, fertility, and protection. Important animals included the dove, goat, bull, cow, and snake."* (historyandarchaeologyonline.com)

266

The religion was a goddess religion, their primary deities were goddesses. The main goddess was the snake goddess.

The goddess had a male companion, a nature god and he had a team of lesser gods who were the intermediaries between the major gods and humans. Sacrifices to the gods were common and the only hope of satisfying the evil beings and this was the hope of the Minoans. Titus saw the temples and fears of the Cretans every day. They lived lives based on a lie. Paul also lived for years in such a culture. The Ephesians built the largest temple in the world to a female deity. The Temple of Artemis was considered the most impressive of all the seven wonders of the ancient world.

These deceptive pagan religions are the design of Satan, God's arch-enemy. Remember, the devil is the father of lies. This is how Jesus described him:

44 You belong to your father, the devil, and you want to carry out your father's desires. He was a murderer from the beginning, not holding to the truth, for there is no truth in him. When he lies, he speaks his native language, for he is a liar and the father of lies. (John 8:44)

Cretans normally had their false temples or caves of worship in forest settings since their goddesses were connected to nature. It was animism, polytheism, and pantheism combined, a blend of evil and lies. Even their prophets knew the reputation of the Cretans was evil:

12 One of themselves, a prophet of their own, said, "Cretans are always liars, evil beasts, lazy gluttons." (Titus 1:12)

Isaiah the prophet described the futility of all who live by idolatry. His words describe the deceptive religion of all pagan worshipers, including the Minoans/Cretans:

9 Those who fashion a graven image are all of them futile, and their precious things are of no profit; even their own witnesses fail to see or know, so that they will be put to shame. 10 Who has fashioned a god or cast an idol to no profit? 11 Behold, all his companions will be put to shame, for the craftsmen themselves are mere men. Let them all assemble themselves, let them stand up, let them tremble, let them together be put to shame.

12 The man shapes iron into a cutting tool and does his work over the coals, fashioning it with hammers and working it with his strong arm. He also gets hungry and his strength fails; he drinks no water and becomes weary. 13 Another shapes wood, he extends a measuring line; he outlines it with red chalk. He works it with planes and outlines it with a compass, and makes it like the form of a man, like the beauty of man, so that it may sit in a house. 14 Surely he cuts cedars for himself, and takes a cypress or an oak and raises it for himself among the trees of the forest. He plants a fir, and the rain makes it grow. 15 Then *it becomes something for a man to burn, so he takes one of them and warms himself; he also makes a fire to bake bread. He also makes a god and worships it; he makes it a graven image and falls down before it. ¹⁶ Half of it he burns in the fire; over this half he eats meat as he roasts a roast and is satisfied. He also warms himself and says, "Aha! I am warm, I have seen the fire." ¹⁷ But the rest of it he makes into a god, his graven image. He falls down before it and worships; he also prays to it and says, "Deliver me, for you are my god."*

¹⁸ They do not know, nor do they understand, for He has smeared over their eyes so that they cannot see and their hearts so that they cannot comprehend. ¹⁹ No one recalls, nor is there knowledge or understanding to say, "I have burned half of it in the fire and also have baked bread over its coals. I roast meat and eat it. Then I make the rest of it into an abomination, I fall down before a block of wood!" ²⁰ He feeds on ashes; a deceived heart has turned him aside. And he cannot deliver himself, nor say, "Is there not a lie in my right hand?" (Isaiah 44:9-20)

Roman temples and pagan worship filled the landscape where Paul and Titus walked. Read Titus 1:2 again and imagine the hope of truth and eternal life it would have given the first-century believers

> *² in the hope of eternal life, which God, who cannot lie, promised long ages ago, (1:2)*

Amid evil, darkness, and lies, comes a shaft of light. There is one great God, who is the living and true God who only speaks the truth. The truth He speaks is a wonderful promise. He alone offers eternal life. He can be trusted unlike the pagan false gods of the land. The promise came from eternity past, long before any false religion. He is truth and He is hope and He will bring light to the darkness of any heart.

PAUL REMINDED TITUS OF THE AUTHORITY HE HAD BEEN GIVEN BY GOD. (1:3)

> *3 but at the proper time manifested, even His word, in the proclamation with which I was entrusted according to the commandment of God our Savior,* (1:3)

Titus had a difficult challenge to bring the gospel to the Cretans and disciple the believers in such a dark society. We previously read about the futility of worship of stone and wood gods who are deaf, dumb, and powerless to save. Paul reminded Titus that his calling was from the true and living God. Titus was now in the line of succession. The torch was being passed to him. The evil of the Cretan society was proof that the gods and goddesses of mythology could not solve the sin in the land. Their only hope was to turn to the one true God. It was the *"proper time"* given by God, entrusted to Paul, and passed on to his disciple. It was time to bring the power of God into the powerless idolatry of Crete. The plan was from God and was *"entrusted according to the commandment of God our Savior."*

> **"The world was uniquely conscious of its need for a Messiah and Savior. "There was never a time when the hearts of men were more open to receiving the message of salvation which the Christian missionaries brought." (Barclay)**

For Titus, the message was not only a hope that the time for Crete had come but that Titus had also been chosen by God for such a time.

THE GODLY HERITAGE OF TITUS, THE COMMON FAITH, AND THE MATCHLESS GRACE OF GOD. (1:4)

> *4 To Titus, my true child in a common faith: Grace and peace from God the Father and Christ Jesus our Savior.* (1:4)

Titus had a tremendous heritage. He had a brother, Luke, who was Paul's historian and also a Gospel writer. He was reminded by Paul that his salvation was influenced by Paul so much that Paul referred to him as a *"true child in a common faith."* Titus had the great privilege to be a partner in the church planting ministry of Paul, *"a fellow worker"* (2 Corinthians 8:23). The great English preacher Charles Spurgeon notes that Titus was *"a man of great common sense; so that, when Paul had anything difficult to be done, he sent Titus."*

With such responsibility on his shoulders, Titus would have needed a double portion of the *"Grace and peace from God the Father and Christ Jesus our Savior"* to sustain him through the perilous journey. With the support of Paul, God the Father, and the Lord Jesus, Titus was ready to venture into the battle for the souls on Crete.

Why Paul sent Titus to Crete and the qualifications of elders he would appoint. (1:5-9)

⁵ For this reason I left you in Crete, that you would set in order what remains and appoint elders in every city as I directed you, ⁶ *namely*, if any man is above reproach, the husband of one wife, having children who believe, not accused of dissipation or rebellion. ⁷ For the overseer must be above reproach as God's steward, not self-willed, not quick-tempered, not addicted to wine, not pugnacious, not fond of sordid gain, ⁸ but hospitable, loving what is good, sensible, just, devout, self-controlled, ⁹ holding fast the faithful word which is in accordance with the teaching, so that he will be able both to exhort in sound doctrine and to refute those who contradict.

PAUL REMINDED TITUS WHY HE WAS ASSIGNED THE MINISTRY IN CRETE. (1:5)

> *⁵ For this reason I left you in Crete, that you would set in order what remains and appoint elders in every city as I directed you,*

Crete, as we have seen was a unique society very different from surrounding cultures. It was a Minoan people, the source of the Philistines who had occupied the southern coastal region of Israel. Their religion was based on goddess worship and their warfare was legendary. But there were believers in Christ in the mid-first century even though they lived on an isolated mountainous island. Where did the believers come from on Crete? They were present in Jerusalem and converted when Peter preached on Pentecost :

> *¹¹ (both Jews and converts to Judaism), Cretans, and Arabs. And we all hear these people speaking in our own languages about the wonderful things God has done!"*
> (Acts 2:11)

After Pentecost, the thousands who were converted from various regions and languages returned as evangelists to their various countries. The church began on Crete with very little background or training. They needed to be discipled. It is hinted in the words of Paul that he did not send Titus to Crete, but he left him behind to finish the work that he and Titus had been doing there.

> *"Paul and Titus likely did a good deal of evangelism on the island in the weeks before Paul commissioned Titus to a leadership position there."* (Swindoll)

After evangelism, the work has only just begun. It is like raising a child. The birth is not the end product. It is the starting point. Discipling and nurturing, training, teaching, and modeling the

Christian life remained to be done. Titus was to finish the task. Paul left to work in other regions. The letter to Titus is like a church planters manual.

Church planting is better caught than taught. Teaching is certainly important but church planters are not raised in Bible schools or seminaries. They are forged on the anvil of experience on the field. They are guided by mentors who are fellow church planters. Paul took Titus to Crete to do battle with evil, evangelize the masses, disciple the new believers, and organize the believers into a strong community of light in the darkness. Paul, after he trained Titus, left him to finish with work and appoint *"elders"* (leaders) and disciple them to carry on after Titus would one day leave. Church planting is mentorship leading to multiplication.

Initially, Timothy's first task was to "set in order" the matters in the church that needed attention. This was not an older or mature church. It was a spontaneous beginning that started with believers returning from Jerusalem on Pentecost with new life and starting the work on Crete. Then, years later, Paul came with Titus and worked with them and did outreach on the island. Then Paul left and put Titus in charge. There was still much that needed to be fixed. The word *"set in order"* is the same language describing a doctor who sets a broken arm, or a gardener who takes a broken branch, straightens it out, and splints it.

There were several large cities in Crete. Travel was very difficult because of the mountains. Titus was assigned the task of appointing leaders in the various population centers and delegating spiritual authority to them. Paul gave Titus a list of leadership qualities so he knew what kind of leaders would be needed to navigate the church on Crete through the storms that would come. When you read the list in the next verses it is abundantly clear that a strong Christian character is essential.

THE QUALIFICATIONS FOR CHRISTIAN LEADERSHIP. (1:6-9)

> *⁶ namely, if any man is above reproach, the husband of one wife, having children who believe, not accused of dissipation or rebellion. ⁷ For the overseer must be above reproach as God's steward, not self-willed, not quick-tempered, not addicted to wine, not pugnacious, not fond of sordid gain, ⁸ but hospitable, loving what is good, sensible, just, devout, self-controlled, ⁹ holding fast the faithful word which is in accordance with the teaching, so that he will be able both to exhort in sound doctrine and to refute those who contradict.* (1:6-9)

Paul gave Timothy a similar list of leadership qualifications. Both Timothy and Titus were given regional leadership roles over the network of house churches in their area. Ephesus no doubt had dozens of house churches. Crete would not have been that large, but the different cities had groups of believers. The first Christians who returned from Pentecost over 20 years before Paul and Titus arrived, most likely, had little training. Crete was a war zone of evil ideology and religious beliefs. Because Crete is an island, the people were isolated with their thinking. It was a big challenge to get the groups on the same page, encourage the family of God to press on, and do good among the pagan population. Titus needed to organize the movement and make them a team with the same goals. One of the first duties was finding gifted leaders and appointing them as Elders. It was still in the early stages of the development of the church on Crete, so Paul makes mention of deacons at that time. Strong and focused leadership was the starting point. These verses list the qualities of godly leaders.

LEADERSHIP QUALIFICATIONS LISTED AND DEFINED. (1:6-9)

Above reproach.

This quality has been described as the last person anyone would think would possess certain bad traits. There is nothing in your life that can be a source of any accusation against his person or the church.

This simply means respectable, good behavior. Elders must not be chaotic in decisions otherwise how can they bring order to the ministry? This was the same word used previously of women who were careful not to dress in excess or immoral fashion. This means the elder is not extreme in his appearance but has a modest appearance. In regards to customs and trends in society, the respectable elder would neither be the first one to get into a new trend nor the last one to get out of an old style. He is not interested in shocking or making a scene. His life is dignified and orderly. He has a high moral character.

He must have a good reputation with those outside *the church* so that he will not fall into disgrace and the snare of the devil. Character is what you are. Reputation is what people think you are. The two things should be the same. An elder or pastor must be an honorable person and live in such a way that others see you the way you are, inside the church and outside.

> *"A good name is to be more desired than great wealth,*
> *Favor is better than silver and gold."* (Proverbs 22:1)

The husband of one wife.

The question always arises, "Can a divorced person pastor a church? The words in the original language describe a man who is a one-woman-man. He is single-minded. His wife is his only passion when it comes to human relationships. In its purest form that rules out divorce and it rules out polygamy. It also rules out women as elders since the word is not "spouse" but "wife." And homosexual marriage is not a biblical arrangement. The ideal may not always be possible and we never want to rule out the grace and forgiveness of God.

There are formerly divorced men who pastor churches. The question is, what do we want, God's best or someone that does not meet the Biblical qualification? Marriage in Ephesians 5 is described as a picture of the church with Christ as the bridegroom and the church as the bride. Jesus is faithful and the only husband in the illustration. The church is to be the faithful wife, seeking no other and being submissive and honoring God. That is Gods' ideal when he says "He must be the husband of one wife." The problem of polygamy seems to have been a problem with the pagan Cretan people. Spurgeon noted this:

> *"For there were many converts there who had two or three wives. Whatever position they might be permitted to occupy in the church, they could not become officers, they must keep in the rear rank."* (Spurgeon)

Having children who believe.

This passage is not teaching that an elder must have children. The point is that if an elder does have children, they must be obedient. A family unified in a common faith is a strong testimony to the unbelievers. Keeping his children under control with all dignity. if a man does not know how to manage his household, how will he take care of the church of God? (1 Timothy 3)). Loving the church begins with loving our spouse and our family. True church leadership is parallel to leadership in the home. The pastorate is very demanding and can consume much of a leader's time. There is a danger in neglecting the training and discipling of our children. A parent that takes time to lovingly nurture his children will be respected by his flock. Children who are disciplined in love will be a crown, not a curse. Married pastors need to be wise and self-controlled, to balance the variety of needs and crises that come to a family and a church. The point of this command is that Godly, well-disciplined children are evidence of a pastor's ability to lead.

The home life of a pastor is the foundation for his public life. How can a pastor teach on loving his wife, or being a spiritual leader when his own home life is not right? Can two walk together and not agree? We become one flesh with our spouse and if that is not a healthy relationship then we are a fractured person. If you are still single, then be careful if you decide to marry to choose wisely. Imagine an ice skating pairs competition if one skater did not come to the event. What if the final runner of a relay race decided to stay home. Becoming one flesh means in every aspect, emotionally, spiritually, purpose, everything. If we are not pulling together, then we are pulling apart. Marriage failure leads to ministry failure.

What if a pastor has a prodigal child? Is that pastor disqualified from ministry"

> *"This text requires that we should look carefully at a man's relationship with his children. Does he model godly behavior in the home? Is he conscientious to train his children in the ways of the Lord? Does he pray and read the Bible with his family? If so, normally most (if not all) of his children will come to believe in Christ. If all or most of his children grow up and reject Christ, there is probably something wrong in that home. We should probably not recognize him as an elder. On the other hand, if most of his children follow*

Christ, but one goes astray, in my estimation, it does not necessarily disqualify the man as an elder. Each situation must be prayerfully considered."
(Bible.org online commentary)

Not accused of dissipation or rebellion.

This applies to the children of the elder. A wayward child is a deep burden to the leader of the flock. It is a word used of the Prodigal Son who left his life at home and wasted his inheritance on riotous living. He not only spent his fortune, but he also spent his life. This is a person with no thought of tomorrow and the consequences of wasteful living. Pleasure means more to him than honor. The result is a life in total rebellion. Titus was warned of any life with those tendencies. It can ruin a leader or cause great emotional distress. If one child in a leader's family wanders in such a way, it must be seriously discussed and prayed about with the church family to decide if the leader will remain in that position or step down. Everyone needs to be at peace with the decision.

For the overseer must be above reproach as God's steward.

The leader must have a clean reputation as one who handles the funds and responsibility of the church. A good steward is a conscientious manager, respecting his role and not abusing his position. A wise pastor will normally appoint honest and trustworthy members of the church to handle church funds. No matter who does it, their reputation must be spotless.

Not self-willed.

When Jesus prayed the night before He was crucified, He surrendered His will to the Father, *"Father, if You are willing, remove this cup from Me; yet not My will, but Yours be done"* (Luke 22:42). As followers of our great Shepherd, we the under-shepherds need to do likewise. This calling to leadership is not about us, it is about the King and His Kingdom. It is about the people we have been entrusted with, leaving no room for selfishness. It is not about us.

> *"Basically, selfish people are disqualified from leadership. They show their* **self-willed** *nature in arrogance, stubbornness, and a proud self-focus. Not one who is determined to have his own way in everything; setting up his own judgment to that of all others; expecting all to pay homage to his understanding."* (Clarke)

Not quick-tempered.

The quick-tempered are also disqualified from leadership. The Greek word translated here is "quick-tempered," or in some versions as "soon angry." It refers more to a steady state of anger, not an infrequent burst of anger. It is a man who is all the time like a pot on the stove ready to boil over.

> *But let everyone be quick to hear, slow to speak, and slow to anger; for the anger of man does not achieve the righteousness of God.* (James 1:19-20)

The mature, godly man is guided by the fruit of the Spirit which includes patience, kindness, and self-control. You can hear the calmness in the words that come from the Holy Spirit. He calms the raging sea of the quick-tempered man.

Not addicted to wine.

Not overindulging in wine, literally, not a drunken person. Not a quarrelsome person or belligerent like a drunk. This is not a prohibition from drinking wine but a warning that an elder should not spend his time sitting around with those who overindulge. The principle can be properly applied today to any addiction, not just alcohol. How can a leader be under the influence of God when under any other influence.

17 So then do not be foolish, but understand what the will of the Lord is. 18 And do not get drunk with wine, for that is dissipation, but be filled with the Spirit.
(Ephesians 5:17, 18)

Not pugnacious, augumentitive.

This refers to having a quarrelsome or combative nature. This trait is similar to what Paul told Timothy. A leader is not to be a bully or a violent man. This can apply to both physical and mental abuse. We have all known people like that, always looking for a complaint, a fight, or a cause to resist. Some people see problems and others see possibilities. Some want to complain and others want to solve the problems. Some are pessimists, only seeing the problems, and others are optimists, seeking solutions.

> *"The Greeks themselves widened the meaning of this word to include, not only violence in action but also violence in speech. The word came to mean one who browbeats his fellow-men, and it may well be that it should be so translated here."* (Barclay)

An elder should not be "a striker." He should not be known as an argumentative or violent person or one who uses his authority to overcome another. He should be a man of peace, a peacemaker. John the Apostle wrote about a church leader who abused his position and damaged his fellowship.

> *9 I wrote something to the church; but Diotrephes, who loves to be first among them, does not accept what we say. 10 For this reason, if I come, I will call attention to his deeds which he does, unjustly accusing us with malicious words; and not satisfied with this, he himself does not receive the brothers either, and he forbids those who want to do so and puts them out of the church."(3 John: 9, 10)*

Titus was to seek the man that is not contentious, not easily provoked or one who provokes others to conflict. A leader should seek conversation, not confrontation. When a disagreement occurs in the body of Christ, the leader should encourage calm, not add fuel to the fire.

When working with others the leader needs to be gentle, It is a fruit of the Spirit. A good Christian leader provides a calming influence. It is not possible to picture Jesus as loud, boisterous, arrogant, or domineering. He treated others with compassion and mercy. When Jesus spoke to the woman caught in adultery, do you hear an angry, judgmental tone in His voice or do you hear a man with a gentle voice guiding the woman out of her shame?

Not fond of sordid gain, not greedy for money.
The things of this world should have no grip on the godly leader. Wealth, position, and titles are seen as passing away without eternal value. The elder needs to have an eternal perspective. Paul would later remind Timothy of the dangerous temptation of wealth. The cure for materialism is contentment.

> *⁸ If we have food and covering, with these we shall be content. ⁹ But those who want to get rich fall into temptation and a trap, and many foolish and harmful desires which plunge people into ruin and destruction. ¹⁰ For the love of money is a root of all sorts of evil, and some by longing for it have wandered away from the faith and pierced themselves with many griefs."*
> (1 Timothy 6:8-10)

A greedy man cannot be trusted. He is always looking out for himself. He has the responsibility for the lives of those in his fellowship. His counsel is cherished by his people but his mind clouded with greed will not give wise counsel

Hospitable.

A lover of strangers. He is open and generous to guests. He is a people person. A leader loves people and serves them. Sometimes we think of Paul as a driven man, unyielding. We remember John Mark being rejected by Paul on his second journey because he deserted Paul on the first journey. But Paul had an open door and worked tirelessly with people even preaching and teaching late into the night. When he was under house arrest awaiting his hearing, we read this: "Now Paul stayed two full years in his rented lodging and welcomed all who came to him" (Acts 28:30). Paul was busy writing four books of the New Testament but he welcomed all who came. Hospitality puts the focus on the importance of people. Paul later forgave John Mark and had good things to say about him. A leader who is not welcoming of outsiders will develop a church that will be the same. The Great Commission is others-centered, not self-centered.

Loving what is good.

Crete was an island filled with evil and godless practices. The godly believer would have stood out as very different. Sin may be attractive for a season but its rewards are counterfeit, not real or lasting. The remedy for gutter thinking is godly thinking.

> *Finally, brethren, whatever is true, whatever is honorable, whatever is right, whatever is pure, whatever is lovely, whatever is of good repute, if there is any excellence and if anything worthy of praise, dwell on these things.*
> (Philippians 4:8)

We will never live well if we don't love good. It starts in the heart and ends up in the walk. Paul told Titus to train his people to do good. In a land where bad people are doing bad things, they needed good people to do good things.

In all things show yourself to be an example of good deeds, with purity in doctrine, dignified, ⁸ sound in speech which is beyond reproach, so that the opponent will be put to shame, having nothing bad to say about us. (Titus 2:7, 8)

Sensible.

A sober minded life. This describes a person who can think clearly. They understand how to deal with serious subjects in a serious way. In the mind of the Apostle Paul, this was an *important* quality in a leader. He used this word ten times in his short letters to Timothy and Titus.

> *"This does not mean he has no sense of humor, or that he is always solemn and somber. Rather it suggests that he knows the value of things and does not cheapen the ministry or the Gospel message by foolish behavior."* (From Wiersbe's commentary on 1 Timothy).

> *"Sensible means to be of sound mind, especially in the sense of not being impulsive. The sensible man is not swayed to extremes by his fluctuating emotions. He doesn't give in to impulses that would be sinful or harmful. He is level-headed. He lives in light of his priorities and commitments."* (Bible.org commentary)

Just.

Micah, the prophet asked an important question:

> *He has told you, O man, what is good;*
> *And what does the Lord require of you*
> *But to do justice, to love kindness,*
> *And to walk humbly with your God? (Micah 6:8)*

We need to be just with others, treat them fairly. A pastor or leader in the church must be **just** (right toward men). When a man is righteous, he is fair-minded to others and honors God. We have been justified by grace through faith. We should never lose sight of the mercy shown to us by God. Elders must be just people, merciful leaders, and humble. He must seek to treat people rightly, without partiality. A good leader is good to everyone.

Devout.

Holy (right towards God). An elder needs to have a clear focus on God. We may walk in a sinful world but we should not participate in the evil in the world. We should love the sinner but not participate in their sin. A godly elder is separate from sin but a friend of sinners. They are looking for light in the wrong places. We show them the right place, at the cross. Paul said to live is Christ, that is the model to follow for an elder, fully devoted to Christ.

Self-controlled.

Self-controlled, disciplined. It implies one who governs and restrains his passions. *"He must be lively and zealous, yet calm and wise"* (Benson Commentary). He is alert to spiritual danger and chooses to avoid it. His priorities are ordered. He is a man of purpose and exercises discipline to achieve his spiritual goals. He avoids distractions, keeping his eyes focused on the high calling of Christ. How can a man govern the body of Christ if he has no control over his passions? God's man is vigilant to guard his heart.

Holding fast the faithful word which is in accordance with the teaching, so that he will be able both to exhort in sound doctrine and to refute those who contradict.

This final character quality has to do with how a leader loves the Word of God, teaches the Scriptures, encourages the body of Christ, and refutes the errors of false teachers.

1. He is a guardian and defender of God's Word.

Elders must have an unshakeable belief in God's Word. No one can defend or give their lives to something they don't fully believe. Paul reminded Titus of the teaching he received from the years of working together. It was time for Titus to teach and pass the truth along to others *"following the teaching."* Paul invested his life in faithful disciples who would carry the process of multiplication with others.

> *² The things which you have heard from me in the presence of many witnesses, entrust these to faithful people who will be able to teach others also.*
> (2 timothy 2:2)

2. He Teaches sound doctrines.

Paul not only wanted Titus to pass the torch on to the next generation, but he also wanted to emphasize how important it was to make sure the things taught were "sound doctrine." The great cities of the Roman Empire were filled with temples and halls where philosophers presented eloquent lectures about their mythology and false teachings. The pagans also passed on what they believed to their students. They discipled their followers. Titus had something they never had; the truth and sound doctrine. Only the Word of God is the foundation that stands firm when the floods come. The others are built on sinking sand.

> *"A preacher must be both soldier and shepherd. He must nourish, defend, and teach; he must have teeth in his mouth and be able to bite and fight."* (Martin Luther)

If a leader does not have a basis in **sound doctrine** to either **exhort** or **convict** an individual, he probably shouldn't do it. Leaders need to stand on the foundation of the Word.

3. He Encourages the church.

The instructions of Paul were clear to Titus. He was to guard the Scriptures, defend them and teach the sound doctrines of the faith. In doing that he "will be able both to exhort" or encourage the believers. The pressures of the ungodly Cretan society were oppressive. Titus and the believers needed to boldly present the gospel which is the power of God to salvation to everyone who believes, Jew and Gentile (Romans 1:16).

> *The Lord is my light and my salvation- whom shall I fear? The Lord is the stronghold of my life- of whom shall I be afraid?* (Psalm 27:1)

4. He refutes those who contradict the truth.

Paul's fourth challenge was to not only stand firm but to shake the land of Crete with the gospel message. The false teachers held strongholds in the land but the gospel of Christ could break up even the hardest of grounds. Titus needed to remember that the God of the armies of heaven was behind His Word. He would go to battle with heavenly support. Those "who contradict" would fail.

> *"The pastor ought to have two voices: one, for gathering the sheep; and another, for warding off and driving away wolves and thieves. The Scripture supplies him with the means of doing both."* (John Calvin)

REVIEW

Both elders and church order was needed in Crete. Elders needed to have a strong faith and good Biblical understanding. They needed to be mature believers, not new converts, as Paul reminded Timothy in his letters. Elders needed to know what they believed and cling to that foundation. Elders needed to obey God instead of compromising with the fallen culture of Crete. It wasn't enough to know the truth; they needed to live the truth. Elders needed to be leaders tuned in to the needs of their church and encourage the body of Christ. Elders needed to stand strong against the false teachers and ungodly idolatry of the Cretans. The church needed that kind of leadership. Crete needed that kind of church to show them the light.

The destructive lifestyles of the Cretans and their false prophets. (1:10-16)

10 For there are many rebellious men, empty talkers, and deceivers, especially those of the circumcision, 11 who must be silenced because they are upsetting whole families, teaching things they should not *teach* for the sake of sordid gain. 12 One of themselves, a prophet of their own, said, "Cretans are always liars, evil beasts, lazy gluttons." 13 This testimony is true. For this reason reprove them severely so that they may be sound in the faith, 14 not paying attention to Jewish myths and commandments of men who turn away from the truth. 15 To the pure, all things are pure; but to those who are defiled and unbelieving, nothing is pure, but both their mind and their conscience are defiled. 16 They profess to know God, but by *their* deeds they deny *Him*, being detestable and disobedient and worthless for any good deed.

HOW TO HANDLE FALSE TEACHERS, GREEDINESS, AND THE DANGEROUS MESSAGE OF THE JUDAIZERS. (1:10, 11)

¹⁰ For there are many rebellious men, empty talkers and deceivers, especially those of the circumcision, (1:10, 11)

One of the most severe opponents to the gospel was a group he was very familiar with. It was the Judaizers. Paul was raised in a devout Jewish home. His father was a Pharisee. He was zealous for the Law of Moses. Then he met Jesus on the Damascus Road. He went through new training, a time with God in the Arabian desert for several years. Paul was then even more zealous but he was zealous for Christ. He had reached a high rank among the Jewish leadership, but that all ended when he joined the ranks of the very people he had been assigned to destroy. The Jewish rulers labeled Paul as a deserter, a renegade. He was like a Christian terrorist to the Jewish traditions and Law.

For many years, the Jewish converts to Christ struggled with the Gentile converts, not knowing where they fit. They were not Jews, they were uncircumcised, they were unclean. They began to demand that the Gentiles adopt the Jewish practices and become circumcised to fellowship with the Jewish converts. Paul dealt with these Judaizers numerous times. The most significant time was when he, Titus, and others traveled to the Jerusalem council to discuss that matter (Acts 15).

> *Some men came down from Judea and began teaching the brothers, "Unless you are circumcised according to the custom of Moses, you cannot be saved." ² And after Paul and Barnabas had a heated argument and debate with them, the brothers determined that Paul and Barnabas and some others of them should go up to Jerusalem to the apostles and elders concerning this issue. ³ Therefore, after being sent on their way by the church, they were passing through both Phoenicia and Samaria, describing in detail the conversion of the Gentiles, and they were bringing great joy*

to all the brothers and sisters. ⁴ When they arrived in Jerusalem, they were received by the church, the apostles, and the elders, and they reported all that God had done with them. ⁵ But some of the sect of the Pharisees who had believed stood up, saying, "It is necessary to circumcise them and to direct them to keep the Law of Moses."
(Acts 15:1-5)

The council agreed with Paul. New proclamations were made stating that the Gentiles did not need to become circumcised to be believers. Peter traveled to Antioch and was confronted by Paul and rebuked for his hypocrisy:

¹¹ But when Cephas came to Antioch, I opposed him to his face, because he stood condemned. ¹² For prior to the coming of some men from James, he used to eat with the Gentiles; but when they came, he began to withdraw and separate himself, fearing those from the circumcision. ¹³ The rest of the Jews joined him in hypocrisy, with the result that even Barnabas was carried away by their hypocrisy. ¹⁴ But when I saw that they were not straightforward about the truth of the gospel, I said to Cephas in the presence of all, "If you, being a Jew, live like the Gentiles and not like the Jews, how is it that you compel the Gentiles to live like Jews? (Galatians 2:11-14)

Many years later, Paul and Titus went to Crete. They were met by the same enemy of grace, the Judaizers. This group had not only maintained the earlier error of the Judaizers, but they had also adopted additional destructive habits from the Cretans. *"¹⁰ For there are many rebellious men, empty talkers and deceivers, especially those of the circumcision."* They had caused confusion among the Jewish Christians who were following Christ along with Gentile converts. Paul told Titus to confront the Judaizers and silence them (with the truth), *"¹¹ who must be silenced because they are upsetting whole families, teaching things they should not teach for the sake of sordid gain."*

Several matters concerned Paul. Jewish converts did not want to give up the old ways. They wanted the Gentile believers to conform to their Jewish system including becoming circumcised. There was some form of greedy financial gain associated with the motive to convert the Gentiles into Jewish traditions. We may not understand what it was but it was troubling to Paul who warned Titus that the upsetting lives and message of these false teachers needed to be stopped.

> *"They tried to persuade them that the simple story of Jesus and the Cross was not sufficient, but that, to be wise, they needed all the subtle stories and the long genealogies and the elaborate allegories of the Rabbis. Further, they tried to teach them that grace was not enough, but that, to be good, they needed to take upon themselves all the rules and regulations about foods and washings which were so characteristic of Judaism." (Barclay)*

Paul then turned his attention to the native Cretan people.

THE CARNALITY OF THE CRETANS. (1:12-14)

> *[12] One of themselves, a prophet of their own, said, "Cretans are always liars, evil beasts, lazy gluttons." [13] This testimony is true. For this reason reprove them severely so that they may be sound in the faith, [14] not paying attention to Jewish myths and commandments of men who turn away from the truth.* (1:12-14)

Living and ministering on Crete presented a two-fold source of challenge to Titus. He had to deal with the Jewish practices and myths and he had to confront the hostile, depraved native Cretan people. We have already seen the Cretans were an ancient Minoan people who were known for their war and brutality along with their worship of mythological goddesses.

For Titus, this was not an ordinary church assignment, but one that only a strong, mature Christian could handle. Titus was chosen for the assignment.

> *"They were a degraded people; and hence, those who would teach them had a most difficult task, and needed great grace. Paul exhorts Titus that only specially fit men, men whose example would have influence, and whose characters would have weight, should be allowed to be elders in such churches."* (Spurgeon)

In describing the characteristics of the Cretans, Paul quotes a Cretan prophet who speaks about his people. Normally, a person who talks about his people, would overlook the negative attributes and highlight the positives. The words of this prophet are blunt and honest.

> *[12] One of themselves, a prophet of their own, said, "Cretans are always liars, evil beasts, lazy gluttons." [13] This testimony is true.* (1:12, 13)

This is why it was important for Titus to appoint strong, godly men to become the leaders of the church. The pressure from the pagan world on Crete would have been intense. It was critical that the characteristics listed of the Cretans not influence the church.

Paul quotes the well-known Cretan prophet because the evaluation of the native people on the island was accurate. Historians have identified the poet as Epimenides, a native Cretan.

> *"So notorious were the Cretans that the Greeks formed a verb* kretizein, to cretize, *which means to lie and to cheat; and they had a proverbial phrase,* kreitzein pros Kreta, *to cretize against a Cretan, which meant to match lies with lies, as diamond cuts diamond."* (Barclay)

The three things which mostly characterized the people of Crete were the total opposite of what should characterize a follower of Christ.

"always liars"

This contrast is as clear as hot and cold, darkness and light, God and Satan. The sum of God's word is truth (Psalm 119:160), the entire vocabulary of the devil is lies (John 8:44). Jesus is the Truth (John 14:6) and those who follow the way of Satan are liars. The Cretans were "always liars." Can any testimony of a people be more horrible? Oddly, a Cretan prophet told the truth for once when he labeled his own people as continual liars.

"evil beasts"

They were not just evil. They were not just beasts. They were evil beasts! Their heartless brutality was legendary. When other nations write about them, it is about their warfare and brutality. The Philistines were Cretans that had settled in southern Israel. The prophet Amos spoke the words of judgment from God against the inhabitants of Philistia because of their brutal assaults and treachery against Israel:

> *Thus says the Lord,*
> *"For three transgressions of Gaza and for four*
> *I will not revoke its punishment,*
> *Because they deported an entire population*
> *To deliver it up to Edom.*
> *⁷ "So I will send fire upon the wall of Gaza*
> *And it will consume her citadels.*
> *⁸ "I will also cut off the inhabitant from Ashdod,*
> *And him who holds the scepter, from Ashkelon;*
> *I will even unleash My power upon Ekron,*
> *And the remnant of the Philistines will perish,"*
> *Says the Lord God.* (Amos 1:6-8)

"lazy gluttons"

Paul wrote to the Philippian church and warned them to avoid certain people who were harmful to the church. He described them in words similar to the Cretans:

> *18 For many walk, of whom I often told you, and now tell you even weeping, that they are enemies of the cross of Christ, 19 whose end is destruction, whose god is their appetite, and whose glory is in their shame, who set their minds on earthly things.* (Philippians 3:18, 19)

The Word of God gives numerous warnings about both laziness and gluttony. *"Diligent hands will rule, but laziness ends in forced labor"* (Proverbs 12,24). *"In the name of the Lord Jesus Christ, we command you, brothers and sisters, to keep away from every believer who is idle and disruptive and does not live according to the teaching you received from us"* (2 Thessalonians 3:6). *"Do not be idolaters, as some of them were; as it is written: 'The people sat down to eat and drink and got up to indulge in revelry.'"* (1 Corinthians 10:7).

These descriptions not only give us insight into the character of the Cretan people but also the character of Titus. God chose a man who could stand against the evil of the land and be victorious. Very few men could have preached to such a hostile crowd day after day. Titus was a great warrior in the army of the Lord.

THE DEFILED CRETANS (1:15, 16)

> *15 To the pure, all things are pure; but to those who are defiled and unbelieving, nothing is pure, but both their mind and their conscience are defiled. 16 They profess to know God, but by their deeds they deny Him, being detestable and disobedient and worthless for any good deed.* (1:15, 16)

There was a lot of conflict and confusion in Crete. All of Paul's letters to Timothy and Titus have warnings about false teachers who had distorted the gospel. They demanded that new believers adhere to the Laws of Moses and abstain from certain foods. Some even were forbidding people to marry (1 Timothy 4:3). Even though these issues and this false teaching had been dealt with at the council in Jerusalem (Acts 15), there were still many who practiced these false teachings. Their teachings destroyed the liberty of believers and put them under bondage to a system of working for salvation.

> *"The 'all things' refers to everything which is non-moral; such as appetite and food, desire and marriage, exchange and commerce, weariness and recreation, and so on through all the varied realm of life. To the pure all these things are pure, and they will be maintained in purity. To the impure, every one of them may be made the vehicle and occasion of impurity."* (Morgan)

This was what was happening in the churches in Crete when Paul and Titus arrived. Titus was given the assignment to get the church back on its feet. He had to confront the Judaizers and teach true Christian doctrines. At the same time, there was a pagan Cretan population that needed the gospel of Christ. They also were a defiled population.

We have seen that the Cretans were liars, polluted by idolatry, lazy, gluttons, and warring people. They are described as "being detestable and disobedient and worthless for any good deed." The Greek words used are very descriptive. They refer to counterfeit coins, having no value. They mean broken pottery is no longer used and is tossed aside. They describe strong pollution and they are used to picture a carved stone that has so many flaws it cannot be used for what it was made.

They remind us of the account of Noah's flood which describes the depraved condition of the heart of the inhabitants of the earth at that time:

> **⁵ Then the Lord saw that the wickedness of man was great on the earth, and that every intent of the thoughts of his heart was only evil continually.** (Genesis 6:5)

Yes, There was a lot of conflict and confusion on Crete. Paul and Titus had great challenges to address in the Jewish world, the confusing church, and the spiritually blind Cretans. It was war. This first chapter gives us a realistic picture of what life was like in Crete and the church.

What can a pastor do in light of all the negative issues and challenges? Where does one begin? That is what Chapter 2 addresses.

Titus 2
How should Christians live?

Chapter 2 Introduction.

Paul's instructions to Titus to get the church matters in order focus on specific groups within the church. Each group of people has its own needs and issues so they are handled individually. These are the target groups in Chapter 2:

- The older men in the church. (2:1,2)
- The older women in the church. (2:3-5)
- The young men in the church. (2:6-8)
- The bondslaves in the church. (1:9, 10)
- General Instructions for all members of the church. (1:11-15)

Instructions for older men in the church. (2:1, 2)

¹ But as for you, speak the things which are fitting for sound doctrine. ² Older men are to be temperate, dignified, sensible, sound in faith, in love, in perseverance.

We have seen how difficult Crete was as a mission field. The church was also in disarray. It was strongly influenced by the Jewish legalists or Judaizers. Many false prophets confused the body of Christ. The world around them was filled with violence and war. It was a world of secular wisdom and philosophy. It seemed like everything was at odds with the Christian worldview. Satan's circus had come to town and had distracted the believers from being the Christians they had been called to be in the lost society of Crete.

It was especially discouraging for the older men. They should be spiritual leaders in the church but many had given up, the battle being so intense. They were old and tired of fighting all the enemies who were attacking every front. It was easier to give in and compromise. Let the younger people fight the battle. Titus needed to get his aging army back in the fight again, they had so much to share. They were experienced soldiers who needed fresh direction and encouragement.

The first thing Titus did was to re-establish them in the great doctrines of the faith. They needed to learn again *"the things which are fitting for sound doctrine"* (2:1). The false prophets and the Judaizers would only be silenced by the truth. The truth was the fresh wind from Heaven that would blow away the dark, storm clouds of doubt and confusion that had covered the besieged church in Crete.

Titus was grounded in the Word of God. No one was more prepared than he was to face the spiritual warfare in the land. Titus's challenge was that he was younger than the ones he was teaching. The culture of the Greeks placed great emphasis on the wisdom of the aged. The philosophers were older so age was respected. Youth were seen as unstable and unlearned. Titus was a young man but Paul was more well-known and his presence gave credibility to the younger Titus. Titus had been discipled, trained, and prepared by the man who wrote one half of the New Testament. Titus was also a strong warrior for the faith. He had faced the fiery darts of the enemy and was a victorious soldier in God's kingdom. The church in Crete was starving for sound doctrine and good news had come, Titus was there and he could be trusted.

Sound doctrine leads to sound living. There were six things the older believers needed to strengthen in their lives (2:2):

- to be temperate.
- to be dignified.
- to be sensible.
- to be sound in the faith.
- to be sound in love.
- to be sound in perseverance.

TO BE TEMPERATE.
This means sober, clear-minded. The literal usage means, "abstaining from wine, either entirely or at least from its immoderate use" (Strongs Concordance). The general principle is to not be under the influence of anything or anyone other than God.

TO BE DIGNIFIED.
They needed to live lives worthy of honor. They had to earn the

right to be heard and share their wisdom. Just being old was not enough, they had to have an honorable character.

TO BE SENSIBLE.
Practical wisdom. Thayers Greek Lexicon defines the Greek word *"sōphrōn"* as "curbing one's desires and impulses, self-controlled, temperate, sober-minded." It is a life marked by "self-control" and discipline."

TO BE SOUND IN FAITH.
Strong's Concordance describes this character trait as:

> "moral conviction (of religious truth, or the truthfulness of God or a religious teacher), especially reliance upon Christ for salvation; abstractly, constancy in such profession; by extension, the system of religious (Gospel) truth itself: —assurance, belief, believe, faith, fidelity."

In other words, older men should not stop in their pursuit of God. They need to grow more grounded every day in God and His Word.

TO BE SOUND IN LOVE.
It was hard to love pagan idolaters. It was also hard to love a compromised church. They needed to know as the sun melts wax, so the love of God can melt the hardest heart, in the church or the world. They needed to know that God loved the church and the Cretans so much He sent Paul and Titus to them to help them return to the true God. The word for love is the highest form of love, God's love. It is supernatural. The older men were to be encouraged to be examples of the love of God to the lost and the church.

TO BE SOUND IN PERSEVERANCE.

Steadfastness, constancy, and endurance. Paul described this attribute in his first letter to the church at Corinth: *"Therefore, my beloved brethren, be steadfast, immovable, always abounding in the work of the Lord, knowing that your toil is not in vain in the Lord"* (1 Corinthians 15:58). The temptation for the elderly was to give up. They were tired of the daily battle. They needed to see that God was not finished with them yet. Crete needed them then more than ever. Hang in there, the finish line is just ahead. Keep pressing on for God and finish well.

Instructions for older women in the church. (2:3-5)

³ Older women likewise are to be reverent in their behavior, not malicious gossips nor enslaved to much wine, teaching what is good, ⁴ so that they may encourage the young women to love their husbands, to love their children, ⁵ *to be* sensible, pure, workers at home, kind, being subject to their own husbands, so that the word of God will not be dishonored.

The next instructions are to the elderly women in the church. We have already seen warnings to Titus to avoid the gossiping women who were using their free time in destructive ways. They, like the men, needed a new challenge to make their lives count for God. They especially needed to invest in the young wives and mentor them into godly women.

We have seen that the false worship of the Cretans was mostly women, the goddesses of mythology. Temples were constructed to worship these fictional women. Women were important in Cretan society but for the wrong reasons. Christian women needed to show what a godly woman was like and lead the Cretans to worship the true God.

TITUS WOMEN.

Many churches today have what are called Titus Women ministries. These ministries are designed to encourage and train older women to be active in discipling young married and single women. The need today for mentoring young women is just as necessary as in the first century. Titus was not told to teach the young women but to have the older women do that. This principle might well be applied today to prevent compromising situations between pastors and young women. These are the disciplines the older women were to both model and teach the younger women:

DEMONSTRATING TO THE YOUNG WOMEN WHAT IS GOOD (2:3)

TO BE REVERENT IN THEIR BEHAVIOR.
The temptations of the pagan society were great to younger women. Beauty was emphasized in the temples and goddesses were worshipped. There was a lot of pressure on young ladies to conform to the immoral culture. The older women were needed to model a life that honored God. The younger women needed to see that a godly life was possible. Only God is worthy of worship and worth. Godly older women needed to let their light shine so the younger women could see the path of
righteousness.

NOT BE MALICIOUS GOSSIPS. (2:3)
In Paul's writings, he warned about the dangers of destructive speech. *"But have nothing to do with worldly*

fables fit only for old women. On the other hand, discipline yourself for the purpose of godliness" (1 timothy 4:7). *"Let no corrupting talk come out of your mouths, but only such as is good for building up, as fits the occasion, that it may give grace to those who hear"* (Ephesians 4:29). *"But avoid irreverent babble, for it will lead people into more and more ungodliness"* (2 Timothy 2:16). *"Besides that, they learn to be idlers, going about from house to house, and not only idlers, but also gossips and busybodies, saying what they should not."* (1 Timothy 5:13).

The matter of laziness and gossip was a problem in the Greek and Roman world. The older women had fallen into the trap of spending their time in unproductive ways. Paul instructed Titus to motivate the older women to use their lives more productively for God and become mentors of the younger women so they would not fall into that same trap. The older women needed to live lives the younger would want to follow.

NOT ENSLAVED TO MUCH WINE. (2:3)

Another problem that resulted from idle time was the drinking of wine. It was quite common in most of the ancient cultures and thus led to abuse. Instead of a dinner beverage, it became excessive when people did not have useful things to do. Paul gave similar warnings to Timothy in Ephesus (1 Timothy 3:11, 1 Timothy 3:8).

> *"Evidently in Crete, the liability to these excesses was more severe than in Ephesus, especially among the women, for the verb (doulo) used here signifies 'bondage' (RSV 'slaves to drink'), a much stronger expression than the corresponding phrase in 1 Timothy."* (Guthrie)

For older Christian women who would not participate in the

pagan culture around them, what could they do? Titus was to challenge them to become active in teaching the younger women. Paul gave Titus seven things the women could teach the younger wives. With all the evil around them, there was much good they could do. There were great opportunities and possibilities available for the older ladies and great value in sharing their experience with those young women just beginning their journey with God.

It is helpful to look at what is known historically about Minoan women since they were a strong influence on the church.

MINOAN WOMEN.

Women were pictured on thrones, they were often larger or in central positions when compared to their male counterparts. Another common theme that reinforced their importance was that they were depicted being attended to by others.

One example is the Snake goddesses excavated from Knossos palace in 1903. These women were treated as prominent deities in the Minoan religion.

The way that the Cretans understand and symbolize power clearly shows that the woman was the real ruler. It is also important to remember, that the Minoan civilization and religion is 1000 years older than the Classical Greek era which explains why the Cretan pantheon is slightly different than the Greek twelfth god system. The Throne Room in Knossos Palace in Crete which holds both a religious and a secular character belongs to the Great Goddess and the Priest-King as well. It was the Great Goddess who was the superior one and the ruler of the pantheon, not the young male god.

TEACHING THE YOUNG WOMEN WHAT IS GOOD. (2:3-5)

TO LOVE THEIR HUSBANDS. (2:4)

The instruction to disciple young women to love their husbands may seem odd to us today. Why would they have to be told, even trained to love their husband? The cultural influence of the Cretan society may have been a big factor. The woman was a goddess who was served by men who worshipped her. Women in the church may have felt that the men were her servants. The Biblical picture of a godly wife was corrupted by the pagan society of the Cretans. The older, godly women of the church would be the example, not society, to teach the proper roles in marriage.

> *22 Wives, subject yourselves to your own husbands, as to the Lord. 23 For the husband is the head of the wife, as Christ also is the head of the church, He Himself being the Savior of the body. 24 But as the church is subject to Christ, so also the wives ought to be to their husbands in everything.*
>
> *25 Husbands, love your wives, just as Christ also loved the church and gave Himself up for her, 26 so that He might sanctify her, having cleansed her by the washing of water with the word, 27 that He might present to Himself the church in all her glory, having no spot or wrinkle or any such thing; but that she would be holy and blameless.* (Ephesians 5:22-27)

TO LOVE THEIR CHILDREN. (2:4)

It is hard to imagine what influences were on the children in the pagan Cretan world. The worship of goddesses, sacrifices to the gods, a distorted picture of mankind, and life in general affected the children. The greatest love a parent can express to his children is to raise them in the nurture and instruction of the Lord and to learn to honor their parents

> **Children, obey your parents in the Lord, for this is right. ² Honor your father and mother (which is the first commandment with a promise), ³ so that it may turn out well for you, and that you may live long on the earth. ⁴ Fathers, do not provoke your children to anger, but bring them up in the discipline and instruction of the Lord.** (Ephesians 5:22-27)

These parental roles must be caught (by example) and taught (by word). The younger wives needed to be lovingly taught these roles and responsibilities by the older women.

TO BE SENSIBLE. (2:5)
The Greek word is sometimes translated as "discreet." Strong's Concordance describes its two primary usages in Scripture:

- To be of a sound mind, sane, in one's senses
- Curbing one's desires and impulses, self-controlled, temperate.

A young woman may be impulsive in her actions and choices. She needs guidance by example and words to develop restraint from ungodly impulses, and develop godly self-control. Immorality was rampant in Cretan society as was temple worship of goddesses. Christian women needed to be separate from the evil practices, not yielding to the temptations around them.

TO BE PURE. (2:5)
We all know that sin has its pleasures and was even rewarded in Cretan society. We also know that it is only

momentary and not a path worth taking. The word means innocent, modest, chaste, and clean. Personal purity was not a value in Cretan life. The kingdom of God has different values which elevate, not desecrate.

> **"Put to death, therefore, whatever belongs to your earthly nature: sexual immorality, impurity, lust, evil desires and greed, which is idolatry"** (Colossians 3:5).

> **Don't let anyone look down on you because you are young, but set an example for the believers in speech, in conduct, in love, in faith, and in purity.** (1 Timothy 4:12)

TO BE WORKERS AT HOME. (2:5)

Literally, to be domestically inclined: "Caring for the house, working at home" (Thayers Greek Lexicon). A mother is a working woman and is the most important working woman. However, there were Christian women in the marketplace, like Lydia and Phoebe. Keeping a home in order and training the children were great priorities in the early church and should be today as well.

> *An excellent wife, who can find her?*
> *For her worth is far above jewels . . .*
> *. . . Her husband is known in the gates,*
> *When he sits among the elders of the land.*
> *. . . She opens her mouth in wisdom,*
> *And the teaching of kindness is on her tongue.*
> *27 She watches over the activities of her household,*
> *And does not eat the bread of idleness.*
> *28 Her children rise up and bless her;*
> *. . . Charm is deceitful and beauty is vain,*
> *But a woman who fears the Lord, she shall be praised.*
> (Proverbs 31:1, 23, 26-28, 30)

TO BE KIND. (2:5)

She is distinguished by doing good to others. She is

thoughtful. Kindness and goodness are both fruits of the Holy Spirit (Galatians 5:22, 23). These were not found in godless cultures like Minoans on Crete. Jesus used the same word in the sermon on the mount:

> **¹¹ So if you, despite being evil, know how to give good gifts to your children, how much more will your Father who is in heaven give good things to those who ask Him!** (Matthew 7:11)

This characteristic is an attribute of God. We are honoring His name and the image of God when we do likewise to others. Older women not only were to display this gift but train the younger women to do likewise.

TO BE SUBJECT TO THEIR OWN HUSBANDS, SO THAT THE WORD OF GOD WILL NOT BE DISHONORED. (2:5)

A wife that does not respect the order of marriage or her husband brings dishonor to God, the gospel, and the name of Christ is blasphemed by the lost. It is a stain to the church since marriage is a picture of the church (Ephesians 5).

> **"That the gospel may not be injuriously spoken of** (Notes, Matthew 9:3)**, on account of the inconsistent lives of those who profess to be influenced by it. The idea is, that religion ought to produce the virtues here spoken of and that when it does not, it will be reproached as being of no value.** (Barnes' notes on the Bible)

PRINCIPLES TO LIVE BY.

The importance of godly young women and wives in the church and society is immense. Older believing women have a great privilege and responsibility to help shape the future generations to glorify God. We still need Titus women today.

Instructions for young men in the church. (2:6-8)

⁶Likewise urge the young men to be sensible; ⁷in all things show yourself to be an example of good deeds, *with* purity in doctrine, dignified, ⁸sound *in* speech which is beyond reproach, so that the opponent will be put to shame, having nothing bad to say about us.

Each group has its weaknesses and strengths. A pastor cannot use a one-size-fits-all approach. Titus is now charged to add young men to his targeted ministry. This group represents future leaders. Discipling them is investing in the future of the church and the gospel outreach to the world. Titus was given ministry goals for older men and older women. Paul gives Titus a list of five key characteristics that need strengthening in the young men in the church. Paul begins by saying "likewise" which connects the different groups.

RIVERBANKS AND YOUNG MEN.

In many parts of the world, the rainy season turns streams into raging rivers. If the riverbanks are not adequate to contain and direct the flow, the river will overflow its banks and flood the countryside causing widespread damage. Think of undisciplined youth like that river and the Law of God and disciplines of the Christian life are the riverbanks. If the riverbanks are strong and adequate, the powerful river can be used to do great things like generating electricity and providing irrigation for a large area. Without the banks, you end up with a swampland. Paul gives Titus five strong riverbanks to help harness the power of young men. Each is important.

YOUNG MEN NEED TO BE SENSIBLE. (2:6)

Of all the young men you have known, how many would you call sensible? Young men may be the greatest single proof of the fallen nature of man. At the same time, they represent a powerful gospel army once they have gone through God's basic training. "Sensible" means making wise decisions, not impulsive mistakes which can handicap their lives. The Greek word refers to curbing one's passions.

> *"The Living Bible translates the thought well: Urge the young men to behave carefully, taking life seriously. This is the only command Titus is told to emphasize to young men, but sometimes a difficult one for younger men." (Blue Letter Bible)*

> *"The word is sophron, and it describes the man with the mind which has everything under control.... strength of mind which has learned to govern every instinct and passion until each has its proper place and no more." (Barclay)*

YOUNG MEN NEED TO BE EXAMPLES OF GOOD DEEDS. (2:7)

One of the typical attributes of youth is a carefree attitude toward life. A great deal of life is spent doing useless things, or as we say, "wasting time." As we age we become more and more aware of the brief journey we call life. Time and how we use it becomes a priority. What if the young people could realize that there is time for good times with friends and there are times to do good things for others which impact their lives? This was Paul's hope, to see young people finding joy in serving others, not just doing the fun things they want to do that please themselves. Not only is the servant the greatest in heaven but also the most joyful. Titus was to become the example to follow.

> *But it is not this way for you; rather, the one who is the greatest among you must become like the youngest, and the leader like the servant.* (Luke 22:26)

YOUNG MEN NEED TO EXHIBIT PURITY IN DOCTRINE. (2:7)

The word translated as "purity" speaks of an uncontaminated mind. It is also translated as "incorruptibility, soundness, the integrity of mind."

> *"Young men are instructed to live as clear examples in two general areas: their good works and their teaching. Here again, Paul's words to Titus resemble his advice to Timothy. Paul had instructed Timothy to study carefully so that others could see his spiritual growth, convicting others and leading them to Christ (1 Timothy 4:15–16)"* (Bibleref.com)

When you think of pure gold, you understand that all contaminations are removed, and what remains is pure metal. It takes work and the heat of a furnace to purify gold and it takes the furnace of life and a purified mentor to disciple a young man in his understanding of God's Word. But the pure gold of a young man whose understanding and application of Scripture is worth the process. Titus was challenged to be the furnace of God to purify the young people into true and effective followers of Christ.

YOUNG MEN NEED TO BE DIGNIFIED. (2:7)

One way to understand the word "dignified" is to look up the opposite meaning. These are words you will find:

- common.
- ignoble.
- informal.
- insignificant.
- ordinary.
- undignified.
- unimpressive.
- unrefined.

These are traits Paul was telling Titus he was not looking for in a young man. When you read words like ordinary, unimpressive, and insignificant, what kind of man does that describe? It sounds like Cretan young men. Cretans were described as "lazy" by one of their historians. They had no great purpose to give them life. Lazy people let life pass them by, they have either given up trying to succeed in something or they don't care. Lazy people don't end up doing anything of value or leaving any significant impact on their world. They are "common," nothing stands out. They follow the crowd and they don't resist the evil in the culture.

Paul was telling Titus to help the young people to avoid a useless life. They were to stand out from local pressure and become dignified workers for God. That means they live a composed or serious manner that is worthy of respect. *"They act in an honorable, worthy way, showing great self-respect and respect for others"* (Online dictionary definition).

YOUNG MEN NEED TO BE SOUND IN SPEECH WHICH IS BEYOND REPROACH, SO THAT THE OPPONENT WILL BE PUT TO SHAME, HAVING NOTHING BAD TO SAY ABOUT US. (2:8)

Young men in the church can be a good or bad testimony of the church to the community. A wayward child can greatly harm the family, the church, and the gospel. A godly child who is active in serving the community is a testimony to the lost and a positive validation of the parents. In Crete and today in our communities, there will always be critics looking for things they can criticize. There will always be opponents. They will usually direct their venom at the weakest part, always looking for some failure to attack. Rebellious young people are often convenient targets.

Young people who become active in good works for the community not only stop the accusations, but their good deeds will humiliate the accusers. It takes away their reasons for accusations. They no longer have anything *"bad to say about us."* The best solution for false accusations is good works, especially when they come from the children of the ones accused.

Instructions for bondslaves in the church. (1:9, 10)

⁹ *Urge* bondslaves to be subject to their own masters in everything, to be well-pleasing, not argumentative, ¹⁰ not pilfering, but showing all good faith so that they will adorn the doctrine of God our Savior in every respect.

UNDERSTANDING BONDSLAVES, OR BONDSERVANTS.

These are the laws given by God for the slaves and bondservants in the time of Moses:

> ² *"If you buy a Hebrew slave, he shall serve for six years; but on the seventh he shall leave as a free man without a payment to you. ³ If he comes alone, he shall leave alone; if he is the husband of a wife, then his wife shall leave with him. ⁴ If his master gives him a wife, and she bears him sons or daughters, the wife and her children shall belong to her master, and he shall leave alone. ⁵ But if the slave plainly says, 'I love my master, my wife, and my children; I will not leave as a free man,' ⁶ then his master shall bring him to God, then he shall bring him to the door or the doorpost. And his master shall pierce his ear with an awl; and he shall serve him permanently.* (Exodus 21:2-6)

In the first century, slavery, servitude, and bondslaves (a voluntary choice) were very common.

> *"During the time of Jesus and the first-century church, as much as one-third of the Roman population were slaves, and another third had been slaves earlier in life. It was common for freeborn men and women to work side-by-side with slaves as street sweepers, dockworkers, doctors, teachers, and business managers. Convicted criminals became bondservants of the state and usually died working in the mines or on galleys."*
> (GotQuestions Bible Commentary)

Jesus used the positions of slaves, servants, and bondservants in his parables (Matthew 25:14-30 and Luke 12:41-48). Paul wrote a complete letter in the New Testament about how a slave owner should handle a runaway slave who had become a believer (Philemon). Believers who called themselves lifetime, voluntary slaves (bondservants), or servants of God included Paul, Timothy, James, Peter, and Jude (Romans 1:1; Philippians 1:1; James 1:1; 2 Peter 1:1; Jude 1:1,). Slavery itself was not condoned, but it was the way of life and could become an avenue of Christian witness for the committed believer.

> *"I do not think for a moment Paul believed that the practice of slavery ought to exist. He believed to the fullest extent that the great principles of Christianity would overthrow slavery anywhere, and the sooner they did so the better pleased would he be; but, for the time being, as it was the custom to have slaves, they must adorn the doctrine of God their Savior in the position in which they were."* (Spurgeon)

What does it mean for a person to become a bondservant of Christ?

"Six of the most outstanding qualities that God builds into His bondservants are:

Diligence – A bondservant works from sun-up to sundown without complaint, knowing that the Master demands and requires a full day of labor.

Courage – Adversity will be faced and conquered to accomplish the task set before them by the Master.

Humility – Not a false humility that was symbolic of the Pharisees, but true brokenness born out of a realistic understanding of our position before a loving and caring Master.

Dependence – A bondservant trusts the Master to provide all the needed supplies including food, clothes, and shelter.

Identity – Bondservants are not ashamed of being identified with their Master or His Family (the Church). They boldly confess that they are Christians and proudly carry the Family Name.

Single-mindedness – The focus of a bondservant is on the priorities of the Master. Christ's desires become the bondservant's desires." (ronpearce.org)

In Titus' day, some bondservants had become believers and were accepted into the church. Paul gave specific instruction to Titus about how these church members should act as bondservants to their masters in the Cretan society. They had special access to the important people and leaders in Crete, an opportunity to shine for Christ in a pagan world. So, they had a double bondservant role, slaves of Christ and slaves of their earthly master. In both cases, they were to serve honorably.

Here are four ways the bondservants were to honor God in their service to their masters:

By being subject to their own masters in everything, (2:9)

When Paul wrote to the church in Collosea he gave similar instructions concerning the slaves in the fellowship:

> *22Slaves, obey those who are your human masters in everything, not with eye-service, as people-pleasers, but with sincerity of heart, fearing the Lord. 23Whatever you do, do your work heartily, as for the Lord and not for people, 24knowing that it is from the Lord that you will receive the reward of the inheritance. It is the Lord Christ whom you serve. 25For the one who does wrong will receive the consequences of the wrong which he has done, and that without partiality.*
> *(Colossians 3:22-25)*

God was aware of every man's situation, including slaves. When a slave honored his master he was at the same time honoring his greater Master, Jesus Christ. So, even the most tedious work assignment the slave was given could be a time of joy knowing he was doing it ultimately for his Lord. This same principle applies to anyone under authority. It can be a boss and a worker at his job. When we do our best for our work we are in essence honoring God, not just the one who employs us. Our work ethic should be the best in the company.

By being well-pleasing, not argumentative. (2:9)

Not only should the work ethic of the bondservant be the best, but so should the work attitude. We should also, like a bondservant that honors his master, honor our employers by being cheerful in our work and uncomplaining. The principle applies we just discussed.

If we resist authority or complain about our work, we are complaining against God. The Hebrew children complained and mumbled against God when traveling across the desert. It did not go well for them when God sent a judgment against them. Read the story in Numbers 21:4-10. God wants our lives to be a living testimony that every man can read. That applies whether we are bond or free.

By not pilfering (stealing). (2:10)

It would have been a temptation for a poor slave to see the wealth of the master and feel jealous. He might reason that the man would not miss a small item. He might feel that he is underpaid and the rich master owed him more money so he was only getting what he deserved when he stole. Whatever the reason, it was no excuse to violate the moral law, *"Thou shalt not steal."* It does not matter what others are doing, the slave was subject to the highest Law. When he honored the Law of God he was representing God to the ungodly around him, including other bondslaves.

In the ancient world, it was almost expected that slaves would steal. Thief and slave were almost synonyms.

> *"It must be remembered that many of the slaves in the Roman empire were employed in other duties besides those connected with the house or on the farm. Some were entrusted with shops, and these being left often quite to themselves, of course, great opportunities for dishonesty and fraud were constantly present."*
> *(Ellicott's commentary)*

The Biblical story of Joseph and Potipher is a good example of how a slave or servant was to respect his master. Joseph proved himself to be a capable and honest man and was given great privilege and trust:

> *⁴ So Joseph found favor in his sight and became his personal servant; and he made him overseer over his house, and put him in charge of all that he owned.*
> (Genesis 39:4)

Potiphar's wife attempted to seduce Joseph, but he kept his integrity as we read:

> *⁷ And it came about after these events that his master's wife had her eyes on Joseph, and she said, "Sleep with me." ⁸ But he refused and said to his master's wife, "Look, with me here, my master does not concern himself with anything in the house, and he has put me in charge of all that he owns. ⁹ There is no one greater in this house than I, and he has withheld nothing from me except you, because you are his wife. How then could I do this great evil, and sin against God?"* (Genesis 39:7-9)

That is the attitude of a godly servant Titus was to instill in bondservants in the church at Crete.

By showing all good faith so that they will adorn the doctrine of God our Savior in every respect. (2:10)

Having faith in God is not based on social status, income, education, or any factor. Faith is faith and is how any person finds salvation, whether bond or free or rich or poor. Titus was to remind those who were in the status of serving others that the windows of Heaven were just as open to them as anyone. They needed to focus on God their Savior and not their outward circumstances. This is a good lesson for all of us today.

Have you ever seen pictures of a royal wedding? Those who attend and participate all wear their finest clothing and most expensive jewelry. It is like a high-end fashion show. They eat the finest of foods at the wedding banquet. With that image in mind, think of a simple wedding in a poor area. Nobody owns fancy clothes and friends help out and make the food to share with the local family, friends, and guests. Wedding clothes are simple, even rented or borrowed.

The question is, are they any less married than the royal couple? Is the relationship between husband and wife any different? When a person becomes a Christian, we are joined to Christ in a permanent bond. He is the bridegroom and we are His bride. The bondslave who trusted Christ was just as much a part of God's forever family the same as a wealthy or privileged person who trusted Christ. The ground is level at the foot of the cross. The great truths of the gospel, of Christ, and the church are now for everyone who believes. They are our wedding garments, our adornments for the wedding feast of Christ. To *"adorn"* means "to take precious jewels and arrange them to show their true beauty" (Draper). This passage is saying that. The bondslave is "adorned" or covered with *"the doctrine of God our Savior in every respect."* The poor believer, the born-again bondslave, may have been poor in the world's eyes but in God's kingdom, they were the bride in the Royal Wedding of the Son of God.

Interestingly, the beauty of fine diamonds is usually displayed against a black background. That is where they shine the brightest and display their beauty. God has chosen to display His glory similarly.

> *26 For consider your calling, brethren, that there were not many wise according to the flesh, not many mighty, not many noble; 27 but God has chosen the foolish things of the world to shame the wise, and God has chosen the weak things of the world to shame the things which are strong.*
> (I Corinthians 1:26, 27)

General Instructions for all members of the church. (2:11-15)

¹¹ For the grace of God has appeared, bringing salvation to all men, ¹² instructing us to deny ungodliness and worldly desires and to live sensibly, righteously and godly in the present age, ¹³ looking for the blessed hope and the appearing of the glory of our great God and Savior, Christ Jesus, ¹⁴ who gave Himself for us to redeem us from every lawless deed, and to purify for Himself a people for His own possession, zealous for good deeds. ¹⁵ These things speak and exhort and reprove with all authority. Let no one disregard you.

A HALLELUJAH CHORUS PASSAGE. (2:11-15)

These last verses of Chapter Two are like joining in with a choir that is singing the majestic "Hallelujah Chorus" from Handel's *Messiah*. The choir is made of all believers. There are the older men, the older women, the young men, the bondslaves, every believer. All of us glorify God and our Savior, Jesus Christ. He is our hope in a hopeless world. He has purchased salvation for all of us, purified us, and claims us as His own possession. We are His and no one is going to take us out of His hands. It is time to sing.

For Titus facing the great challenges of the Cretan culture and a church that was greatly needing guidance, this passage must have lifted his soul into the heavenlies as it should ours. Let's look at it more closely.

FOR THE GRACE OF GOD HAS APPEARED, BRINGING SALVATION TO ALL MEN. (2:11)

The grace of God is for all people. Even the Cretans, that

godless, idolatrous, warring people? Yes, even the Cretans. To the Jewish Christians on the island who held prejudices against all idolatry, they needed this reminder. All people are invited to the Great Wedding Feast of God. They can be changed by grace like anyone else. The sin of man, no matter how dark, cannot extend beyond the grace of God. This grace appeared when God the Son appeared and walked among us

> *"There is a beauty and energy in the word epiphaino, hath shined out, that is rarely noted; it seems to be a metaphor taken from the sun. As by his rising in the east and shining out, he enlightens, successively, the whole world; so the Lord Jesus, who is called the Sun of righteousness,(Malachi 4:2), arises on the whole human race with healing in his wings."* (Clarke)

> [14] *And the Word became flesh, and dwelt among us, and we saw His glory, glory as of the only begotten from the Father, full of grace and truth.* (John 1:14)

INSTRUCTING US TO DENY UNGODLINESS AND WORLDLY DESIRES AND TO LIVE SENSIBLY, RIGHTEOUSLY, AND GODLY IN THE PRESENT AGE. (2:12)

Living a godly life in an ungodly world was not just for older men or older women. It was not a special challenge for the young men or what would seem to be a major hurdle for the bondservants. No, our God saves all who come in faith to Him. He frees the imprisoned spirit to rise above the noise around us and soar into the heights where the air is clean and the view is above all the evil beneath. Every soul can live to honor God. Every soul can say "no!" to sin and the vices that have snared them. Every soul, regardless of social standing, can deny sin and fleshly desires. There is a God in Heaven who will come to your cry if you call Him (Jeremiah 33:3).

Titus was to instruct all the church to deny, avoid the numerous temptations in the Cretan society. The pressures of the pagan culture resulted in decisions being made that were unsensible, unrighteous, and ungodly. Titus' task was to teach godliness and disciple the people by word and example

LOOKING FOR THE BLESSED HOPE AND THE APPEARING OF THE GLORY OF OUR GREAT GOD AND SAVIOR, CHRIST JESUS. (2:13)

The church needed great hope, something to look forward to. It was hard to resist the fleshly temptations of the Cretan world, but there was hope. A great day was coming. Jesus who had given them life was coming again one day to make all things right. It would be worth it all. The Cretans were liars, but God is the truthteller. The gods of Crete were stone and wood, but Jesus is *"our Great God and Savior,"* the way the truth and the life. His promises would come to pass. The church in Crete, though persecuted, was on the winning team. Jesus would have the final word. It was something to look forward to then and it is today as well. The world is an enemy of God with temptations all around us calling us to give up our hope. Every believer should live in the daily expectation of the greater day that is coming. It gives us strength for the journey.

- "He came the first time to save the soul of man; He will come a second time to resurrect the body.
- He came the first time to save the individual; He will come a second time to save society.
- He came the first time to a crucifixion; He will come a second time to a coronation.
- He came the first time to a tree; He will come a second time to a throne.
- He came the first time in humility; He will come a second time in glory.
- He came the first time and was judged by men; He will

come a second time to judge all men.
- He came the first time and stood before Pilate; He will come a second time and Pilate will stand before Him." (Enduring Word Commentary)

NOTE – This verse contains one of the clearest declarations about the deity of Christ. There is only one definite article in Greek. It is not talking about two persons, one being Jesus and the other being the Father, the Great God. This verse is talking about "the" One, and "the" One is our Savior who is, in essence, our great God and Savior. Christ is both Savior and God incarnate.

WHO GAVE HIMSELF FOR US TO REDEEM US FROM EVERY LAWLESS DEED. (2:14)

Titus reminded the church of another great privilege, that of being purchased from the slave market of sin and freed to live victoriously. Redemption means to be bought out of slavery by paying a ransom. Before we trusted Christ we were dead in trespasses and sins, slaves to sin.

> *¹ And you were dead in your trespasses and sins, ² in which you formerly walked according to the course of this world, according to the prince of the power of the air, of the spirit that is now working in the sons of disobedience. ³ Among them we too all formerly lived in the lusts of our flesh, indulging the desires of the flesh and of the mind, and were by nature children of wrath, even as the rest. ⁴ But God, being rich in mercy, because of His great love with which He loved us, ⁵ even when we were dead in our transgressions, made us alive together with Christ (by grace you have been saved).* (Ephesians 2:1-4)

There are five main thoughts in this verse in Ephesians which help us understand the immensity of our redemption.

According to Ephesians 2:1-4, we were:

- **DEAD:** [1] *And you were dead in your trespasses and sins,*
- **DECEIVED:** [2] *in which you formerly walked according to the course of this world, according to the prince of the power of the air, of the spirit that is now working in the sons of disobedience.*
- **DEPRAVED:** [3] *Among them we too all formerly lived in the lusts of our flesh, indulging the desires of the flesh and of the mind,*
- **DOOMED:** *and were by nature children of wrath, even as the rest.*
- **DELIVERED:** [4] *But God, being rich in mercy, because of His great love with which He loved us,* [5] *even when we were dead in our transgressions, made us alive together with Christ (by grace you have been saved).*

When we consider our desperate condition before Christ redeemed us, we sense the immensity of our redemption. It was all God, we are recipients of His immeasurable love, mercy, and grace. The believers on Crete needed, as we do, a reminder to never forget our great redemption. We are His special purchased possession and we now have the Holy Spirit to empower us to overcome and move away from our "lawless deeds."

The believers on Crete had many reasons to rejoice. God had given them a new birth and new life through the Holy Spirit. They had been redeemed from the curse of the Law by the blood of Christ.

Have you thanked God for these things today?

TO PURIFY FOR HIMSELF A PEOPLE FOR HIS OWN POSSESSION. (2:14)

"The Greek term literally means "one's own" or "one's own possession," which is why His people are special. They are God's own, and so are therefore distinctive because nobody else owns the called-out ones." (The Berean Commentary)

When Christ died on Calvary, He defeated Satan and his armies from Hell. Jesus, the King of kings and Lord of lords, had now taken His captives back, the souls of those He purchased with His blood. We are now His rightful spoils of battle, the prize from the victory over sin and Satan. We are His possession set apart for Himself.

Therefore there is now no condemnation for those who are in Christ Jesus. ² For the law of the Spirit of life in Christ Jesus has set you free from the law of sin and of death. (Romans 8:1, 2)

Because of the work of Christ and the cleansing work of the Holy Spirit we are being conformed into the purified people God intends. He plans that *"He might present to Himself the church in all her glory, having no spot or wrinkle or any such thing; but that she would be holy and blameless"* (Ephesians 5:27).

TO BE ZEALOUS FOR GOOD DEEDS. (2:14)

If God's total purpose for us was to be saved from sin and born into His family, He would have taken us to Heaven the moment we were saved. We have been left here with a great purpose to share the good news of the gospel across the world. We are the ambassadors for the Kingdom of God. We were saved by grace through faith to be active participants in His Great Commission. There are specific assigned works we are to do. These good works are a result of salvation, not what makes us saved. They are the fruit on the tree. We have been called to do good works for God.

> *⁸ For by grace you have been saved through faith; and this is not of yourselves, it is the gift of God; ⁹ not a result of works, so that no one may boast. ¹⁰ For we are His workmanship, created in Christ Jesus for good works, which God prepared beforehand so that we would walk in them.”* (Ephesians 2: 8-10)

Titus was calling the Cretan believers to stop their lazy tendencies and become active in impacting their community with the gospel. They should let their light shine before men.

> *¹⁴ “You are the light of the world. A city set on a hill cannot be hidden; ¹⁵ nor does anyone light a lamp and put it under a basket, but on the lampstand, and it gives light to all who are in the house. ¹⁶ Let your light shine before men in such a way that they may see your good works, and glorify your Father who is in heaven.* (Matthew 5:14-16)

There is great joy in working when our work matters, and makes a difference. There is no work more fulfilling than God's work. Titus' assignment was to mobilize the church and motivate them to be active in changing the Cretan world from paganism to Christian. They were to become zealous in this assignment of good deeds. This is what Jesus was saying to His disciples:

> *³⁴ A new commandment I give to you, that you love one another, even as I have loved you, that you also love one another. ³⁵ By this all men will know that you are My disciples, if you have love for one another.*
> (John 13:34, 35)

THESE THINGS SPEAK AND EXHORT AND REPROVE WITH ALL AUTHORITY. LET NO ONE DISREGARD YOU. (2:15)

Titus had been given a challenging assignment. He was the man for the job. Paul reminded him that he had authority from God to do these things and no man should derail that calling. There will always be critics and opposition. Just as Titus stayed on track doing the will of God despite the enemy attacks, we need to take heart in the work God has called each of us to do.

> [58] *Therefore, my beloved brethren, be steadfast, immovable, always abounding in the work of the Lord, knowing that your toil is not in vain in the Lord.* (1 Corinthians 15:58)

The prophet Jeremiah was given a similar task. His audience was a rebellious nation that was in the judgment of God. He was to be the one to call the nation back to God. He felt inadequate for the task and afraid of the people. Maybe, Titus had some reservations. He understood the depth of sin on Crete and the reputation of that warring people. God reassured Jeremiah that He would be with him so he needed not to fear his accusers.

> *"[5] Before I formed you in the womb I knew you,*
> *And before you were born I consecrated you;*
> *I have appointed you a prophet to the nations."*
> *[6] Then I said, "Alas, Lord God!*
> *Behold, I do not know how to speak,*
> *Because I am a youth."*
> *[7] But the Lord said to me,*
> *"Do not say, 'I am a youth,'*
> *Because everywhere I send you, you shall go,*
> *And all that I command you, you shall speak.*
> *[8] "Do not be afraid of them,*
> *For I am with you to deliver you," declares the Lord.*
> (Jeremiah 1:5-8)

The God of Jeremiah was the God of Titus. Oh, yes, He is our God also.

¹ The Lord is my light and my salvation;
Whom shall I fear?
The Lord is the defense of my life;
Whom shall I dread?
² When evildoers came upon me to devour my flesh,
My adversaries and my enemies, they stumbled and fell.
³ Though a host encamp against me,
My heart will not fear;
Though war arise against me,
In spite of this I shall be confident. (Psalm 27:1-3)

Titus 3

DOING GOOD IN A BAD WORLD.

Being a good citizen. How should a believer respect the government? (3:1)

¹ Remind them to be subject to rulers, to authorities, to be obedient, to be ready for every good deed,

Jesus walked the earth in a region that was under the control of the Roman government. The religion was pagan, polytheistic idolatry. The rule was strict. Slaves were taken from conquered people and used to build the Roman cities. Immorality was a national pastime. Torture and suffering of people and animals were entertainment. It was the most powerful empire on the earth at that time. Even with all the advances that came from the Romans, it was still a repressive and fearsome empire. That was the political power that ruled the world when Jesus and Paul lived.

The question always comes if a Christian should pay taxes and support an evil government. This verse and others answer that question. The answer is yes. If we are citizens of a country we are expected to be good citizens and follow the rules of that government unless we are commanded to break the laws of God. We are also expected to show proper respect to the ruling authorities even if they have not earned respect. *"¹⁸ If possible, so far as it depends on you, be at peace with all men"* (Romans 12:8). When we are peaceable, not resistive of the government, we earn the right to minister to the people. We are citizens of a country but more importantly, we are citizens of God's kingdom. We obey the laws of the land where we live so we can bring the good news of the greater kingdom to the people.

Let's consider taxes as an example:

JESUS PAID TAXES TO THE ROMAN EMPIRE.

Jesus taught the people to give to Caesar what was required, but give to God what we should give.

> *¹⁵ Then the Pharisees went and plotted together how they might trap Him in what He said. ¹⁶ And they sent their disciples to Him, along with the Herodians, saying, "Teacher, we know that You are truthful and teach the way of God in truth, and defer to no one; for You are not partial to any. ¹⁷ Tell us then, what do You think? Is it lawful to give a poll-tax to Caesar, or not?" ¹⁸ But Jesus perceived their malice, and said, "Why are you testing Me, you hypocrites? ¹⁹ Show Me the coin used for the poll-tax." And they brought Him a denarius. ²⁰ And He said to them, "Whose likeness and inscription is this?" ²¹ They said to Him, "Caesar's." Then He said to them, "Then render to Caesar the things that are Caesar's; and to God the things that are God's."*

²² And hearing this, they were amazed, and leaving Him, they went away. (Matthew 22:15–22)

Jesus paid taxes:

²⁴ Now when they came to Capernaum, those who collected the two-drachma tax came to Peter and said, "Does your teacher not pay the two-drachma tax?" ²⁵ He *said, "Yes." And when he came into the house, Jesus spoke to him first, saying, "What do you think, Simon? From whom do the kings of the earth collect customs or poll-tax, from their sons or from strangers?" ²⁶ When Peter said, "From strangers," Jesus said to him, "Then the sons are exempt. ²⁷ However, so that we do not offend them, go to the sea and throw in a hook, and take the first fish that comes up; and when you open its mouth, you will find a stater. Take that and give it to them for you and Me." (Matthew 17:24-27)

PAUL INSTRUCTED THE BELIEVERS IN ROME TO PAY THEIR TAXES AND FEES.

¹ Every person is to be in subjection to the governing authorities. For there is no authority except from God, and those which exist are established by God. ² Therefore whoever resists authority has opposed the ordinance of God; and they who have opposed will receive condemnation upon themselves. ³ For rulers are not a cause of fear for good behavior, but for evil. Do you want to have no fear of authority? Do what is good and you will have praise from the same; ⁴ for it is a minister of God to you for good. But if you do what is evil, be afraid; for it does not bear the sword for nothing; for it is a minister of God, an avenger who brings wrath on the one who practices evil. ⁵ Therefore it is necessary to be in subjection, not only because of wrath, but also for conscience' sake. ⁶ For because of this you also pay taxes, for rulers are servants of God, devoting themselves to this very thing. ⁷ Render to all what is due them: tax to whom tax is due; custom to whom custom; fear to whom fear; honor to whom honor. (Romans 13:1-7)

Daniel respected the Babylonian rulers, but he and his believing friends refused to bow down to false gods or stop worshipping the God of heaven and earth. They accepted the consequences of their action. The three children were thrown into a burning furnace and Daniel into a den of lions. God honored their resolve to worship only Him (Daniel chapter 3 and Daniel chapter 6).

Paul gave the same instruction to Titus to teach the church. They were to respect the authorities on Crete and be good citizens. This would open doors of ministry on the island. The next verse expands on how we are to treat people as Christians even when we disagree with them.

What should a believer's testimony be like in the world? (3:2)

² to malign no one, to be peaceable, gentle, showing every consideration for all men.

WE ARE TO NEVER MALIGN (SLANDER) ANYONE.

Words should be used to build up, not to destroy the reputation of another. Crete as a society had a gossip problem. Paul previously warned Titus about this problem in the church in Crete (Titus 2:3), particularly among the older women.

> *"The idea is, that we are not to slander, revile, or defame anyone. We are not to say anything to anyone, or of anyone, which will do him injury. We are never to utter anything which we know to be false about him or to give such a coloring to his words or conduct as to do him wrong in any way. We should always so speak to him and of him in such a way that he will have no reason to complain that he is an injured man."* (Barnes Notes on the Bible)

WE ARE TO BE PEACEABLE.

This is referring to avoiding arguments, unnecessary confrontation. The word also is used to describe one who does not get into fights or brawling. A peacemaker can calm the agitated and the hot-tempered. This is a person who brings a calming influence to a situation.

> *A gentle answer turns away wrath,*
> *But a harsh word stirs up anger.* (Proverbs 15:1)

WE ARE TO BE GENTLE.

Christians should be fair-minded. We should speak in a fashion to others that draws them to the Savior. Jesus said, *"16 Let your light shine before men in such a way that they may see your good works, and glorify your Father who is in heaven"* (Matthew 5:16). Gentleness is one of the fruits of the Holy Spirit (Galatians 5:22, 23). The opposite of gentleness is brutality. Remember how the Cretans were described in Chapter One, *"2 One of themselves, a prophet of their own, said, 'Cretans are always liars, evil beasts, lazy gluttons'"* (1:12). Paul was concerned that the church was acting like the pagan Cretans and needed to get back to acting like Christians.

It is the same today. We live in societies that are based on the Word of God. There is much violence, corruption, and evil all around us. The church should stand strong in the virtues of the Christian faith. Conformity to the world will only lead to ruin in the body of Christ. We are called to be a light to our cold dark world.

> *2 And do not be conformed to this world, but be transformed by the renewing of your mind, so that you may prove what the will of God is, that which is good and acceptable and perfect.* (Romans 12:2)

WE ARE TO SHOW CONSIDERATION TO EVERY MAN.

This means we should see others like Jesus sees them. Each person is treated respectfully as valuable to God. James warned about the sin of partiality, *"an attitude of personal favoritism"* (James 2:1). One commentator put it this way, "This is a distinctively Christian kindness, coming not from simple good manners, but from knowing who we are and who others are in the heart of Jesus" (David Guzik).

> *3 Do nothing from selfishness or empty conceit, but with humility of mind regard one another as more important than yourselves; 4 do not merely look out for your own personal interests, but also for the interests of others.*
> (Philippians 2:3, 4)

SUMMARY – Christians should live to honor God, respect others, and treat them in a fashion that draws them to Jesus. On the island of Crete, this was just what they needed to see from the church.

Our great salvation. (3:3-7)

3 For we also once were foolish ourselves, disobedient, deceived, enslaved to various lusts and pleasures, spending our life in malice and envy, hateful, hating one another. 4 But when the kindness of God our Savior and *His* love for mankind appeared, 5 He saved us, not on the basis of deeds which we have done in righteousness, but according to His mercy, by the washing of regeneration and renewing by the Holy Spirit, 6 whom He poured out upon us richly through Jesus Christ our Savior, 7 so that being justified by His grace we would be made heirs according to *the* hope of eternal life.

THE WAY WE ALL USED TO LIVE. (3:3)

> *³ For we also once were foolish ourselves, disobedient, deceived, enslaved to various lusts and pleasures, spending our life in malice and envy, hateful, hating one another.* (3:3)

In this section of his letter, Paul encouraged Titus to remind the believers that they were once lost and no different from the Cretans. They were foreigners wandering in the desert of sin. Before they became too critical of the pagan world of the Cretans, they needed a reminder that they were in the same condition before God showed mercy on them. They were no better than the Cretans. The difference was the grace of God. The same God who pardoned them could pardon the Cretans.

It was time to review the great salvation of God which was available to all men. That is what the next verses describe.

GOD SAVED US DESPITE OURSELVES. (3:4, 5)

> *⁴ But when the kindness of God our Savior and His love for mankind appeared, 5 He saved us, not on the basis of deeds which we have done in righteousness, but according to His mercy,* (3:4, 5)

Our salvation is a gift from God. It is because of His kindness and love. While we were helpless and dead in our sins (Ephesians 2:4), He reached down and mercifully rescued us. Did He rescue us because we deserved it, or because of our good deeds, or because of anything good in us? No, it was because of His sovereign act of showing mercy on a people that did not deserve mercy. It was the kindness of God and His overflowing love that moved upon us. The church in Crete needed that reminder and we today need that same reminder.

None of us deserve to be saved. We would all be far less judgmental if we keep in mind that we are all part of the same fallen human race and deserving only of the wrath of God (Romans 3:23; 6:23).

> *And you were dead in your trespasses and sins, ² in which you formerly walked according to the course of this world, according to the prince of the power of the air, of the spirit that is now working in the sons of disobedience. ³ Among them we too all formerly lived in the lusts of our flesh, indulging the desires of the flesh and of the mind, and were by nature children of wrath, even as the rest. ⁴ But God, being rich in mercy, because of His great love with which He loved us, ⁵ even when we were dead in our transgressions, made us alive together with Christ (by grace you have been saved).* (Ephesians 2:1-6)

An old hymn used these words, "Nothing in my hand I bring, simply to the cross I cling." That is all we have, nothing to boast in but Christ the King. Once understood, the Cretan church would look upon the pagan world around them with eyes of compassion and not be judgmental. They would also be encouraged that the Cretan culture was not so fallen that the grace of God could not reach them.

> "**Not by works of righteousness which we have done***: Our salvation isn't based on any* **works of righteousness which we have done.** *In and of itself, response to an altar call does not save. Saying the sinner's prayer does not save. Baptism does not save. Church attendance does not save. Giving does not save. Reading the Bible does not save. Each of these may be wonderful* **works of righteousness,** *but they do not save us. Instead,* **according to His mercy, He saved us.**" (Enduring Word Commentary)

THE BENEFITS OF SALVATION. (3:5-7)

> *... by the washing of regeneration and renewing by the Holy Spirit, ⁶ whom He poured out upon us richly through*

Jesus Christ our Savior, [7] so that being justified by His grace we would be made heirs according to the hope of eternal life. (3:5-7)

We have received the washing of regeneration and renewing of the Holy Spirit. (3:5)

The controversy. Some think this means a person is washed of his sins by physical baptism. Others see this as a spiritual baptism. Others see this as a spiritual event done by the Holy Spirit. It means the Holy Spirit is the instrument of the New Birth, we are born of the Spirit and cleansed from our sins at that new birth. So, which is correct?

Since this is described as a function of the Spirit, it is not a reference to a physical event even though a physical event like water baptism may be used as a symbol of what has happened spiritually.

> *"Through the washing of regeneration: These words are commonly taken as a reference to baptism, and this passage is sometimes quoted in support of the idea of baptismal regeneration. Yet we cannot say that Paul specifically mentions baptism here, and the only other use of the ancient Greek word translated washing here is connected with the spiritual cleansing of the believer by the Word of God through faith."* (Ephesians 5:26: The Enduring Word Commentary)

Regeneration is a description of the new birth, we are transformed, given new life when we are born again. The best way to view the phrase "washing of regeneration" is to see it as a spiritual cleansing by the Holy Spirit that takes place at our salvation. We are born into the family of God, given a full cleansing of our sins, and transformed (regenerated) into a child of God. Paul used the concept of washing when describing salvation elsewhere:

> *¹¹ Such were some of you; but you were washed, but you were sanctified, but you were justified in the name of the Lord Jesus Christ and in the Spirit of our God.*
> (1 Corinthians 6:11)

"Washing" and "renewing", are a description of forgiveness, removal of sins changing our hearts into a new heart, a transformed heart.

> *¹⁷ Therefore if anyone is in Christ, he is a new creature; the old things passed away; behold, new things have come.*
> (1 Corinthians 5:17)

> *And do not be conformed to this world, but be transformed by the* renewing *of your mind, that you may prove what is that good and acceptable and perfect will of God.*
> (Romans 12:2)

Water baptism is a beautiful image that symbolizes a new believer being buried, dying to our old sinful man, and being raised as a new creation in Christ. But we should not confuse the inward spiritual event of being washed, regenerated, and renewed, with the outward symbol of water baptism. Salvation is a work of the Spirit, baptism is a public proclamation of our new life in Christ.

The next benefit is our justification.

WE HAVE BEEN JUSTIFIED BY HIS GRACE. (3:7)

Justification is a major theme in the Epistle to the Romans. Justification is the declaring of a person to be just, or righteous. It does not mean a person is innocent. It is a legal term signifying the acquittal of a crime. It is a legal pardon. It means we are no longer held accountable for our crimes. God remains just and the justifier of the ungodly. His justice has been satisfied in Christ's substitutionary death on the cross. God poured out His just wrath on His Son, who paid the complete penalty for our sin. That was possible because He was fully man and also fully God. Now that the punishment is over, God can credit our spiritual accounts with the righteousness of His Son. We, as guilty sinners who have been pardoned, now stand before God as righteous, just as if we had never sinned. Our role in all this is to simply trust the work of Christ and accept His justification as a gift.

Justification illustrated.

One way to understand this is to picture a vile murderer sitting on death row, rightfully condemned to pay the ultimate penalty for his crime. He had taken a life, now he must forfeit his own. As he sits on death row awaiting his final doom, he knows he is guilty and deserves his punishment. He is a dead man, staring at the gallows, awaiting the actual moment that will end his sinful life.

The unthinkable happens. The sovereign of the land, the king himself, has mercy on the man and sends a letter of pardon and reprieve. The execution is canceled. Why? Did the sinner deserve it, or do something to earn this favor? No, it was a sovereign decision by the king who has the legal authority to pardon a man.

> *¹ Therefore there is now no condemnation for those who are in Christ Jesus. ² For the law of the Spirit of life in Christ Jesus has set you free from the law of sin and of death.* (Romans 8:1, 2)

WE HAVE BEEN MADE HEIRS OF CHRIST. (3:7)

> *¹⁶ The Spirit Himself testifies with our spirit that we are children of God, ¹⁷ and if children, heirs also, heirs of God and fellow heirs with Christ, if indeed we suffer with Him so that we may also be glorified with Him.* (Romans 8:16, 17)

Each of these benefits of salvation is immense. In Romans 8, we are called *"children and heirs of God."* In Titus, we are *"made heirs"* of Christ through the grace of God. When Paul wrote to the church of Ephesus he told the believers:

> **Blessed be the God and Father of our Lord Jesus Christ, who has blessed us with every spiritual blessing in the heavenly places in Christ, 4 just as He chose us in Him before the foundation of the world, that we would be holy and blameless before Him. In love 5 He predestined us to adoption as sons through Jesus Christ to Himself, according to the kind intention of His will, 6 to the praise of the glory of His grace, which He freely bestowed on us in the Beloved.**
> (Ephesians 1:3-6)

Let's summarize what God's Word is telling us about ourselves. These great thoughts were no doubt what the discouraged church in Crete needed to hear just as we need to hear it today. Before the world began God chose us in Christ to be a part of His forever family. He sent His Son to pay for all our sins on the cross and then He legally could pardon our guilty souls because the penalty for our sins was fully paid at Calvary. The Holy Spirit cleansed our souls, filled our spirits with His presence, and empowers us to fulfill the gifts he has assigned to us. God adopted us into His family as children and therefore we are now joint-heirs with Christ in the eternal riches of God. Amen and amen. An old preacher once said, "If that doesn't light your fire, your wood is wet!"

WE HAVE THE HOPE OF ETERNAL LIFE. (3:7)

God has placed eternity in the hearts of every man.

> **He has made everything beautiful in its time. He has also set eternity in the human heart; yet no one can fathom what God has done from beginning to end.**
> **(Ecclesiastes 3:11)**

The pages of Scripture are filled with eternity and hope that awaits the family of God. We are eternal creations. We had a beginning, but believers have a bright future with God. We don't know everything about heaven, but we have enough hints to know that no one will be disappointed or bored. Hope is a comforting word, but eternal hope, that one is beyond description. For the struggling Christians in Crete, overwhelmed with the darkness around them, the hope of victory was good news.

Do good to all men. (3:8)

⁸ This is a trustworthy statement; and concerning these things I want you to speak confidently, so that those who have believed God will be careful to engage in good deeds. These things are good and profitable for men.

Faith alone saves, but the faith that saves is never alone. We know from Ephesians 2:8-10 that we are saved by grace through faith, but then we also are told we are God's masterpiece created to do good works. These works are the evidence of our salvation. They are the fruit on the tree. They show us that it is alive and well. James described a person that claimed to be a Christian but had no evidence, nor good works to show for his salvation. That person is dead; his faith is not genuine:

> ¹⁴ *What use is it, my brothers and sisters, if someone says he has faith, but he has no works? Can that faith save him?* ¹⁵ *If a brother or sister is without clothing and in need of daily food,* ¹⁶ *and one of you says to them, "Go in peace, be warmed and be filled," yet you do not give them what is necessary for their body, what use is that?* ¹⁷ *In the same way, faith also, if it has no works, is dead, being by itself.* (James 2:14-17)

Some confuse the words of James, *"faith without works is dead,"* to mean that we need to do good works to be saved. That is not what he is saying. He is saying that if good works are not evident in a person's life, then salvation is not real. A faith that claims to be genuine is dead if it has no good works to back it up. Faith comes first, then works. Works prove that faith is real.

Paul was instructing Titus to take confidence in these matters and be diligent to let their light shine before men. The pagan Cretan culture was dark in false religion and goddess worship. It was a great opportunity for the church to demonstrate the love of Christ. People know we are Christians by our love for each other and our compassion for the lost. That is what they see.

The theme of doing good works is a major message of the letter to Titus. As some have noted, we begin by grace, but we show gratitude to God by demonstrating our love for those around us. Paul mentions "good works" 14 times in his letters to Timothy and Titus. He knew how important it was for the believers in Ephesus and Crete to not just talk about Christ, but to demonstrate Christ to the lost. Think of the relationship of faith and works as what happens when we breathe. We breathe in and breathe out. We can't just do one of them. Breathing in is taking in, it is learning from God, study, and prayer. We are breathing in. Breathing out is sharing it with others by example, good works, and words. It is demonstrating the love of Christ not just talking about it. That is breathing. We need both breathing in and breathing out to have a healthy body. *"These things are good and profitable for men"* (3:8).

The reason Paul and Titus needed to remind the church of these matters is that they had become distracted from their purpose by confused leaders. The people were arguing and speculating about useless things. That is found in the next verses.

Things and people to avoid. (3:9-11)

⁹ But avoid foolish controversies and genealogies and strife and disputes about the Law, for they are unprofitable and worthless. ¹⁰ Reject a factious man after a first and second warning, ¹¹ knowing that such a man is perverted and is sinning, being self-condemned.

These verses give us a glimpse into the Cretan society and the challenges that confronted the church in Crete. There was a similarity between the Cretans, the Romans, and the Greeks. They each put great emphasis on intellectual debate. When Paul traveled through Athens, Greece, he encountered a people that loved to debate new things and philosophies (Acts 17). Athens was the hub of Greek Mythology. It spread throughout the region, everywhere Rome conquered. Temples for worshipping the Greek gods were built all over the Roman Empire. Libraries were constructed to assemble the teachings. Halls and schools helped propagate the false views of their religion of Mythology. Crete had its form of mythology with a strong emphasis on worshipping goddesses.

It was easy for the church to be distracted and derailed from the message of the true God. It was also a fearful thing to go against the long-standing beliefs of local people. They were like a David facing Goliath. Paul and Titus were confident that the God that helped David defeat Goliath would give the church victory over the darkness.

The church needed to see how far they had departed from their calling. They needed to see how intellectuals and false teachers had deceived them. They needed to stop the useless arguments and work as a team to evangelize the Cretans by both word and deed.

Paul listed several things the church needed to do to get back on track again. These were:

- Stop foolish controversies and useless genealogies. (3:9)
- Stop arguing and disputing about the Law, for they are unprofitable and worthless. (3:9)
- Stop listening to those who stir up trouble. Reject and discipline these troublemakers. (3:10, 11)

STOP FOOLISH CONTROVERSIES AND DISCUSSIONS ABOUT GENEALOGIES. (3:9)

Paul dealt with this continually among the Jewish community. Many were proud of their tribe or family line. Instead of being of this bloodline or that tribal heritage, it was all of no value when compared to being in Christ. Paul wrote this very thing in his letter to the church in Philippi:

> *³ for we are the true circumcision, who worship in the Spirit of God and glory in Christ Jesus and put no confidence in the flesh, ⁴ although I myself might have confidence even in the flesh. If anyone else has a mind to put confidence in the flesh, I far more: ⁵ circumcised the eighth day, of the nation of Israel, of the tribe of Benjamin, a Hebrew of Hebrews; as to the Law, a Pharisee; ⁶ as to zeal, a persecutor of the church; as to the righteousness which is in the Law, found blameless. ⁷ But whatever things were gain to me, those things I have counted as loss for the sake of Christ. ⁸ More than that, I count all things to be loss in view of the surpassing value of knowing Christ Jesus my Lord, for whom I have suffered the loss of all things, and count them but rubbish so that I may gain Christ.* (Philippians 3:3-8)

Genealogies, Paul said, were rubbish, compared to the only family line that mattered, being a child of God. That family line is a work of God, not man, so what is there to boast about. Boast only in God's grace.

"The Jewish Rabbis spent their time building up imaginary genealogies for the characters of the Old Testament.... It is much easier to discuss theological questions than to be kind and considerate and helpful at home, or efficient and diligent and honest at work." (Barclay)

STOP ARGUING AND DISPUTING ABOUT THE LAW, FOR THEY ARE UNPROFITABLE AND WORTHLESS. (3:9)

The Pharisees in Jesus' time were consumed with the ceremonial law and even added hundreds of their statutes. They spent their time disputing these laws. Jesus rebuked them:

> [23] *"Woe to you, scribes and Pharisees, hypocrites! For you tithe mint and dill and cumin, and have neglected the weightier provisions of the Law: justice and mercy and faithfulness; but these are the things you should have done without neglecting the others.* [24] *You blind guides, who strain out a gnat and swallow a camel!*
> (Matthew 23: 23, 24)

The church at Crete had become like the Pharisees. They spent their time in useless discussions about details in the Law and neglected the lost around them. They would rather win an argument than win the lost souls around them. Satan will use any means to get the church to focus on meaningless things and miss the greatest things. Crete needed to return to the Great Commission and stop wasting their lives on useless arguments.

STOP LISTENING TO THOSE WHO STIR UP TROUBLE. REJECT AND DISCIPLINE THESE TROUBLEMAKERS. (3:10, 11)

There are always those who cause trouble, strife, and division. The church in Crete had tolerated these people who were causing trouble. Like a cancerous tumor that kills the body, it had to be cut out. The troublemakers needed to be dealt with, not ignored. They had to be publically rejected or disciplined.

As with cancer, radical surgery was necessary.

This warning is not for people that have stumbled into an error in their understanding. These are heretics, who have willingly chosen error over truth and are leading the church astray. They are wolves in sheep's clothing. The church is commanded to deal with them as such. The guidance for disciplining a sinning member of the church is given in Matthew 18:

> [15] *"If your brother sins, go and show him his fault in private; if he listens to you, you have won your brother.* [16] *But if he does not listen to you, take one or two more with you, so that by the mouth of two or three witnesses every fact may be confirmed.* [17] *If he refuses to listen to them, tell it to the church; and if he refuses to listen even to the church, let him be to you as a Gentile and a tax collector.*
> (Matthew 18:15-17)

The early church struggled with legalism from its beginning. The Judaizers insisted that Gentile converts become like Jews in practices like circumcision and adherence to the ceremonial Law, especially the food laws. The role of Titus was to set things in order, to right the wrongs, and to bring the people back to Christ from legalism and false teachers. Once the course was corrected, they could use their energy in productive ways.

New assignments are coming for Titus and some of his associates. (3:12, 13)

[12] When I send Artemas or Tychicus to you, make every effort to come to me at Nicopolis, for I have decided to spend the winter there. [13] Diligently help Zenas the lawyer and Apollos on their way so that nothing is lacking for them.

The massive task of getting the church back on track was

accomplished in a very short time frame. Titus was on Crete between 6 months to one year according to some historians. This tells us a lot about Titus. He was a tireless worker, confident in the gospel and strong in his faith. He was able to stand against the pagan world and the false teachers who had invaded the church.

These two verses inform Titus that a change of assignment is coming. Zenas, a lawyer, and Apollos, a valued co-worker of Paul had carried Paul's letter to Crete with the new assignment. Titus was to send them on, providing for their needs. Meanwhile, Paul would be sending a replacement for him so Titus could leave and travel north to Nicopolis. The one coming, according to Paul, would be either Artemas or Tychicus. We know Tychichus was later sent by Paul to Ephesus to take over the work so Timothy could visit Paul in prison before he died.

> *12 But I have sent Tychicus to Ephesus. 13 When you come, bring the overcoat which I left at Troas with Carpus, and the books, especially the parchments.* (2 Timothy 4:12)

We can assume that Artemas was sent to Crete to replace him so he could travel to Dalmatia and Nicopolis. Nicopolis was a new church planting region that Paul knew he could not complete. He wanted Titus to finish the church planting of the area which included Dalmatia. The work of Titus was coming to an end and he, being a strong pioneer church planter, was headed to another difficult region, this time to do pioneer work.

Paul's final instructions and emphasis on the believers in Crete needing to be doing good. (3:14-15)

¹⁴ Our people must also learn to engage in good deeds to meet pressing needs, so that they will not be unfruitful. ¹⁵ All who are with me greet you. Greet those who love us in *the* faith. Grace be with you all.

Titus was once again given the assignment to challenge the church in Crete: "Do good works." This was one of the most dominant themes in the book of Titus. Hopefully, they would get the message. For them, the Great Commission had become the Great Ommission. They needed to stop fighting each other and get back into the real war for the souls of men.

Paul seemed to sense the urgency of the message. He knew his days were numbered. He was an enemy of the state in Rome. His arrest would come shortly after this. His emphasis on the urgency of the gospel and to not be "unfruitful" probably echoed the challenges Christ gave to His disciples:

> *³⁵ Jesus was going through all the cities and villages, teaching in their synagogues and proclaiming the gospel of the kingdom, and healing every kind of disease and every kind of sickness. ³⁶ Seeing the people, He felt compassion for them, because they were distressed and dispirited like sheep without a shepherd. ³⁷ Then He *said to His disciples, "The harvest is plentiful, but the workers are few. ³⁸ Therefore beseech the Lord of the harvest to send out workers into His harvest."* (Matthew 9:35-38)

> *³⁵ Do you not say, 'There are yet four months, and then comes the harvest'? Behold, I say to you, lift up your eyes and look on the fields, that they are white for harvest. ³⁶ Already he who reaps is receiving wages and is gathering fruit for life eternal; so that he who sows and he who reaps may rejoice together.* (John 4:35-36)

Finally, Paul ends where he started the letter, praying for God's grace for Titus and all in the church. Our salvation is all grace and by grace we serve God. It is all God's amazing grace. Amen.

> *"Through many dangers, toils and snares,*
> *I have already come;*
> *'Tis grace hath brought me safe thus far,*
> *And grace will lead me home."*

(Amazing Grace, Hymn, John Newton)

Made in the USA
Columbia, SC
30 November 2022

72199962R00209